PAPER CRAFTS & STAMP IT!
MAGAZINE®

the ultimate paper crafts
collection

Clever cards and paper crafts for every occasion

> No INFLUENCE is so POWERFUL as that of a MOTHER.
> *Sarah Josepha H*

> MOTHERHOOD:
> All love begins and ends there.
>
> *Robert Browning*

Presenting over 650 inspiring projects and ideas from *Paper Crafts* magazine and its *Stamp It!* special editions, with a wealth of keepsake cards, albums, tags and other paper crafts to make for loved ones on all occasions

A TREASURY OF FAVORITES PRODUCED EXCLUSIVELY FOR LEISURE ARTS

PaperCrafts

Editorial
Editor-in-Chief Stacy Croninger
Managing Editor Vee Kelsey-McKee
Special Issues Editor Jennafer Martin
Sr. Special Issues Editor Marissa Dorny
Creative Editor Catherine Edvalson
Assistant Editors Natalie Jackman, Melinda Frewin
Contributing Editor Valerie Pingree
Copy Editor Erin Poulson
Editorial Assistant Brenda Peterson
Web Site Manager Emily Johnson
Web Site Editor April Tarter

Design
Art Director Stace Hasegawa
Designer Junko Barker
Photographer Skylar Nielsen

Events
Events Director Paula Kraemer
Events Coordinator David Ray

Advertising
Publisher Tony Golden
Advertising Manager Becky Lowder
Advertising Assistant Kristi Larsen
Advertising Sales U.S. & International Donna Summers, 815/389-3289
Advertising Sales AZ, CO, NM, UT Barbara Tanner, 801/942-6080

Operations
VP, Group Publisher Dave O'Neil
Circulation Marketing Director Kristy LoRusso
Promotions Director Dana Smith
Finance Director Brad Bushlack
Director, Sales and Marketing Tara Green
Senior Production Director Terry Boyer
Production Manager Gary Whitehead

Subscriptions/address change/product customer service
Subscriptions and customer service PO Box 420235, Palm Coast, FL 32142
Phone 800/727-2387
E-mail papercrafts@palmcoastd.com
Back issues and special issues www.PaperCraftsMag.com or 800/727-2387

Offices
Editorial Paper Crafts Magazine, 14850 Pony Express Road, Bluffdale, UT 84065-4801
Phone 801/984-2070
Fax 801/984-2080
E-mail editor@PaperCraftsMag.com
Web site www.PaperCraftsMag.com

TRADEMARKED NAMES mentioned in this book may not always be followed with a trademark symbol. The names are used only in an editorial fashion and to the benefit of the trademark owner, with no intention of infringement of the trademark.

PRIVACY—Occasionally, our subscriber list is made available to reputable firms offering goods and services that we believe would be of interest to our readers. If you prefer to be excluded, please send your current address label and note requesting to be excluded from these promotions to PRIMEDIA, Inc., 745 Fifth Avenue, New York, NY 10151 Attn.: Privacy Coordinator.

PRIMEDIA

The Ultimate Paper Crafts Collection
Softcover ISBN 1-57486-573-0
Library of Congress Control Number 2005932069
Printed in the United States of America.

Published by Leisure Arts, Inc., 5701 Ranch Drive, Little Rock, Arkansas 72223-9633. 501-868-8800. www.leisurearts.com.

Leisure Arts Editorial
Vice President and Editor-in-Chief Sandra Graham Case; Executive Director of Publications Cheryl Nodine Gunnells; Senior Publications Director Susan White Sullivan; Special Projects Director Susan Frantz Wiles; Graphic Design Supervisor Amy Vaughn; Graphic Artist Katherine Atchison; Director of Retail Marketing Stephen Wilson; Director of Designer Relations Debra Nettles; Senior Art Operations Director Jeff Curtis; Art Imaging Director Mark Hawkins; Publishing Systems Administrator Becky Riddle; Publishing Systems Assistants Clint Hanson, Josh Hyatt and John Rose

Leisure Arts Operations
Chief Operating Officer Tom Siebenmorgen; Director of Corporate Planning and Development Laticia Mull Dittrich; Vice President, Sales and Marketing Pam Stebbins; Director of Sales and Services Margaret Reinold; Vice President, Operations Jim Dittrich; Comptroller, Operations Rob Thieme; Retail Customer Service Manager Stan Raynor; Print Production Manager Fred F. Pruss

Creative excuses needed

I loved art when I was in grade school. I'd pull out my favorite crayon colors and create what I thought was the most beautiful picture. I was sure everyone else could see the beauty too, especially when it was hung in the place of honor, the kitchen refrigerator. Even today, I love to

make things and share them. The joy I see on the recipient's face is worth every minute I spent designing and creating. Luckily there are many occasions for sharing with those I love—birthdays, weddings, new babies, graduations, and more.

This book compiles favorite projects for every occasion from past Paper Crafts magazines. It includes cards, bags, tags, home décor, and more. You'll never need an excuse to be creative as long as this book is handy!

So, the next time you need a creative outlet, find an idea and get to work. Have fun paper crafting!

StacyC

Note: Because these projects are from past issues, some products may not be available. Luckily, the Internet provides a wonderful way to search for similar items so you can still create a beautiful project using these inspiring techniques. So, if you can't find a product, use your creativity to adapt the project or find a replacement.

CONTENTS

PAPER CRAFTS

16

107

127

60

27

74

148

272

200

238

216

222

226

246

197

Birth

day Wishes

Make them come true with a special gift. And add extra love with a handmade card and gift tag.

Happy Birthday Card and Tag

Designer: Alison Beachem

SUPPLIES

FOR CARD:

White cardstock

Light green textured cardstock: *K I Memories*

Wish charm: *Once Upon a Charm*

Dimensional adhesive: Diamond Glaze, *Judi-Kins*

Other: slide mount, craft knife, hole punch, colored string

FOR TAG:

Mauve tag: *K I Memories*

Metal-rimmed tags: *Avery*

Other: polka dot tulle ribbon, satin ribbon, watch crystals, mini glass balls

FOR BOTH:

Blue patterned paper: *K I Memories*

Birthday punch-outs: *K I Memories*

Eyelets: *American Tag and Label Inc.*

Finished sizes:
  card 6½" x 5"
  tag 2¼" x 5"

MAKE CARD

❶ Make card base from white cardstock. Cover with blue patterned paper.

❷ Cut frame from birthday punch-out. Glue to slide mount.

❸ Cut out candle image and glue behind slide mount window.

❹ Apply thick layer of dimensional adhesive to window to make plastic pane. Let dry at least one hour. *Note: To test whether the adhesive is dry, feel the back of the glued area. If it feels cool and damp, it needs to dry longer. Do not touch the top or your fingerprints will show.*

❺ Punch hole and set eyelet.

❻ Thread string through eyelet and charm. Tie a bow.

❼ Matte slide mount on green cardstock. Glue to card front.

MAKE TAG

❶ Cut and tear patterned paper. Glue to bottom of tag.

❷ Cut circles from punch-outs around "happy" and "birthday". Glue to metal-rimmed tags.

❸ Place tiny glass marbles in the watch crystals. Glue metal-rimmed tags to backs.

❹ Glue watch crystals to paper tag.

❺ Tie bow at bottom. Loop ribbon through eyelet.

Frame

Slide mount

Punch-out

Green cardstock

Tag

Punch-out

Watch crystal & glass marbles

Raspberry Birthday

Designer: Jana Millen

SUPPLIES

Cardstock: black, light green textured, pink, white, *Bazzill Basics Paper*

Rubber stamps:
  Berries, *Art Impressions*

  "happy birthday", *Impress Rubber Stamps*

Pigment ink: crimson, green; Anna Griffin, *All Night Media*

Dye ink: Black, *Stewart Superior*

Pink gingham ribbon: *Offray*

Light green brads: *Lasting Impressions for Paper*

Mini adhesive dots: *Glue Dots International*

Finished size 5½" x 4"

INSTRUCTIONS

❶ Make card base with white cardstock.

❷ Cut light green textured and pink cardstocks to fit card front. Overlap the two pieces and adhere. Add brads to bottom corners. Tie ribbon around piece where colors meet and secure with adhesive dots. Adhere piece to card base.

❸ Stamp "happy birthday" below ribbon with black ink.

❹ Stamp raspberries on white cardstock, using green and crimson ink. Trim and double-mat with pink and black cardstock. Adhere to card.

Simple Sentiments

Clever birthday quips for your card:

Birthdays are good for you.
Statistics show that the people who
have the most
live the longest.

—Larry Lorenzoni

Birthdays are nature's
way of telling us
to eat more cake.

Set in CK Primary

Birthday Rules:
Stay Cute. Wish Big.
Never Let Anybody Count
Your Candles!

A birthday is just the first day of
another 365-day journey around
the sun. Enjoy the trip.

Heavenly Hydrangeas

Designer: Nichole Heady

SUPPLIES

FOR CARD:

Naturals Ivory cardstock: *Stampin' Up!*
Brown chalk: *Craf-T Products*
Other: brown ink, black pen

FOR BOX:

Script stamp: *Stampin' Up!*
Shrinkable plastic: Shrink It!, *Duncan*
Other: green ink, hole punch, pink string

FOR BOTH:

Mellow Moss cardstock: *Stampin' Up!*
Hydrangea stamp: *Stampin' Up!*
Stickers: Nostalgiques, *Sticko*
Other: watercolor pencils, blender pen

Finished sizes:
   card 5½" x 4¼"
   box 3" x 3" x 1½"

CARD

1 Make Mellow Moss card base.

2 Stamp hydrangea on Naturals Ivory cardstock and color with pencils. Blend with blender pen.

3 Tear out and crumple. Chalk edges. Adhere to card.

4 Spell "HAPPY" with stickers and write "birthday" across bottom of card.

BOX

1 Make box and lid with Mellow Moss cardstock, using pattern. Stamp script background.

2 Stamp hydrangea on shrinkable plastic. Color and blend; cut out. Punch holes in sides. Shrink according to manufacturer's instructions. Tie to box; add stickers.

enlarge 200%

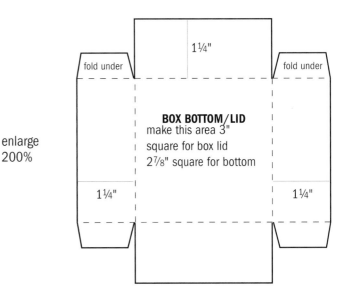

fold under

1¼"

BOX BOTTOM/LID
make this area 3"
square for box lid
2⅞" square for bottom

fold under

1¼"

1¼"

1¼"

Whimsical Gift

Designer: Julie Hillier

SUPPLIES

Rubber stamps: Anita's Art Stamps, Sugarloaf Products (Gift); Anna Griffin, All Night Media, *Plaid* (A Very Happy Birthday sentiment)

Pigment ink: black, VersaColor, *Tsukineko*

Embossing powder: clear, *Magenta Rubber Stamps*

Patterned paper: *Creative Imaginations* (Karen Foster Design, red; Debbie Mumm, Cracked Wood)

Other: cardstock (white, tan), pewter brads, scissors, adhesive, embossing heat tool

Finished size: 4¼" x 5½"

INSTRUCTIONS

❶ Make white card.

❷ Cut rectangles from Red and Cracked Wood paper. Adhere to tan cardstock; trim to fit card front.

❸ Stamp Gift and sentiment with black on Cracked Wood; emboss.

❹ Secure brads to corners of patterned paper.

❺ Adhere tan cardstock to card front.

Bright & Cheery Birthday

Designer: Leslie Elvert

SUPPLIES

Rubber stamps: *Hero Arts* (Square shadow); Special Occasion Super Set, *Close To My Heart* (Happy Birthday sentiment)

Dye ink: *Close To My Heart* (Tropical Blue, Star Spangle Blue); *Stampin' Up!* (Basic Black, Green Galore, Yoyo Yellow)

Cardstock: *Stampin' Up!* (Ultrasmooth White, Yoyo Yellow, Green Galore); *Close To My Heart* (Star Spangle Blue)

Eyelets: yellow, *Making Memories*

Other: adhesive, eyelet-setting tools, scissors

Finished size: 5½" x 4¼"

INSTRUCTIONS

❶ Make Green Galore card.

❷ Stamp shadow with Tropical Blue, Green Galore, Star Spangle Blue, Yoyo Yellow, Tropical Blue on Ultrasmooth White cardstock.

❸ Stamp sentiment with Basic Black on yellow square.

❹ Cut rectangle from Star Spangle Blue cardstock; mat with Yoyo Yellow and trim. *Note: Leave excess at bottom of yellow and tear.*

❺ Adhere stamped strip to cardstock rectangles; set eyelets above stamped strip. Adhere to card front.

Happy, Happy

Designer: Livia Mcree

SUPPLIES

Rubber stamps: Happy Dreams sentiment, *Double D Rubber Stamps*

Dye ink: Luau, Kaleidacolor, *Tsukineko*

Flower accents: Jolee's by You, *EK Success*

Other: cardstock (cream, yellow, orange), white card, adhesive, scissors

Finished size: 5" x 7"

INSTRUCTIONS

❶ Stamp Happy Dreams sentiment with Luau on cream cardstock. Cut words apart, angling edges.

❷ Cut candle from cream cardstock, flame from orange. Cut three graduated rectangles, angling ends, for cake.

❸ Adhere cake, candle, and sentiment to card front. Embellish cake with flower accents.

Bonus Idea

Make a matching envelope! Use extra embellishments for the front or back flap of your envelope. Make sure to leave plenty of space for the mailing and return addresses.

Celebrate

Designer: Erin Tenney

SUPPLIES

Rubber stamps: House-Mouse Designs, Stampabilities (birthday mouse); *PSX* (Love Letters alphabet)

Dye ink: Coal Black, Ancient Page, *Clearsnap*

Cardstock: *Bazzill Basics Paper* (yellow, light blue)

Other: orange fibers, watercolor pencils, adhesive, blender pen, glue

Finished size: 5½" x 4¼"

INSTRUCTIONS

❶ Make yellow card.

❷ Stamp birthday mouse with Coal Black on light blue cardstock.

❸ Color image with watercolor pencils; blend with blender pen. Cut image to fit front of card; adhere.

❺ Stamp "celebrate" with Coal Black.

❻ Adhere fibers to edge of stamped image.

Celebrate with You

Designer: Nichole Heady

SUPPLIES

Rubber stamps: (Mostly Flowers set, Flexible Phrases set) *Stampin' Up!*

Watermark ink: (White) VersaMark, *Tsukineko*

Embossing powder: (White) Stampin' Up!

Cardstock: (white)

Paper: (ribbed yellow) *Robin's Nest*

Craft foam: 2 mm white adhesive-backed

Adhesive: glue stick

Tools: scissors, heat tool

Finished size: 4¼" x 5¼"

INSTRUCTIONS

❶ Make card from white cardstock.

❷ Heat foam until pliable. Immediately press Mostly Flowers stamp into foam. Hold until foam is cool. Remove stamp; trim.

❸ Trim and adhere ribbed yellow paper to card front.

❹ Stamp celebrate; emboss.

❺ Adhere foam block to card.

Vintage Birthday

Designer: Stacy McFadden

SUPPLIES

Rubber stamps: *Hero Arts* (Printer's Type alphabet, Small Blocks alphabet)

Patterned papers: Vintage Floral, \Scrappy Chic, *me & my BIG Ideas* (stripe, vintage floral, gray diamond)

Gold metal frame: *7gypsies*

Other: black ink, brown cardstock, white thread, scissors, adhesive, sewing machine

Finished size: 6" x 4"

INSTRUCTIONS

❶ Make brown card.

❷ Cut patterned paper rectangles to fit card front. Overlap stripe with vintage Floral; adhere.

❸ Straight stitch around edge of vintage floral.

❹ Stamp "HAPPY BIRTH-DAY" above striped paper on card and "TO YOU" on gray diamond paper.

❺ Trim "TO YOU" to size of frame; adhere to card.

Butterfly Birthday

Designer: Lori Bergmann

SUPPLIES

Rubber stamps: (Butterfly Birthday) All Night Media, *Plaid*; (butterfly) Hampton Art

Solvent ink: (Royal Purple) StazOn, *Tsukineko*

Specialty ink: (Clear Resist) *Ranger Industries*

Dye ink: (Butterscotch, Eggplant, Lettuce, Stonewashed) Adirondack, *Ranger Industries*

Cardstock: (white, dark purple)

Glossy paper: (White) *Ranger Industries*

Accent: (purple 22-gauge wire) *Artistic Wire*

Adhesive: (pop-up dots) *Glue Dots International*; glue stick

Tools: (round-nose pliers) *NSI Innovations*; heat tool, ruler, scissors

Other: non-alcohol baby wipes, sponge

Finished size: 7¼" x 4¼"

INSTRUCTIONS

❶ Make card from white cardstock.

❷ Randomly stamp largest butterfly image onto 3¾" x 7¼" piece of white glossy with Clear Resist. Heat set.

❸ Starting with lightest color first, sponge ink randomly over stamped glossy paper. Repeat with remaining colors until entire surface is colored. Use baby wipe to gently blend together.

❹ Stamp sentiment on colored paper with Royal Purple.

❺ Stamp smaller butterfly onto scrap of glossy paper that has been colored as above. Cut out. Add antennae by wrapping wire around body. Curl ends.

❻ Adhere butterfly to colored background with pop-up dots.

❼ Mat colored background with dark purple. Adhere to card.

Funky Birthday

Designer: Julie Medeiros

SUPPLIES

Rubber stamps: (cake, party hat, present from Let's Party set) *Stampin' Up!*; (Alphabet Blocks) Hero Arts

Dye ink: (Blue) Hero Arts

Cardstock: (light green, olive green, sky blue, deep red)

Adhesive: glue stick

Tools: scissors, ruler

Finished size: 6¼" x 4¼"

INSTRUCTIONS

❶ Make card from olive green cardstock.

❷ Stamp birthday images on light green cardstock; trim stamped images into varying squares.

❸ Mat images with sky blue; cut varying angles.

❹ Stamp "HAPPY BIRTHDAY" on sky blue; trim to size. Mat with red.

❺ Cut ¼" strip of red cardstock; adhere to card.

❻ Adhere birthday images to strip. Adhere sentiment to card.

Wild and Crazy Friend

Designer: Leslie Elvert

SUPPLIES.

Rubber stamps: (At the Zoo) *Close To My Heart*; (Circle Pop Alphabet, Printers Type Alphabet) *Hero Arts*; (Buttons Alphabet) PSX, *Duncan*; (Classic Alphabet) *Stampin' Up!*

Dye ink: (More Mustard, Really Rust) *Stampin' Up!*; (Indian Corn Blue) *Close To My Heart*

Cardstock: (Ultrasmooth Vanilla) *Stampin' Up!*

Patterned paper: (Sunroom) Scrapbook Walls, *Chatterbox*

Gatefold card: (Buttercup Polka Dot) *Making Memories*

Adhesive: glue stick

Tools: scissors, paper trimmer, small circle punch, ruler

Other: sponge

Finished size: 5½" square

INSTRUCTIONS

❶ Stamp animals on 5" strip of Ultrasmooth Vanilla with all ink colors. Trim to size.

❷ Cut 2" x 5" strip of Sunroom; adhere to card. Adhere animals to strip.

❸ Stamp sentiment with various alphabets on Ultrasmooth Vanilla with Really Rust and More Mustard. Trim and ink. Adhere to card.

❹ Ink edges of card with Really Rust.

❺ Sponge circle closures with Really Rust.

Party Hat

Designer: Kathleen Paneitz

SUPPLIES

Rubber stamps: (hat from Party Hats set) *Hero Arts*

Dye ink: (Black) *PrintWorks*

Pigment ink: (Orchid) VersaColor, *Tsukineko*

Cardstock: (White) *Bazzill Basics Paper*

Textured cardstock: (Limeade) *Bazzill Basics Paper*

Patterned paper: (Raspberry Bangles) Lava Lamp, Collection III, (Summer Simple Stripe) Summer Collection IV, *KI Memories*

Color media: (yellow, pink pens) ZIG Writer, *EK Success*; (green chalk) *Craf-T Products*

Paper accents: (pink daisy) Blossoms, *Making Memories*; (mini envelope) *Impress Rubber Stamps*

Accents: (pink bookplate) Art Warehouse, *Creative Imaginations*; (pink staples) *Making Memories*

Rub-ons: (Happy Day, My Friend) Sticky Little Words, *All My Memories*

Fasteners: (pewter decorative brad) *Making Memories*; (pink mini brads) *Magic Scraps*; (pink eyelet) *Impress Rubber Stamps*

Fiber: (pink gingham ribbon) *Offray*; (orange rickrack)

Adhesive: glue stick, low-tack tape

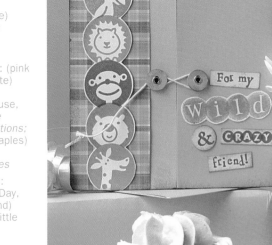

Tools: scissors, stapler, eyelet-setting tools, chalk applicator

Finished size: 4¼" x 5¼"

BACKGROUND

❶ Make card from White cardstock.

❷ Adhere Raspberry Bangles to top half. Adhere Summer Simple Stripe to bottom half. Cover center seam with orange rickrack. Secure with pink staples.

❸ Insert brad through daisy; secure to card.

❹ Stamp party hat on envelope with Black. *Note: Mask off party hats to isolate one image.*

❺ Color party hat with pens and chalk.

❻ Ink edges of rub-ons with Orchid. Adhere "happy day" to mini envelope.

EMBELLISH

❶ Make mini tag from Limeade cardstock.

❷ Cut small strip of Summer Simple Stripe; adhere to tag.

❸ Attach pink eyelet and ribbon.

❹ Insert tag into envelope.

❺ Apply "my friend" rub-on to white cardstock; trim and adhere to card. Adhere bookplate over sentiment. Secure with brads.

Ladybug Birthday

Designer: Alison Beachem

SUPPLIES

Cardstock: white, orange

Pink textured cardstock: *Bazzill Basics Paper*

Alphabet and ladybug stickers: *Paper Fever*

Ribbon: *Offray*

Finished size 4½" x 3"

INSTRUCTIONS

❶ Make orange card base.

❷ Cut 3" square from white cardstock. Mat with pink.

❸ Adhere matted piece to card.

❹ Add ladybug sticker. Spell "HAPPY BIRTHDAY" with alphabet stickers.

❺ Near bottom, cut small slit in card fold; thread ribbon through; tie.

Butterfly Dreams

Designer: Gretchen Schmidt

SUPPLIES

White cardstock: *Making Memories*

Pink vellum: *DMD Industries*

Butterfly stamp: *Embossing Arts*

Metal frame: *Making Memories*

Paint pens: Pink, Yellow, White; Zig Posterman, *EK Success*

Dimensional adhesive: Diamond Glaze, *Judi-Kins*

Font: MaszynaAEG, *www.scrapvillage.com*

Square punch: *Marvy Uchida*

Black ink: *Tsukineko*

Black embossing powder: *Ranger Industries*

Chalk: *Craf-T Products*

Ribbon: *Offray*

Adhesive dots: *Glue Dots International*

Other: paintbrush, embossing heat tool, craft knife

Finished size 5½" x 4¼"

INSTRUCTIONS

❶ Print "Happy Birthday" on cardstock. Make card base. Punch window.

❷ Stamp and emboss butterfly on vellum; color with chalk. Glue behind window.

❸ Paint spots of color on frame; blend with brush. Glaze with dimensional adhesive.

❹ Near bottom, cut small slit in card fold; thread ribbon through; tie bow. Adhere frame around card window with adhesive dots.

Happy Birthday to You!

Designer: Melissa Deakin

SUPPLIES

ALL CARDS:

Rubber stamp: (Polka Dot Cake) *Savvy Stamps*

Textured cardstock: (white)

Fasteners: (silver brads) Mini Brads, *Making Memories*

Font: (2Ps Typo) *www.twopeasinabucket.com*

Adhesive

Tools: computer and printer, scissors, hole punch

ORANGE CARD:

Pigment ink: (Pearlescent Orange) Brilliance, *Tsukineko*

Textured cardstock: (Apricot) *Bazzill Basics Paper*

Cardstock: (Super Hero Original Stripes) *Scrapworks*

Fibers: (orange gingham ribbon) *Offray*

PINK CARD:

Pigment ink: (Pink) ColorBox, *Clearsnap*

Textured cardstock: (Romance) *Bazzill Basics Paper*

Cardstock: (Hot Girl Squiggle Worm) *Scrapworks*

Fibers: (pink satin ribbon) *Offray*

BLUE CARD:

Pigment ink: (Sky Blue) ColorBox, *Clearsnap*

Cardstock: (Cool Boy Solid, Cool Boy Squiggle Worm) *Scrapworks*

Fibers: (blue dot ribbon) *May Arts*

Finished sizes: 5" square

INSTRUCTIONS

❶ Cut 5" square of solid colored cardstock for card base.

❷ Print sentiment on patterned cardstock; trim.

❸ Adhere patterned cardstock to base; secure with brads.

❹ Make mini card from white cardstock.

❺ Stamp cake on mini card.

❻ Punch hole, thread ribbon through hole, and tie bow.

❼ Adhere mini card to base.

Pretty In Plaid

Designer: Erin Tenney

SUPPLIES

Textured cardstock: Olive, Gold, *Bazzill Basics Paper*

Ribbon: *Offray*

Pen: Zig Millenium, *EK Success*

Chalk: *Craf-T Products*

Other: hole punch, tag template, jumbo eyelet, vellum metal-edged tag, string

Finished sizes:
  card 5½" x 4"
  tag 4¼" x 2½"

CARD

❶ Make olive card base. Chalk edges.

❷ Cut 2" x 3" piece of Olive cardstock. Chalk edges; tie ribbon. Mat with Gold cardstock. Chalk edges and adhere to card.

❸ Write "celebrate" on a ¾" x 2¼" piece of Gold cardstock. Chalk edges. Adhere to card.

TAG

❶ Make card from olive cardstock, using template. Chalk edges.

❷ Mat tag on Gold cardstock. Chalk edges.

❸ Write "happy birthday" on a ¾" x 3¼" strip of Gold cardstock. Chalk edges.

❹ Set eyelet, catching in one end of "happy birthday" strip.

❺ Cut two ⅜" squares of Gold cardstock. Chalk edges and adhere to tag. Write "to:" and "from:" on squares. Add names.

❻ Write message on vellum tag. Punch hole and add string.

❼ Tie ribbon through eyelet. Tie string to ribbon.

Rub-ons:
   (Happy birthday from Kids Transfers) Studio K,
   K&Company
   (letters from Journey) Simply Stated Mini, *Making Memories*
   (Black Date/Numbers) *Autumn Leaves*
Stickers: (Birthday, With Love Word Circles Embossed, Round Tags Alphabet Embossed) Studio K, *K&Company*
Fasteners: (silver eyelets)
Fibers: (waxed linen twine, white thread)
Adhesive: (dimensional glaze) Glossy Accents, *Ranger Industries*
Tools: ruler, scissors, sewing machine, eyelet-setting tools, needlenose pliers

Finished size: 3¾" x 9¼"

CARD & ENVELOPE

❶ Adhere piece of Stitched Squares paper inside card. To make pocket, trim acetate sheet slightly larger than paper piece and stitch in place along sides and bottom. Trim edges of acetate. Apply Happy birthday rub-on.

❷ Trim Polka Dots paper slightly smaller than card; cut into two pieces to fit card flaps and adhere.

❸ Mat word circles with blue from Stitched Squares. Apply "16" rub-ons to birthday circle. Attach circles to card flaps with eyelets, Set eyelets loosely to allow room for wrapping twine.

❹ Tie twine around top circle and wrap around both circles to close card. Spell "On your" above top circle with letters trimmed from Journey rub-on.

❺ To line envelope, trim Diagonal Striped paper slightly smaller than inside, place in envelope, and adhere to inside of top flap only.

KEY CHAIN

❶ Adhere alphabet sticker behind metal frame and trim. Adhere Diagonal Striped paper behind sticker.

❷ Apply dimensional glaze inside frame; let dry. Remove chain from key ring; attach ring to frame with jump rings.

❸ Place key ring in card pocket.

On Your 16th Birthday

Designer: Alice Golden

SUPPLIES

Patterned paper: (Diagonal Striped, Small Orange Polka Dots, Stitched Squares) Studio K, *K&Company*

Card and envelope: (Olive Green Gatefold) *DieCuts with a View*

Transparency sheet or page protector

Key ring: (Key Chain) *Hirschberg Schutz & Co.*

Accents:
   (yellow metal Colored Frame charm) Studio K, *K&Company*
   (silver jump rings)

Happy Birthday Gift Pocket

designer: Susan Neal

SUPPLIES

Rubber stamps: *JudiKins* (Jeans, Jean Pocket); *Hero Arts* (Little Happy Birthday)

Dye ink: Midnight Blue, Memories, *Stewart Superior Corp.*

Cardstock: *Bazzill Basics Paper* (Coral, Kraft)

Punch: Shipping Tag, *Quickutz*

Snaps: Antique Brass, *The Stamp Doctor*

Other: jute, adhesive foam squares, scissors, adhesive, eyelet-setting tools, money or gift card

Finished size: 4½" x 5½"

PREPARE & STAMP

1 Make Coral card.

2 Stamp Jeans on card.

3 Stamp pocket on Coral; cut out.

4 Punch out tag from Coral and circle from Kraft. Adhere Kraft circle to Coral tag hole.

5 Stamp sentiment on tag.

ASSEMBLE

1 Attach jute to tag.

2 Adhere tag to pocket; adhere ends of jute behind pocket.

3 Attach snaps to top corners of pocket; attach pocket to card with foam squares.

4 Insert money or gift card in pocket.

Happy 18th

Designer: Gretchen Schmidt

SUPPLIES

Rubber stamps: (Officially Independent) Art Warehouse, *Limited Edition Rubberstamps*; (18) Hartin II, *Ma Vinci's Reliquary*; (Happy Birthday To You) *Hero Arts*

Dye ink: (Crimson) Memories, *Stewart Superior Corp.*; (Black) Stampabilities

Cardstock: (Black) *Making Memories*; (Maroon, Grey) *SEI*

Adhesive: glue stick

Tools: scissors

Finished size: 5½" x 4½"

INSTRUCTIONS

1 Make card from Black cardstock.

2 Randomly stamp Officially Independent with Crimson on Maroon cardstock.

3 Stamp 18 with Black on Maroon. Adhere to card.

4 Stamp "Happy Birthday To You" with Black on Grey cardstock. Trim and adhere to card.

Photo Tri-fold

Designer: Nichol Magouirk

SUPPLIES

Cardstock: blue, gold, green

12" x 12" striped cardstock: *SEI*

"happy birthday to you!" stamp: *Savvy Stamps*

Mini buttons: *Karen Foster Design*

Star buttons: *Hillcreek Designs*

Printed accent squares: cupcake, hat, "Make a wish", *Pebbles in My Pocket*

Other: photo, black ink, sewing machine, white thread

Finished size
    5½" x 12" open
    5½" x 4" closed

INSTRUCTIONS

❶ Cut, score, and fold card base.

❷ Cut three 3¼" squares of colored cardstock.

❸ Adhere photo and accents, then zigzag-stitch borders.

❹ Adhere buttons to card.

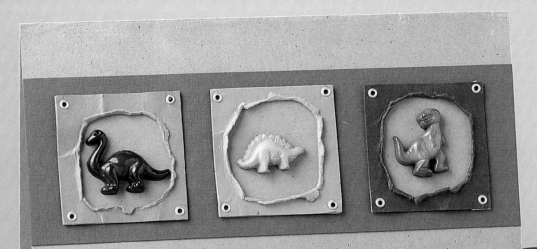

Dino-Mite Kid

Designer: Sheila Toppi

SUPPLIES

Cardstock: olive, brown, mustard, gray, dark gray

Dinosaur buttons: *Dress It Up*

Font: Scrap Sweetness, Scrap Sloppy, *www.twopeasinabucket.com*

1¼" Square punch: *Marvy Uchida*

Other: silver eyelets, ⅛" paper punch or piercing tool, pliers

Finished size 5½" x 7"

INSTRUCTIONS

❶ Make gray card base.

❷ Print "happy birthday To A Dino-Mite Kid!" on front. Adhere 2½" x 7" dark gray strip.

❸ Punch squares from cardstock. Cut centers and tear openings. (see figures a and b).

❹ Curl torn edges between fingers (see figure c).

❺ Back squares with light gray. Set eyelets.

❻ Cut shanks from buttons with pliers and adhere.

❼ Adhere squares to card.

DESIGNER TIP

In areas where a punch won't reach, use a paper piercer to make holes for small eyelets and brads.

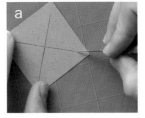

Cut

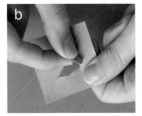

Tear

Roll

Ladybug Birthday Invitation

designer: Jennifer Mayer Fish

SUPPLIES

Foam stamps: ladybug, leaf

Acrylic paint: Celery Green, Country Red, Lamp (Ebony) Black, Leaf Green

Antiquing medium

Paintbrushes: 1" sponge, ¼" flat

8½" x 11" cardstock:
    Red
    White

4¼" x 5½" kraft note card

Ladybug button

Miscellaneous items: clear craft glue, double-sided tape, black fine-tip marker, palette or paper plate, wire cutters, computer with printer (optional)

INSTRUCTIONS

STAMP THE IMAGES

❶ Mix two parts Celery Green with one part antiquing medium. Repeat this with Leaf Green. *Note: This will extend the drying time of your paint and give your design a soft, translucent look.*

❷ Apply a small amount of the Celery Green mix to the top half of the leaf stamp with the sponge brush. Apply the Leaf Green mix to the other half of the leaf stamp, blending the two colors slightly.

❸ Stamp the image on white cardstock, lifting the stamp straight up after pressing. Let the leaf dry completely.

❹ Apply Country Red to the ladybug bodies with the sponge brush and Lamp Black to the heads with the flat brush.

❺ Stamp the ladybugs over the leaf design and let them dry completely.

❻ Remove the shank from the ladybug button with wire cutters and attach it to the top of the leaf with craft glue.

ASSEMBLE THE INVITATION

❶ Trim the stamped cardstock and then mat it with red.

❷ Trim the note card slightly and adhere it to a slightly larger piece of white cardstock. Adhere the stamped piece to the front of the note card.

❸ Write or print, "It's a Birthday Party!" on the front of the card and "Fly on Over!" on the inside.

❹ Write or print the party details on white cardstock, trim around them, and adhere them inside the card.

BONUS IDEAS

▪ Use the same stamping technique to cover a kraft gift box or bag.

▪ Fill cellophane bags with candy and attach a stamped card to the top for fun party favors.

Designer Candi Gershon used the following verse for her invitation. Substitute your child's name and age, and change the wording to rhyme with your child's age, if necessary. Below the verse, print the party date, time, address, and RSVP phone number.

Gracie is having a princess party.

She is turning four!

Please wear your favorite princess

dress and this

pretty necklace to our door!

A TIP FROM CANDI

The ink on the shrink film may not appear evenly distributed after printing. Once the film has been baked, however, the color will even out.

Bonus Ideas

■ Make a football invitation for a boy's party, or adapt the design to any party theme your child would like.

■ Make a charm for another theme—an umbrella for a baby shower, a diamond ring for an engagement party, a house for a "we've moved" announcement, or a bandage for a get well card.

Princess Party Invitation

Designer: Candi Gershon

SUPPLIES

All supplies from Chatterbox unless otherwise noted.

Light pink cardstock

Pink striped paper

Pink floral patterned vellum

Pink rivets

Pink flower fasteners

Inkjet shrink film: *Grafix*

Pink satin ribbon: *Offray*

Silver split rings: *Making Memories*

Fonts:

   2Ps Miss Priss, D W Dingbats (flower), *www.twopeasinabucket.com*

   CK Handprint, "Creative Clips & Fonts by Becky Higgins" CD, *Creating Keepsakes*

Other: ⅛" hole punch, inkjet color printer, conventional oven, baking sheet

Finished size 7½" x 5"

CHARM

❶ Print flower on ink jet shrink film. Note: Size the flower 50% larger than you would like the charm to be.

❷ Cut out flower. Punch 1–2 holes for split ring(s).

❸ Bake, following manufacturer's instructions.

INVITATION

Invitation does not open.

❶ To make invitation base, cover a 7½" x 5" piece of cardstock with striped paper.

❷ Print text on cardstock (see "Invitation Text"). Mat with floral vellum. Attach to invitation with fasteners at top corners and rivets at bottom corners.

❸ Attach charm to a necklace-length ribbon with split ring(s). Thread ribbon through rivets and tie ends in back.

Beach Party

Designer: Marla Bird

SUPPLIES

FOR INVITATION:

Vellum

Seed beads: *Magic Scraps*

Font: CK Elegant, "Fresh Fonts"
CD, Creating Keepsakes

Other: glass vial with stopper,
sand, hole punch, string

FOR PLACE CARD:

Cardstock: brown, black,
Pebbles in My Pocket

Fonts: CK Elusive, CK
Stenography, CK Newsprint, CK
Chemistry, "Fresh Fonts" CD,
Creating Keepsakes

Other: tape, netting

FOR BOX:

Brown cardstock

Clear acetate sheet (transparency
film): *3M*

Fonts: CK Elusive, CK
Stenography, CK Newsprint, CK
Chemistry; "Fresh Fonts" CD,
Creating Keepsakes

Dimensional adhesive: Diamond
Glaze, *Judi-Kins*

Other: gable box, cream tulle
ribbon, hole punch, brads, sand,
netting

FOR NAPKIN RING:

Beads: *Magic Scraps*

Other: wire, small shells

FOR ALL:

Acrylic beach accents: *Dress It Up*

Finished sizes:
    invitation in vial approx. 3" long
    place card 2" x 3½"
    box 5" x 4" x 2"
    napkin ring approx. 1½" in
    diameter

INVITATION

❶ Print invitation on vellum. Punch hole
in corner. Tie to sand dollar.

❷ Place sand and beads in bottle. Roll
up invitation and place inside. Adhere
sand dollar to bottle.

PLACE CARD

❶ Print name on brown cardstock; trim
to 2" x 3½" and mat on black.

❷ Cut a 1½" x 6" black strip and fold
into triangle; tape ends together (see
Figure a). Adhere to back of card (see
Figure b). Adhere netting and sand dollar
to front.

BOX

❶ Fold box; adhere netting.

❷ Print name on transparency and cut
to 1" x 3¼". Cut a matching strip from
brown cardstock. Stack pieces and
punch holes in top corners.

❸ Cover brown strip with adhesive;
sprinkle with sand. Shake off excess;
dry.

❹ Stack pieces and insert brads. Adhere
piece and shells to box.

❺ Place gift in box and tie ribbon around
handle.

NAPKIN RING

❶ String shells on a 4½" piece of wire.
Add seed beads at ends. Form ends of
wire into small loops.

❷ Twist wire together to make ring (see
photo). Adhere starfish.

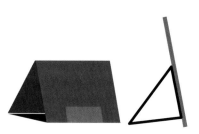

a Make base   b Adhere card

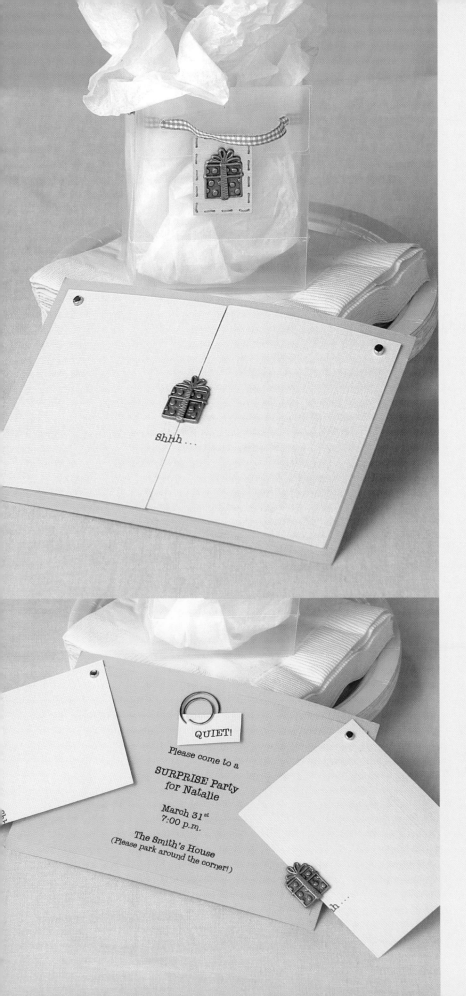

B'rthday Wishes

Surprise!

Designer: Marla Bird

SUPPLIES

Textured cardstock: orange, peach, *Bazzill Basics Paper*

Brads, spiral clip, metal plaque, charms: *Making Memories*

Font: CK Stenographer, "Fresh Fonts" CD, *Creating Keepsakes*

Other: gingham ribbon, floss, gift bag, foam adhesive squares, hole punch, embroidery needle

Finished sizes:
   card 4½" x 6½"
   bag 3½" x 3"

MAKE CARD

❶ Print invitation on orange cardstock and cut 4" x 6" rectangle around it. Mat on orange cardstock.

❷ Adhere clip to invitation. Print "QUIET!" on peach cardstock. Cut out and place in clip.

❸ Print "Shhh…" on peach cardstock. Cut 4" x 6" rectangle around it. Cut rectangle in half crosswise to make doors and attach to invitation with brads (see photo).

❹ Glue gift charm to center of card. *Note: Apply glue to one half of charm and glue it to only one door so the card can freely open and close.*

MAKE BAG

❶ Stitch a running stitch through holes in metal plaque.

❷ Glue gift charm to center and adhere to bag.

❸ Punch holes in top and sides of bag and thread ribbon through. Trim ribbon and knot at side, leaving extra ribbon for handles (see photo).

Box of Cards

Designer: Nichol Magouirk

SUPPLIES

Patterned papers: Chic Plaid, Lemonade Mini Bangles, Peachy Blossom, Rhinestone (white dot), Rhinestone Reverse (peach dot), Runway (striped); Beautiful Collection III, *KI Memories*

Box with lid

Alphabet stickers: uppercase, lowercase Bubbletters; Sweet 'N Sour, *KI Memories*

Accents:
   Mini buckle: Icicles; Collection III, *KI Memories*
   Die cut labels: Beautiful Funky Frames & Labels; Collection III, *KI Memories*
   Handle charm: Collage, *Frost Creek Charms*
   Brown/Pink Ribbon: *Impress Rubber Stamps*

Rounded corner punch: *Marvy Uchida*

Decoupage adhesive: Mod Podge, *Plaid*

Other: awl, black permanent marker, adhesive, paintbrush, sewing machine, thread

Finished size 4" x 5½" x 3½"

BOX & LID

1 To cover box with striped paper and lid with peach dot paper, apply decoupage adhesive to box and adhere. Brush adhesive over the paper and let dry. *Note: If needed, trim edges with craft knife when dry.*

2 Center handle charm on box lid, mark, and make two holes with awl. Push charm prongs through holes and bend prongs toward center on inside of lid.

3 Spell "correspondence" with letter stickers on box. Brush decoupage adhesive over letters to secure.

4 Thread ribbon through buckle. Brush light layer of decoupage adhesive on box and quickly wrap ribbon around box. Secure ribbon ends with small amount of adhesive.

DIVIDERS

1 Cut patterned paper pairs to 3½" x 5¼" and adhere wrong sides together.

2 Round corners with punch.

3 Sew die cut labels to divider tops. Write section names for types of cards on tabs with pen, e.g., birthday, congratulations.

CARDS

1 Make greeting cards for each section. Place in box between dividers.

2 Include matching envelopes.

A TIP FROM NICHOL

If the lid sticks a bit after the decoupage adhesive is dry, sand lightly where the lid and box meet to decrease the tackiness.

Pastel Phrases

Designer: Jennifer Miller

SUPPLIES

Cardstock: (White) *Bazzill Basics Paper*

Paper: (Grape, Lemonade, Lipstick, Splash) *KI Memories*

Patterned paper: (Grape Capri Stripe, Grape Lines, Lemonade Capri Stripe, Lipstick Capri Stripe, Splash Capri Stripe, Splash Lines) *KI Memories*

Rubber stamps: (Mostly Flowers, Simple Sayings I and II sets) *Stampin' Up!*

Dye ink: (Lovely Lilac, More Mustard, Pink Passion, Tempting Turquoise) *Stampin' Up!*

Adhesive:
   (pop-up dots) All Night Media, *Plaid*
   (glue stick)

Tools: ruler, scissors

Finished size: 5½" x 4"

INSTRUCTIONS

❶ Make card from cardstock.

❷ Cut 5½" x 3" piece of patterned paper; adhere to card.

❸ Stamp message on coordinating paper with coordinating ink; trim and adhere to bottom of card.

❹ Cut ¼" strip of patterned paper, with stripes running perpendicular to those on card. Adhere where papers meet.

❺ Stamp flower image on coordinating paper; trim and mat with cardstock. Adhere to card with pop-up dots.

Bonus Ideas

■ Place the cards and matching envelopes in a clear stationery box (available from Impress Rubber Stamps) and tie it closed with ribbon and tag.

■ For a nice personal touch, stamp "Handmade by" on the back of each card and sign your name. You can purchase such stamps from Stampin' Up!

Build-a-Card Portfolio

Designer: Alice Golden

SUPPLIES

Cardstock: (Parakeet, White) *Bazzill Basics Paper*

Patterned paper: (Green Curly Qs, Green Paisley, Lime Green Stripe) *Anna Griffin*

Cards: (white) *Halcraft USA*

Envelopes:
(white) *Halcraft USA*
(glassine) *Limited Edition Rubberstamps*

Accents:
(Daisy White flowers) *Making Memories*
(green/yellow bead mix) Art Accentz, *Provo Craft*

Fibers: (cream grosgrain ribbon)

Fonts:
(Beautiful ES) *www.freefonts.fateback.com*
(Bradley Hand ITC) *www.myfonts.com*

Adhesive: (craft glue, double-sided tape, pop-up dot)

Tools:
(Card Portfolio template) PSX, *Duncan*
(Large Birch Leaf punch) *The Punch Bunch*
(ruler, pencil, scissors, craft knife, scoring tool, computer and printer)

Finished sizes:
portfolio 4½" x 6" x ½"
card 5½" x 4"

PORTFOLIO

❶ Cut and score portfolio from Parakeet cardstock, using template. Cut slits in sides with craft knife.

❷ Cut strip of Lime Green Stripe paper and adhere to wider strip of Green Paisley paper. Adhere to portfolio cover.

❸ Adhere beads to center of flower with craft glue; let dry. Punch three leaves from Green Curly Qs paper. Adhere leaves to strip on cover; adhere flower with pop-up dot.

❹ Cut two 12" lengths of ribbon. Thread end of one length through slit in front, and one length in back of portfolio. Adhere flap over ribbon end.

❺ Cut Green Curly Qs to line inside of portfolio; adhere. Assemble portfolio following template instructions.

CARDS

❶ To make card accents, adhere beads to center of flowers. Print sentiments on White cardstock (see "Designer Tips"); trim and mat with Parakeet. Place accents in separate glassine envelopes and tuck inside left portfolio pocket.

❷ Cut patterned paper to fit card front (see photo). Adhere top and bottom paper pieces first. Adhere middle strip where papers meet. *Note: Alternate placement of papers on each card.* Tuck cards in right pocket.

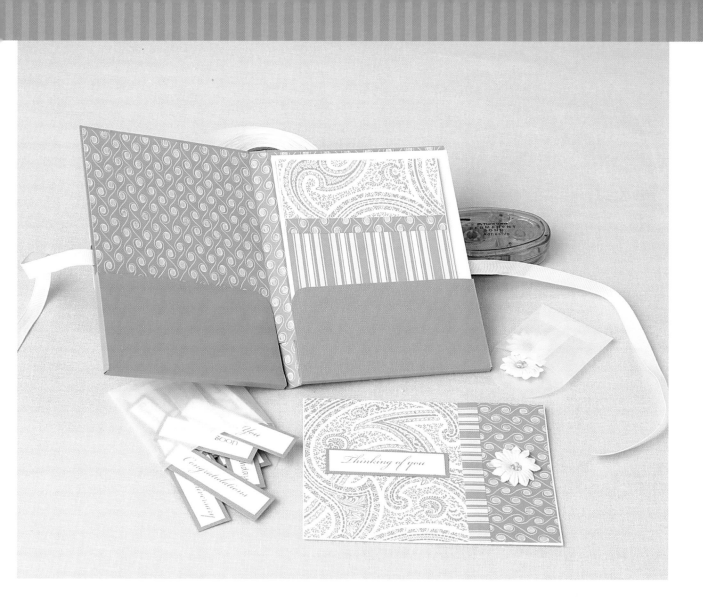

DESIGNER TIPS

■ I used various fonts to convey different emotions with each sentiment. I chose one formal, one handwritten, and one whimsical font.

■ I used a variety of sentiments for different card-giving occasions: Congratulations, Thinking of You, Thank You, Happy Birthday, Get Well Soon, Happy Anniversary, and Hello!

ENVELOPE LINERS

Line the envelopes with patterned paper to match the cards.

❶ Trace an open envelope on patterned paper.

❷ Cut approx. ¼" inside the traced line to create a slightly smaller liner that will easily slide into the envelope. *Note: You may wish to cut liner further inside traced line so it won't cover gummed portion of envelope flap.*

❸ Adhere the top section of the liner (above the fold line) inside the envelope. *Note: Bottom part of envelope liner will stay put without adhesive. Plus, envelope will fold more smoothly without adhesive on fold or bottom portion.*

Bonus Ideas

■ Stamp or use stickers for the sentiments instead of printing them.

■ Tuck the envelopes in one pocket of the portfolio, the cards in the other pocket, and store the accents separately.

■ Make a deeper portfolio to hold more cards. Using the portfolio template as a guide, increase the width of the spine and bottom edges.

■ Use other coordinated paper sets to create card portfolios with different styles.

Hi There

Designer: Carolyn Hurst

SUPPLIES

Rubber stamps: (Cheryl's Postcards, Hi There Large, Ink Bottle, Ink Splash) *Serendipity Stamps*

Dye ink: (Vintage Photo) Distress Ink, *Ranger Industries*

Pigment ink: (Graphite Black) Brilliance, *Tsukineko*

Textured cardstock: (dark green, light green)

Patterned paper: (Nature Trails) *Autumn Leaves*; (Stamp Collage Paper) *K&Company*

Transparency sheet

Chipboard

Adhesive: foam tape, glue stick

Tools: (Slide Mount #1 die, die-cut machine) AccuCut Systems; (craft brush) Color Duster, JudiKins; (Swirl Corner punch) *Posh Impressions*; scissors, ruler

Other: scrap paper

Finished size: 4¼" x 5½"

SLIDE MOUNT

❶ Adhere Nature Trails paper to piece of chipboard and die-cut slide mount.

❷ Lightly brush slide mount with Vintage Photo ink (see "Designer Tips"). Stamp Cheryl's Postcards with Graphite Black.

❸ Adhere transparency sheet behind slide mount. Cut stamp from Stamp Collage Paper and adhere behind transparency.

CARD

❶ Make card from light green cardstock.

❷ Cut 3½" x 4¾" piece of Nature Trails paper. Brush edges with Vintage Photo. Punch swirl in top right corner. Randomly stamp Hi There Large, Ink Bottle, and Ink Splash with Graphite Black. Stamp Cheryl's Postcards with Vintage Photo.

❸ Mat with dark green and adhere to card.

❹ Adhere slide mount to card with foam tape.

DESIGNER TIPS

Brush the craft brush across the ink pad several times. Place the slide mount or patterned paper on a piece of scrap paper and, touching the bristles of the craft brush to the scrap paper, lightly brush the edges of the slide mount or patterned paper.

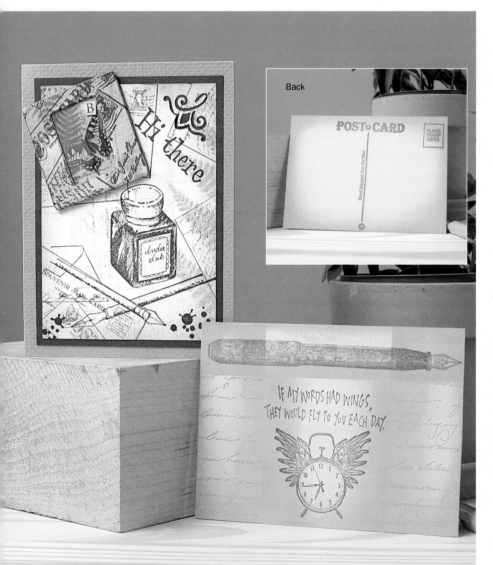

Words with Wings

Designer: Susan Neal

SUPPLIES

Rubber stamps: (Flying Clock, Pen, Words Had Wings sentiment) *Inkadinkado*; (Manuscript background) *Hero Arts*; (Postcard) *River City Rubber Works*

Chalk ink: (Yellow Ochre) ColorBox, *Clearsnap*

Dye ink: (Coal Black) Ancient Page, *Clearsnap*

Cardstock: (Gold) *Bazzill Basics Paper*

Adhesive

Tools: sponge, scissors

Other: scrap paper

Finished size: 5" x 3½"

INSTRUCTIONS

❶ Cut two pieces of cardstock to finished size and adhere together to make postcard.

❷ Stamp Pen, sentiment, and Flying Clock on postcard with Coal Black. Place scrap paper over card, exposing pen; sponge with Yellow Ochre. Repeat, forming lines on each side of sentiment and Flying Clock.

❸ Stamp Manuscript background on each side of sentiment with Yellow Ochre.

❹ Stamp Postcard with Coal Black on reverse side; sponge edges with Yellow Ochre.

Just a Note—
Butterfly Card

Designer: Janelle Clark

SUPPLIES

Cardstock: (black)

Patterned cardstock: (Stamp Collage Embossed) Life's Journey, *K&Company*

Patterned paper: (Gold Plumes) *Anna Griffin*

Specialty paper: (Straw Weave) *Me and My Big Ideas*

Card: (oatmeal)

Rubber stamp: (just a note) *Savvy Stamps*

Dye ink: (Coal Black) Ancient Page, *Clearsnap*

Fibers: (gold embroidery floss) *DMC*

Adhesive: (glue stick, transparent tape)

Tools: needle tool, needle, ruler, scissors

Finished size: 5½" x 4¼"

INSTRUCTIONS

❶ Cut 2½" x 4¼" piece of black card-stock and 2¼" x 4¼" piece of Gold Plumes paper. Adhere to card.

❷ Cut butterfly and framed woman images from Stamp Collage Embossed cardstock, leaving small border around each. Adhere to card.

❸ Stamp phrase on Straw Weave paper and adhere to card.

❹ Accent card with stitching. *Note: Punch holes through card with needle tool first.*

❺ Secure floss ends in back with tape. Line inside of card with paper or cardstock to hide floss ends.

Bonus Ideas

Create coordinating cards, using different images from the Stamp Collage Embossed cardstock. Cut or tear the paper pieces and arrange the stitching as desired.

Floral Just For You

Designer: Nichol Magouirk

SUPPLIES

Rubber stamps: *Hero Arts* (Artist's Flowers set, Just for You)

Dye ink: black, Memories, Stewart *Superior Corp.*

Watermark ink: VersaMark, *Tsukineko*

Card: sage, *Impress Rubber Stamps*

Patterned paper: *K&Company*

Handmade paper: sage, Artistic Scrapper, *Creative Imaginations*

Tag: pink, *Karen Foster Design*

Powdered paint: Moonglow Powder, *Impress Rubber Stamps*

Fixative spray: *Krylon*

Other: hemp, sandpaper, scissors, glue stick, paintbrush

Finished size: 4¼" x 5½"

INSTRUCTIONS

❶ Trim patterned paper to fit sage card front; adhere.

❷ Trim handmade paper and adhere to floral paper.

❸ Stamp sentiment around border with black.

❹ Lightly sand tag. Stamp flower on tag with watermark ink. Paint flower with powder; brush off excess.

❺ Spray tag with fixative.

❻ Tie hemp in bow on tag; adhere tag to card.

Bonus Ideas

Stamp a set of tags to use on a scrapbook page or for gift tags.

Make a matching set of cards as a gift.

Be Happy Every Day

Designer: Janelle Clark

SUPPLIES

Rubber stamps: Savvy Stamps (stripes background, flower); *Hero Arts* (Be Happy Every Day)

Dye ink: Memories, *Stewart Superior Corp.* (Soft Leaf); Ancient Page, *Clearsnap* (Cardinal)

Markers: *Marvy Uchida* (green, red, yellow gold)

Other: cardstock (sage, dark red, cream), adhesive, scissors

Finished size: 4¼" x 5½"

INSTRUCTIONS

❶ Stamp stripes background on cream cardstock with Soft Leaf.

❷ Apply marker ink to flower stamp and stamp over background. *Note: Huff on stamp before stamping to remoisten ink for a brighter image.*

❸ Reapply ink and stamp flower again; stamp three more times without reinking.

❹ Stamp sentiment with Cardinal.

❺ Trim cream cardstock; mat with red. Adhere to card.

INSTRUCTIONS

❶ Make card from Green Tea Solid cardstock.

❷ Paint sections of white cardstock with Nightfall Blue, Pigskin, Truly Teal, and Olive Yellow; let dry.

❸ Cut rectangle of Together Runway paper; adhere to bottom of card front.

❹ Stamp flip-flop on each painted cardstock section. *Note: Only ink flip-flops.*

❺ Punch out stamped images and adhere to Together Rhinestone paper; cut out and mat with Boogieboard Flower paper. Punch hole at top left corner.

❻ Ink "relax" on flip-flop stamp; stamp repeatedly across bottom of card and once on white mini tag.

❼ Thread charm and stamped tag on ribbon and ribbon through hole at top of matted paper; tie bow and adhere to card front.

Bonus Idea

Say a lot with another little stamp from the A Little Love set from Stampin' Up! Use the same card design and create a card for a special someone, a baby shower, a girlfriend, or just because.

Flip-Flop Fun

Designer: Linda Beeson

SUPPLIES

Rubber stamps: (flip-flop from A Little Love set) *Stampin' Up!*

Solvent ink: (Jet Black) StazOn, *Tsukineko*

Acrylic paint: (Nightfall Blue, Pigskin, Truly Teal, Olive Yellow) Ceramcoat, *Delta*

Cardstock: (Green Tea Solid) Colorways, Collection I, *KI Memories*; (white)

Patterned paper: (Together Runway, Together Rhinestone, Boogieboard Flower) Collection III, *KI Memories*

Paper accent: (white mini tag) *Making Memories*

Accent: (sand dollar charm)

Fibers: (blue and white striped ribbon)

Adhesive

Tools: scissors, square punch, sponge paintbrushes, ⅛" hole punch

Finished size: 5½" square

We've Moved

Designer: Jenny Grothe

SUPPLIES

Rubber stamps: (Rummage alphabet) Magnetic Date Stamp, *Making Memories*; (house from Frame Fill-ins set) *Close To My Heart*; (pansy, daisy outline, daisy solid from Burst into Bloom set) *Stampin' Up!*

Pigment ink: (Pink Grapefruit, Sugarcane, Malted Mauve, Hint of Pesto) VersaMagic, *Tsukineko*

Cardstock: (white, sage)

Blank card: (Plum Solid/Shopping Bag Matchbook) *Making Memories*

Color media: (green, brown, pink, yellow chalk) *Pebbles Inc.*; (brown colored pencil)

Fasteners: (silver brads, silver eyelet) *Making Memories*

Adhesive: glue stick

Tools: scissors, eyelet-setting tools, chalk applicators

Finished size: 4¾" x 5½"

INSTRUCTIONS

❶ Cut four strips of sage cardstock; adhere to card front.

❷ Stamp pansy with Pink Grapefruit randomly on card front.

❸ Stamp house on white cardstock; chalk image. Stamp "we've moved" below house; chalk edges and adhere to card front. *Note: Draw in apostrophe with colored pencil.*

❹ Stamp daisy solid with Hint of Pesto, pansy with Sugarcane, and daisy outline with Malted Mauve; cut out. Attach to card front with brads and eyelet.

INSTRUCTIONS

❶ Make card from black cardstock. Line inside of card with white cardstock.

❷ Stamp mouse foot with Silver; emboss.

❸ Stamp Special Friend on 3¾" x 4½" piece of white cardstock with Black. Line edges of cardstock with leafing pen; adhere to card.

❹ Stamp Amanda 117 on 3" x 2" white cardstock; chalk image. Highlight feet, pen, and ink bottle with marker and set with acrylic spray.

❺ Line edges with leafing pen; mat with black cardstock and adhere to card.

❻ Add glitter and adhere bow.

Special Friend

Designer: Stephanie Church

SUPPLIES

Rubber stamps: (mouse foot) Stamps by Judith; (Amanda 117) House-Mouse Designs, *Stampabilities;* (Special Friend) WordPrint, *Hero Arts*

Dye ink: (Black) ColorBox, *Clearsnap*

Pigment ink: (Silver) ColorBox, *Clearsnap*

Embossing powder: (silver)

Cardstock: (black, white)

Accent: (glitter)

Fibers: (ribbon)

Acrylic spray: (UV-resistant Clear) *Krylon*

Leafing pen: (Silver) *Krylon*

Color media: (Bliss Blue marker) Stampin' Write Marker, *Stampin' Up!;* (brown, yellow, pink, blue chalk) *Craf-T Products*

Adhesive: (double-sided tape)

Tools: heat tool, scissors, ruler

Other: chalk applicator

Finished size: 4¼" x 5½"

The Best Antiques

Designer: Julie Hillier

SUPPLIES

Rubber stamps: (antique bike and car from Journey set) *Club Scrap;* (heart) All Night Media, *Plaid*

Dye ink: (Brown) *Delta Rubber Stampede*

Cardstock: (white, black, beige)

Patterned paper: (Timberwood) *Karen Foster Design;* (script background) *Amscan;* (Rusty Star) *Carolee's Creations*

Accents: (flat marble) *Making Memories*

Font

Color medium: (brown chalk) *EK Success*

Adhesive

Tools: (circle punch) *Marvy Uchida;* scissors, computer and printer

Other: chalk applicator

Finished size: 5½" x 4¼"

INSTRUCTIONS

❶ Make card from white cardstock.

❷ Tear various pieces of patterned paper and adhere to beige cardstock. Mat with black cardstock and adhere to card.

❸ Print "Old Friends are the Best Antiques" on beige cardstock. Tear and chalk edges; adhere to card.

❹ Stamp antique bike and car on beige cardstock; chalk edges and adhere to card.

❺ Stamp heart on white cardstock and punch out with circle punch. Adhere to card; mount flat marble on image.

Live Well

Designer: Summer Ford

SUPPLIES

Rubber stamps: (Spring Garden set, square from Little Shapes set) *Stampin' Up!*

Dye ink: (Mellow Moss, Pale Plum, Perfect Plum) *Stampin' Up!*

Cardstock: (White) *The Paper Company*; (Plum) Paper Reflections, *DMD, Inc.*

Fibers: (green ribbon) *Offray*

Adhesive

Tools: (tag template #44-5274) Coluzzle, *Provo Craft*; scissors

Other: scrap paper

Finished size: 5" x 6½"

BACKGROUND

① Make card from White cardstock.

② Stamp square repeatedly on card front with Mellow Moss. *Note: Stamp off onto scrap paper first for lighter squares.*

③ Stamp butterflies randomly with Pale Plum and Perfect Plum.

ACCENTS

① Cut rectangle of White cardstock for card center; ink and tear edges. Mat with Plum cardstock and tear edges.

② Stamp flowers, overlapping, on White rectangle with all ink colors.

③ Stamp sentiment on White cardstock with Perfect Plum; cut into tag shape using template.

④ Crumple tag and tear one end; ink with Mellow Moss.

⑤ Tie ribbon around torn rectangles, attach tag, and tie bow. Adhere to card.

Bonus Idea

Create a matching bookmark to give as a gift or attach as a gift tag.

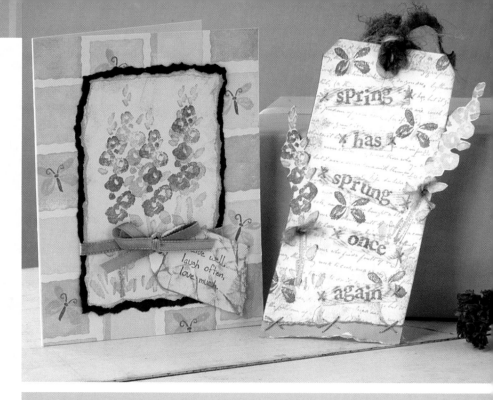

Sunflower

Designer: Alison Bossinas

SUPPLIES

Rubber stamps: (Sunflower Thank You set) *Dream Impressions*

Dye ink: (brown, moss)

Pre-cut cardstock: (Moss Green, White) *Art2Start*

Color medium: (brown, golden yellow, orange watercolor pencils)

Adhesive: (clear-drying) Designer "Dries Clear", *Art Institute Glitter*

Tools: water brush

Finished size: 5½" x 4¼"

INSTRUCTIONS

① Make card from Moss Green pre-cut cardstock.

② Stamp seeds on card with moss. *Note: Only stamp around outside edges.*

③ Randomly stamp leaves, seeds, sunflowers on large White rectangle with moss; adhere to card.

④ Stamp sentiment on small White rectangle with moss; mat with Moss Green and adhere to card.

⑤ Stamp sunflower on White square with brown; color with pencils and mat with Moss Green.

⑥ Blend sunflower leaves; adhere to card.

Many Thanks

Designer: Nancy Church

SUPPLIES

Cardstock: kraft, navy blue, red, white

Vellum envelope

Red mini buttons: *Hillcreek Designs*

Mini adhesive dots (for buttons): *Glue Dots International*

Font (for "many thanks"): CK Fraternity, "Creative Clips and Fonts" CD, *Creating Keepsakes*

Other: assorted fonts (for "thanks" strips)

Finished size 5½" x 4¼"

INSTRUCTIONS

1 Make kraft card base.

2 Mat red cardstock rectangle with navy blue. Adhere to card base.

3 *Note: you may purchase an envelope template from* Lasting Impressions. Adhere to card.

4 Print "thanks" several times on white cardstock, using assorted fonts. Cut into strips. Insert in envelope.

5 Finish card as shown in photo.

Thankzzzz

Designer: Marlo Knox

SUPPLIES

Rubber stamps: (dragonfly and thankzzzz from Cute as a Bug set) *Stampin' Up!*

Watermark ink: VersaMark, *Tsukineko*

Dye ink: (Basic Black) *Stampin' Up!*

Cardstock: (Red, White) *Making Memories*

Patterned paper: (plaid) *Karen Foster Design*

Color medium: (blue, yellow, red watercolor pencils) *Stampin' Up!*

Accent: (glitter) Dazzling Diamonds, *Stampin' Up!*; (black wire) *Making Memories*

Adhesive: (pop-up dots) All Night Media, *Plaid;* (glue pen) 2 Way Glue Pen, (foam squares) Herma Vario, *EK Success*

Tools: scissors, ruler, paintbrush

Other: water

Finished size: 5½" x 4¼"

CARD

❶ Make card from Red cardstock.

❷ Stamp dragonfly at random on card with watermark ink.

❸ Cut strip of White cardstock; stamp dragonfly and Thankzzzz! at random with Basic Black.

❹ Trace around dragonfly with blue watercolor pencil, re-trace with wet paintbrush and blue watercolor pencil.

❺ Tear edges of patterned paper. Mat white strip with patterned paper and adhere to card.

ACCENTS

❶ Stamp dragonfly twice on White with Basic Black. Color with watercolor pencils; brush with water. Let dry and cut out.

❷ Apply glue to center of one dragonfly and over entire image of other. Sprinkle both with glitter. Adhere two pieces of wire to back of each dragonfly for antennae. Curl ends.

❸ Adhere one dragonfly to card with pop-up dots. Adhere second dragonfly with glue pen.

Triple Daisy

Designer: Leslie Elvert

SUPPLIES

Rubber stamps: (Flower, Thank You from All Natural Set) *Stampin' Up!*

Watermark ink: VersaMark, *Tsukineko*

Dye ink: (More Mustard, Really Rust) *Stampin' Up!*; (black)

Embossing powder: (white)

Cardstock: (Ultrasmooth White) *Stampin' Up!*

Textured cardstock: (Leapfrog, Sienna) *Bazzill Basics Paper*

Patterned paper: (Sunroom Cabana Stripe) *Chatterbox*

Fibers: (moss grosgrain ribbon) *Stampin' Up!*; (polka-dot green ribbon) *Offray*

Adhesive: (mini dots) Glue Dots International; double-sided tape

Tools: heat tool, scissors

Other: sponge, sponge dauber, cotton swab

Finished size: 5½" x 4¼"

INSTRUCTIONS

❶ Make card from Leapfrog cardstock.

❷ Stamp Flowers three times on Ultrasmooth White cardstock with watermark ink; emboss.

❸ Sponge More Mustard around flowers. Apply Really Rust with sponge dauber to middle of embossed image. *Note: Wipe excess colored ink from embossed image with cotton swab.*

❹ Stamp Thank You with black. Tear bottom of cardstock.

❺ Mat stamped cardstock with Sunroom Cabana Stripe and Sienna; tear bottom edge of mat and adhere to card.

❻ Tie ribbons around card.

I'm Thinking of You

Designer: Kathleen Paneitz

SUPPLIES

Rubber stamp: (Background IV) *Hero Arts*
Pigment ink: (Marigold, Split Pea, Smoke

Blue) VersaColor, *Tsukineko*
Textured cardstock: (Fiesta) *Bazzill Basics Paper*
Cardstock: (white)
Patterned paper: (Surf Mosaic) Collection II, *KI Memories*
Accent: (Get Well) Ice Candy, Collection III, *KI Memories*

Rub-on: (I'm thinking of you) Script Itty Bitty Everyday Rub-ons, *Wordsworth*
Fibers: (green ribbon)
Adhesive: glue stick
Tools: scissors

Finished size: 5" x 4¼"

INSTRUCTIONS

❶ Make card from white cardstock.

❷ Cut Surf Mosaic paper to fit card front and adhere.

❸ Stamp Background IV on white cardstock with Marigold, Split Pea, and Smoke Blue. Trim and mat with Fiesta cardstock; adhere to card.

❹ Adhere Get Well accent to card.

❺ Apply rub-on.

❻ Knot ribbon and attach to card.

Bonus Idea

Attach this card to a secure container of your favorite chicken soup. Or better yet, use the following recipe for a steaming bowl of comfort from the cold.

Chicken Soup in a Bowl

Designer: Janelle Clark

SUPPLIES

Rubber stamps: (Donut, Chicken Soup, Under the Weather) *The Cat's Pajamas*

Dye ink: (Coral Red) Ancient Page, *Clearsnap*
Watermark ink: VersaMark, *Tsukineko*
Textured cardstock: (Fiesta, Lemonade, Pomegranate) *Bazzill Basics Paper*

Accents: (blue, orange buttons) Fabulous Findings, *Blumenthal Lansing Co.*
Fibers: (yellow embroidery floss) *DMC*
Adhesive: glue stick
Tools: scissors, needle

Finished size: 5½" x 4¼"

INSTRUCTIONS

❶ Make card from Fiesta cardstock.

❷ Stamp Donut with watermark ink on card.

❸ Trim rectangle of Pomegranate cardstock; sew buttons on with embroidery floss and adhere to card.

❹ Cut rectangle of Lemonade cardstock. Stamp Chicken Soup and Under the Weather with Coral Red. Mat with Fiesta and adhere to card.

Homemade Chicken Soup

(courtesy of allrecipes.com)

1 (3 lb.) whole chicken
4 carrots, halved
4 stalks celery, halved
1 large onion, halved
water to cover
salt and pepper to taste
1 tsp. chicken bouillon granules (optional)

Place chicken, carrots, celery, and onion in large soup pot; cover with cold water. Heat and simmer, uncovered, until chicken meat falls off bones (skim off foam when needed). Remove pot contents; strain broth, pick meat off bones, and chop carrots, celery, and onion. Season broth with salt, pepper, and chicken bouillon, if desired. Place contents back into broth and stir together. Serve hot.

The World Can Wait

Designer: Michelle Tardie

SUPPLIES

Pigment ink: ColorBox, *Clearsnap* (black, silver)

Walnut ink: *7gypsies*

Embossing powder: silver, *PSX*

Cardstock: Watermelon, *Bazzill Basics Paper*

Patterned paper: Pamela Woods, *Creative Imaginations* (Gold Foundation, Burgundy Foundation)

Mesh: silver, *Magic Mesh*

Punch: Primitive heart, *Emagination Crafts*

Font: Fat Finger, downloaded from the Web

Poem: Unknown, *www.scrapangels.com /inspiration/index.php*

Foam tape: Scotch, *3M*

Other: white cardstock, scissors, embossing heat tool, computer and printer, adhesive foam squares

Finished size: 6½" x 4"

INSTRUCTIONS

1. Make card from Watermelon cardstock.

2. Cut rectangle of Gold Foundation and strip of silver mesh; adhere both to card.

3. Print poem on Burgundy Foundation; tear and ink edges with black.

4. Punch two hearts from white cardstock; ink and emboss with silver.

5. Apply walnut ink to hearts; heat set.

6. Adhere hearts to printed verse and printed verse to card with foam squares.

Three Flowers

Designer: Michelle Tardie

SUPPLIES

Rubber stamps: Hero Arts (flower); *PSX* (Antique Alphabet)

Pigment ink: Dauber Duos, *Tsukineko* (Petal Pink, Orchid, Marigold, Cool Mint)

Cardstock: Beach, *Bazzill Basics Paper*

Paper: Sweetwater, *Farmyard Creations* (cream, pink, Yellow Antique, Pink Flower Antique patterned)

Mesh: Rose, *Magic Mesh*

Square punch: *Emagination Crafts*

Adhesive: *Glue Dots International*

Other: swirl paper clip, staples, stapler, scissors

Finished size: 6" x 4"

1. Make card from Beach cardstock.

2. Cut Pink Flower Antique to fit card front; adhere.

3. Adhere mesh strip to card.

4. Stamp flower with Petal Pink on Yellow Antique, Cool Mint on pink, and Marigold on cream.

5. Punch out flowers and adhere to mesh strip.

6. Stamp "GET WELL SOON" with Orchid at bottom of card.

7. Staple on each side of flowers and attach swirl paper clip.

Vintage Sunflower

Designer: Kathleen Paneitz

SUPPLIES

Foam stamp: Sunflower, *Duncan*

Pigment ink: blue, VersaColor, *Tsukineko*

Patterned paper: Shorthand, *Design Originals*

Twill tape: *Wrights*

Other: bleach, paper towels, plastic plate, adhesive, scissors, cardstock (blue, yellow gold)

Finished size: 4½" x 6"

INSTRUCTIONS

1. Make blue card.

2. Adhere patterned paper to card.

3. Cut yellow gold cardstock to fit card.

4. Stamp sunflower on yellow gold cardstock with bleach; let dry. Ink edges with blue.

5. Tie twill tape around yellow gold cardstock; adhere to card.

Embossed Leaf Trio

Designer: Jana Millen

SUPPLIES

Rubber stamp: Take Care, *Rubber Moon Stamp Co.*

Dye ink: Black, Memories, *Stewart Superior Corp.*

Cardstock: *Bazzill Basics Paper* (white, light green, medium green)

Clear embossing powder: *JudiKins*

Pewter sticker: *Magenta Rubber Stamps*

Other: green pigment ink, scissors, embossing heat tool, adhesive

Finished size: 4" x 5½"

INSTRUCTIONS

1. Make white card.

2. Cut light green cardstock to fit card front; adhere.

3. Cover pewter sticker with green pigment ink; sprinkle with embossing powder. Heat powder to enamel-like finish.

4. Mat sticker with white and medium green cardstock; adhere to card.

5. Stamp sentiment with black.

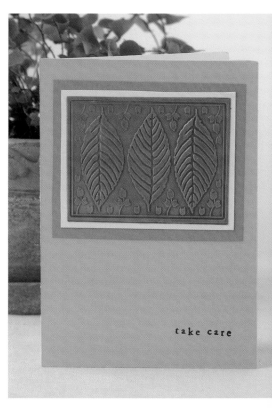

Sympathy Leaves

Designer: Julie Hillier

SUPPLIES

Rubber stamps: *Delta Rubber Stampede* (Fern Frond from Pressed Leaf Collection); Anna Griffin, All Night Media, *Plaid* (With Sympathy from Salutations set)

Watermark ink: VersaMark, *Tsukineko*

Pigment ink: green, VersaColor, *Tsukineko*

Chalk: green, Chalklets, *EK Success*

Patterned paper: green, *Anna Griffin*

Tag: *Avery Dennison*

Snap: brown, *Making Memories*

Other: black ink, cardstock (white, black), eyelet-setting tools, adhesive, ruler, scissors, cotton swab or make-up applicator

Finished size: 5½" x 4¼"

INSTRUCTIONS

❶ Make card from white cardstock.

❷ Cut patterned paper to 5¼" x 4".

❸ Stamp Fern Frond on patterned paper using watermark ink.

❹ Stamp Fern Frond on tag with green; chalk edges.

❺ Secure tag to patterned paper with snap; stamp With Sympathy with black below tag.

❻ Mat patterned paper with black; adhere to card.

Golden Sympathy

Designer: Jana Millen

SUPPLIES

Rubber stamps: *Hero Arts* (Greeting set); *River City Rubber Works* (crackle background)

Dye ink: Raisin, Adirondack, *Ranger Industries*

Chalk ink: Autumn Pastels, ColorBox, *Clearsnap*

Cardstock: *Bazzill Basics Paper* (white, Mustard)

Other: ribbon, mini brad, round tag, adhesive, make-up sponges, ruler, scissors

Finished size: 4" x 5½"

INSTRUCTIONS

❶ Make card from white cardstock.

❷ Sponge chalk inks on white cardstock.

❸ Stamp crackle background with Raisin on chalked paper.

❹ Cut stamped cardstock to 3⅜" x 3⅞" and mat with white.

❺ Sponge chalk ink on tag. Stamp greeting with Raisin; attach tag to stamped cardstock with mini brad.

❻ Tie ribbon around cardstock and mat with Mustard. Adhere to card.

ConGRADulations

Designer: Alisa Bangerter

SUPPLIES

Rubber stamps: *Hero Arts* (block letters); *Stampin' Up!* (leaf background); *PSX* (alphabet)

Pigment ink: Craft Pad, Stampin' Up! (Basic Black); *Delta Rubber Stampede* (Wheat)

Embossing powder: black, *Stampin' Up!*

Ink pen: VersaMark Pen, *Tsukineko*

Metal numbers: *Making Memories*

Mounting squares: *Therm O Web*

Adhesive: *Glue Dots International*

Other: ribbon, cardstock (black, white, gold), pencil, adhesive, scissors, embossing heat tool, craft knife

Finished size: 6⅞" x 5"

INSTRUCTIONS

1 Make gold card.

2 Cut black cardstock to fit inside card; adhere to card interior. Trim ⅜" from bottom of gold card front.

3 Stamp leaf background on card front with Wheat.

4 Stamp "GRAD" on gold cardstock with block letters; emboss with black.

5 Cut out squares and place on card interior. Draw a rectangle around letters with pencil and cut window with craft knife. Adhere letter blocks to interior of card.

6 Stamp "con" and "ulations" on either side of window with Basic Black.

7 Adhere ribbon. Thread metal numbers through separate piece of ribbon; tie bow. Make miniature diploma from white cardstock and attach. Adhere bow to ribbon.

Draped Tassel

Designer: Alisa Bangerter

SUPPLIES

Rubber stamps: *PSX* (diploma, graduation cap, alphabet)

Dye ink: Basic Black, Classic Stampin' Pad, *Stampin' Up!*

Floss: black, *DMC*

Brads: black triangles, *Magic Scraps*

Fibers: yellow, *Adornaments*, EK Success

Adhesive: *Glue Dots International*

Other: yellow vellum, black cardstock, scissors, adhesive, bleach, paper towels, plastic plate

Finished size: 5½" x 4¼"

BLEACH STAMPING TIPS

■ Clean and dry stamps before applying bleach.

■ Pour a small amount of bleach onto several paper towels and place on a plate. Gently tap stamp on bleach and lightly blot on dry paper towel before stamping.

■ Experiment on scrap paper before stamping your card. Not all cardstock will produce the same color when bleached.

■ Rinse stamps well with water immediately after stamping.

INSTRUCTIONS

1 Make black card.

2 Randomly stamp diploma and cap using bleach.

3 Stamp "congratulations" on vellum with alphabet stamps.

4 To make tassel, wrap fiber around 3" square of cardboard strip eight times. Tie knot with piece of fiber through loops; cut fibers off cardboard opposite knot. Tie black floss below knot; trim bottom of tassel.

5 Drape fiber across top of card; adhere tassel to fiber.

6 Attach stamped vellum with brads.

IT'S GRADUATION DAY.

A MILESTONE—

A TIME TO LOOK BACK

WITH FOND MEMORIES

A TIME TO LOOK FORWARD

WITH HOPES AND DREAMS.

2004

CARD

1. Make card base with white cardstock.

2. Cut patterned paper to 3¾" x 8¾". Chalk edges with black. Adhere to card.

3. Cut white cardstock to 7½" x 3". Chalk edges with black. Adhere to card (see photo).

4. Place vellum quote over white cardstock. Attach with flat top eyelets.

5. Adhere number charms to card.

6. Set round eyelet in corner and loop tassel through.

MONEY POCKET

1. Cut vellum to 7" x 9¾". Fold into thirds, seal along front.

2. Cut 3¼" x 1½" vellum strip. Trim diagonal corners; adhere to bottom of folded vellum.

3. Set flat top eyelet in center of vellum strip.

4. Punch half circle with 1¼" circle punch through top of vellum.

5. Adhere money pocket to inside of card.

DESIGNER TIP

Mini adhesive dots work great for adhering tiny embellishments such as the metal number charms.

Elegant Tassels Card

Designer: Maria Larson

SUPPLIES

White cardstock

Black striped paper: Snip Its, *Pebbles Inc.*

Chalk: *Pebbles Inc.*

Black double tassel: *Provo Craft*

Black flat top eyelets: *Moonshine Design*

Black round eyelet: *doodlebug design*

Metal number charms: 2, 0, 4, Making Memories

Graduation quote: Quote Stacks, *Die Cuts with a View*

Finished size 9¼" x 4"

Inside

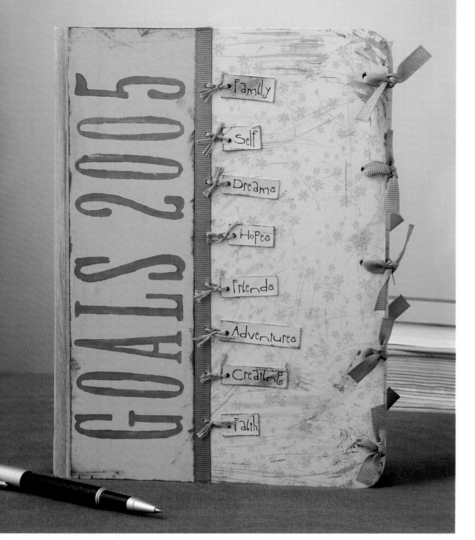

Goals, Hopes, and Dreams Book

Designer: Gretchen Schmidt

SUPPLIES

Cardstock:
   Green: *Bazzill Basics Paper*
   Pastel Pink, White: *Making Memories*

Floral patterned paper: Rosey Floral; Cottage Collection, *Chatterbox*

Composition book

Ink:
   Brown: Close to Cocoa, *Stampin' Up*
   Walnut stain: Distress, *Ranger Industries*

Foam alphabet stamps: Philadelphia, *Making Memories*

Acrylic paint:
   Wedgewood Green, Wild Rose: *Delta*
   Titanium White: Van Gogh, *Royal Talens*

Sage green grosgrain ribbon: *Offray*

Violet floss: *DMC*

Font: OhGoody CBX, *www.twopeasinabucket.com*

Eyelets: *Making Memories*

Adhesives:
   Decoupage: Royal Coat Decoupage Finish, *Plaid*
   Mini adhesive dots: *Provo Craft*

Narrow double-sided tape: Terrifically Tacky Tape, *Provo Craft*

Hole punches: small, medium; *McGill*

Other: brayer, clear fingernail polish, craft knife, eyelet-setting tools, needle, paintbrush, paper towels, pencil, spray bottle, water

Finished size 9¾" x 7½"

SPINE

❶ Paint spine with two coats of white; let dry between coats.

❷ Brush spine with green paint and wipe off with paper towel, working small sections at a time. Let some white show through (see Figure a).

COVERS

❶ Cut paper and cardstock as follows:

Patterned paper: 9¾" x 4" (front cover)

Green cardstock: 9¾" x 3" ("GOALS 2005") and 9¾" x 6½" (back cover)

Pink cardstock: two pieces 9¾" x 7¼" (inside covers)

❷ Age all papers with walnut stain or brown ink. Pat crumpled paper towel on ink pad, spray towel with water, and rub across the paper, repeating as needed (see Figure b); or, apply ink pad directly to paper (see Figure c). *Note: USE dry paper towel each time you press into an ink pad to avoid damaging the ink pad.*

❸ Ink edges of green cardstock strip (see Figure d). Stamp title, using Wild Rose paint and foam stamps.

❹ Brush decoupage adhesive on book cover; adhere paper and cardstock pieces, one at a time. Use brayer to smooth out air bubbles or creases.

❺ Punch medium holes in front and back covers. Cut 5" lengths of ribbon and tie through holes; brush ends with nail polish to prevent fraying.

GOALS

❶ Print goal words on aged white cardstock. Cut out word strips, leaving space for eyelet. Ink edges with brown. Punch small hole in each strip and set eyelet.

❷ Cut 9¾" length of ribbon. Punch small holes in ribbon and tie each word strip to ribbon with floss. Adhere ribbon to cover with tape and adhere words with adhesive dots.

Brush on and wipe off paint.

Apply walnut ink with paper towel.

Pat or lightly drag ink pad across paper.

Ink paper edges, using pad.

Cheers...You Did It!

Designer: Beth Opel

SUPPLIES

All supplies from Making Memories unless otherwise noted.

Foam stamps: (Philadelphia Lowercase alphabet)

Solvent ink: (Jet Black) StazOn, *Tsukineko*

Card: (Pinstripe Manila) Upright Slot

Textured cardstock: (Maraschino, Pear) *Bazzill Basics Paper*

Patterned paper: (Stripes) Embellishment

Vellum: (Light Green) *Hot Off The Press*

Acrylic paint: (Manila) Cityscape, Scrapbook Colors

Accents: (Martini) Charmed Plaque; (Tiffany concho) *Scrapworks*

Rub-ons: (Congrats, You did it!) Simply Stated

Fibers: (light green, burgundy)

Adhesive: (dots); (double-sided tape) no source

Fasteners: (Uppercase alphabet) Eyelet Alphabet

Tools: (scissors, eyelet-setting tools, paintbrush) no source

Finished size: 3¾" x 9¼"

TIPS FROM GRETCHEN

- To flatten paper or cardstock that has curled during the aging process, use an iron.
- Rubber-stamp the words instead of printing on a computer.
- Omit eyelets and floss and adhere words overlapping the ribbon.

INSTRUCTIONS

❶ Adhere strip of Stripes paper to bottom of card insert; spell "TO YOU" with eyelets on paper. Ink edges of insert.

❷ Apply rub-ons to card insert. Cut rectangle of vellum slightly smaller than insert and attach at top with concho and fibers.

❸ Stamp "cheers" with Manila paint on Cardinal cardstock and cut out letters; adhere to insert.

❹ Adhere Martini accent to Kiwi cardstock; mat with Cardinal. Trim and adhere to strip on card.

DESIGNER TIP

Designing your own card is simple and fun with Making Memories' pre-made cards and envelopes. Mix and match colors and embellishments for a truly personalized way to say you care.

On The Job

WISH A WARM WELCOME, SAY SO LONG, OR SHOW APPRECIATION WITH THESE GEARED-FOR-CAREER IDEAS.

New Job Survival Kit

Designer: Heather Erickson

SUPPLIES

Cardstock:
(Garden, White) *Bazzill Basics Papers*
(Yellow/Plaid) *O'Scrap!*

Textured cardstock: (Olive Green Corrugated) *Xpedx*

Patterned paper: (Butter & Olive Stripe) *Chatterbox*

Paper accent: (mini memo book)

Accents:
(Metal-rimmed tags) *Making Memories*
(paper clips)

Fasteners: (brads, eyelets) *Making Memories*

Stickers: (Simple Joys) Build a Flower, (Best Friends) Simple Things II, (Kindness) Simple Squares, *O'Scrap*

Fibers:
(Olive ribbon) *Making Memories*
(beige, tan ribbon) *Offray*
(twill ribbon, jute)

Fonts: (Labelmaker, Monument) "Journaling Fonts" CD, *Chatterbox*

Adhesive: double-sided tape

Tools: awl, computer and printer, scissors, ruler, stapler

Other: aspirin, gum, hand sanitizer, pencils, corrections fluid

Finished size: closed 8½" x 10" x 2", open 27½" x 10"

COVER PIECES

❶ Cut inside and outside covers from corrugated cardstock (see diagram).

❷ Slip paper clip on twill ribbon and adhere along one edge of outside cover (see photo); attach brads. Adhere Olive ribbon beside twill.

INSTRUCTION PAMPHLET

❶ Cut four inside pages from Garden cardstock. First page is 5½" x 7¼"; each additional page is approx. ½" longer than previous one. Staple pages together at top.

❷ Print labels on Plaid cardstock, using Labelmaker font; trim and adhere to page corners.

❸ Cut White cardstock to 5½" x 6¾" for front cover. Cut patterned paper to 5½" x 7". Adhere to front cover, leaving ½" at top for binding.

❹ Cut White cardstock to 5½" x 9" for back cover.

❺ Stack pages on back cover; adhere at top. Place front cover on top, fold binding over pages, and adhere to back cover. Adhere to inside corrugated cover.

ASPIRIN POCKET

❶ Cut Plaid cardstock to 4" x 2½". Cut strip from patterned paper, mat with White cardstock, and adhere to pocket top. Apply circle sticker. Tie ribbon to tag and adhere to pocket. Adhere pocket to corrugated piece. Tuck in aspirin packets. Insert sentiment.

ASSEMBLY

1 To attach kit pieces, pierce holes through inside cover and tie or adhere pieces as directed (see "Kit Pieces" and photo for placement).

2 Print, mat, and adhere sentiments (see "Sentiments").

3 Place cover pieces back to back with ribbon edge on outside; score, fold, and adhere.

4 Make closure with ribbon. Attach matted sentiment with paper clips.

KIT PIECES

GUM: Remove outer wrapper only. Mat patterned paper with White and adhere around gum; tie with jute. Cut 2½" x 10" corrugated cardstock strip, fold lengthwise, and adhere to inside cover next to fold. Adhere gum packet.

HAND SANITIZER: Remove labels. Cut Plaid cardstock to cover bottle front. Apply sticker to center. Tie to inside cover with jute.

MEMO BOOK: Cover with patterned paper. Adhere White cardstock piece, flower, leaf, and tag to cover. Tie to inside cover with jute.

PENCILS: Tie to inside cover with ribbons.

CORRECTION FLUID: Remove labels. Apply sentiment sticker. Tie to inside cover with jute and ribbon.

SENTIMENTS

Print sentiments on White cardstock and mat with Yellow cardstock.

- ASPIRIN: For your first official "work" headache! Take two and call me in the morning.

- GUM: Mint gum for that fresh taste.

- HAND SANITIZER: Hand Sanitizer ... to keep you healthy!

- INSTRUCTION PAMPHLET: Instruction Pamphlet for your first day!

- CORRECTION FLUID: For those little mistakes!

- GREETING: Print personal note on Garden. Mat with white and adhere sticker. Adhere to cover

HOW TO MAKE THE COVER

COVER ASSEMBLY
Adhere back-to-back,
score, fold
Cut 2

| 8½" | 1½" | 8¾" | 1½" | 7¼" | 10" |

8½"
10"
18¾"
20¼"
27½"

27¼" for inside, 27½" for outside

New Job Card

Designer: Sheila Toppi

SUPPLIES

Manila folder

Walnut ink with dauber: (EZ) *Fiber Scraps*

Color medium: (black marker)

Paper accents:
(Post-It note) *3M*
(While You Were Out note, notebook paper)

Accent: (label tape) *Dymo*

Stickers: (shirt, briefcase from At The Office) Jolee's Boutique, *EK Success*

Font: (Stan's Hand) *www.abstractfonts.com*

Adhesive: double-sided tape

Tools:
(pencil medium die cut) Sizzix, *Provo Craft/Elison*
(label maker) *Dymo*
computer and printer, die cut machine, ruler, scissors

Other: cup

Finished size: 5" x 7"

INSTRUCTIONS

❶ Cut card from manila folder, using pattern.

❷ Stamp coffee stain on card front and inside, using walnut ink and cup bottom.

❸ Write "Meeting at . . ." on scrap of notebook paper. Adhere to card.

❹ Write "on your new job" on Post-It note. Adhere to card.

❺ Die-cut pencil and adhere.

❻ Adhere stickers.

❼ Make "Congratulations" label, using label maker, and adhere to card tab.

❽ Adhere "While You Were Out" note inside card.

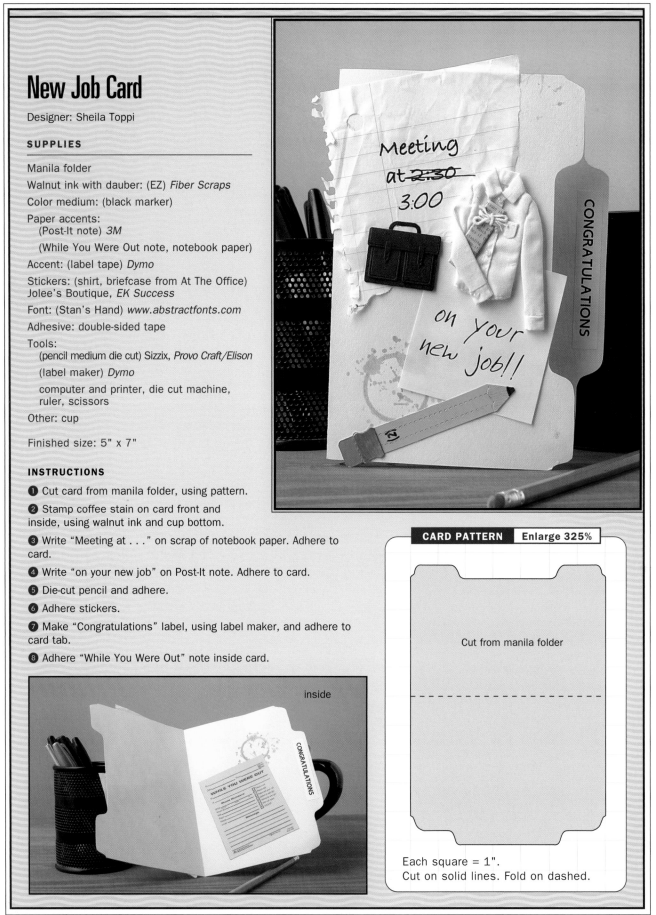

inside

CARD PATTERN   **Enlarge 325%**

Cut from manila folder

Each square = 1".
Cut on solid lines. Fold on dashed.

Ladder of Success Card

Designer: Alisa Bangerter

SUPPLIES

Textured cardstock: (Fawn, Vanilla, Walnut) *Bazzill Basics Paper*

Color medium: (light brown chalk) *Craf-T Products*

Paint: (brown, tan) Ceramcoat, *Delta*

Accent: (brown chenille stems)

Fasteners: (brads, eyelet) *Making Memories*

Fibers: (natural string)

Font: (Monotype Corsiva) *Microsoft*

Adhesive:
   (Foam Mounting Squares) *Therm O Web*

   craft glue

Tools: computer and printer, eyelet-setting tools, heat tool, paintbrush, scissors, ruler, tweezers, wedge sponge

Finished size: 4¼" x 5½"

INSTRUCTIONS

❶ Make card from Walnut cardstock. Drybrush edges with tan paint.

❷ Cut Fawn cardstock to 3½" x 4½"; dry brush edges with brown paint. Attach to card with brads.

❸ To make ladder, cut two 5¼" and five 2" lengths of chenille. Shrink using heat tool (see "Shrinking Chenille"). Adhere pieces together to form ladder and adhere to card with craft glue.

❹ Print sentiment in brown on Vanilla cardstock and cut into tag shape. Tear bottom and chalk edges. Set eyelet in tag, and tie to ladder with string. Adhere tag to card with foam squares.

SHRINKING CHENILLE

To reduce chenille stem fuzziness and size, hold the chenille with tweezers and shrink, using heat tool. Don't overheat or the fibers will lose texture.

Happy Secretaries' Day Coupons

Designer: Jennifer Miller

SUPPLIES

Textured cardstock: (Canteen, Fresh, Lipstick, Mulberry, White) *Bazzill Basics Paper*

Patterned Paper: (Green Tea Bitty Blossom, My Girl Chic Plaid, My Girl Chic Stripe, My Girl Simple Stripe from My Girl) Collection IV, *KI Memories*

Accents: (clear acrylic gems) *Westrim Crafts*

Fastener: (green eyelet)

Fibers: (pink polka-dot organdy ribbon)

Font: (CAC Camelot) *www.techtalknet.com/fonts2.html*

Adhesive: (adhesive machine) *Xyron*

Tools:
(Daisy punch) Paper Shapers, *EK Success*

computer and printer, eyelet-setting tools, ruler, scissors, small hole punch

Finished sizes:
card 5½" x 4"
coupon book 4¼" x 2½"

CARD

❶ Print sentiment on Fresh cardstock. Make card.

❷ Cut strip of Chic Plaid and adhere to card top.

❸ Cut two thin strips of Lipstick cardstock and adhere to card (see photo).

❹ Punch Mulberry and Canteen daisies, adhere gems to centers, and adhere to card.

COUPONS

❶ Print sentiments on assorted cardstock. Cut to 4¼" x 2½". Punch hole in upper left corner of each.

❷ Trim front cover to 4" x 2⅛", round corners, and mat with contrasting cardstock. Set eyelet in upper left corner.

❸ Embellish coupons with patterned paper, cardstock strips, and punched daisies.

❹ Tie together with ribbon.

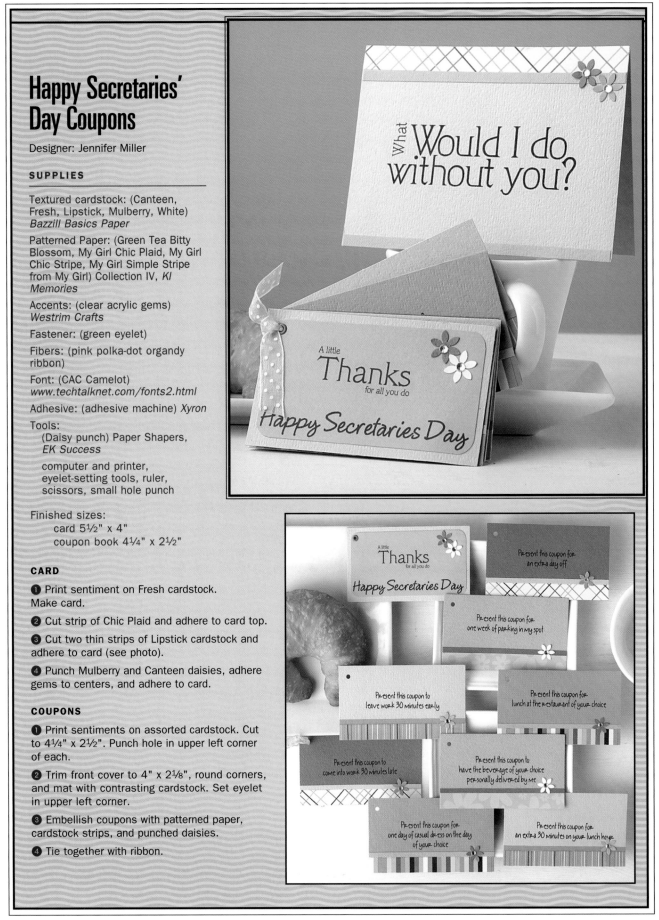

Greatest Boss In The World Card

Designer: Michelle Tardie

SUPPLIES

Patterned Paper: (Maps from Sonnets By The Sea) *Creative Imaginations*

Card: (Kraft) *DMD, Inc.*

Pigment ink: (black) ColorBox, *Clearsnap*

Accent: (metal-rimmed round tag) *Avery*

Rub-ons: (Headline from Small Alphawear) Scrapperware, *Creative Imaginations*

Stickers: (Alphastamps Embossed, Sidewalk Café black) Sonnets, (Cork Alphabet Circles) Artistic Scrapper, (Skid, Sophisticate from Clear Alphabet) Shotz, (globe from School) Debbie Mumm, *Creative Imaginations*

Fibers: (tan gingham ribbon) *Jordan Paper Arts*

Adhesive: (adhesive squares) Scotch, *3M*

Tool: ruler, scissors

Finished size 4" x 5½"

INSTRUCTIONS

❶ Ink card edges.

❷ Trim Maps paper slightly smaller than card, ink edges, and adhere.

❸ Apply rub-ons and stickers to create sentiment.

❹ Tie ribbon near card fold.

❺ Apply globe sticker to tag. Adhere tag to ribbon knot.

V is for Valuable Card

Designer: Jennifer Miller

SUPPLIES

Cardstock: (Natural) *Bazzill Basics Paper*

Patterned paper: (Cream/Red Type, Cream on Red Newspaper, Red on Cream Newspaper) *Mustard Moon*

Paper accents: (Valuable Synonym Tab) *Autumn Leaves*

Accents: (Red buttons) *Making Memories*

Fibers: (red ribbons) *May Arts*

Bonus Idea

Synonym cards are available for every letter of the alphabet. Make different cards for the different words. For example, create a thank you card with the letter "T" for "Thoughtful".

Adhesive

Tools: hole punch, ruler, scissors

Finished size: 4" x 5½"

INSTRUCTIONS

❶ Make card from cardstock.

❷ Cover card, using both Newsprint papers.

❸ Cut Type paper into strip and adhere across seam.

❹ Punch two holes in Synonym Tab, tie ribbons, and adhere to card.

❺ Adhere buttons to corner.

Good Luck Folder Card

Designer: Rhonda Palmer

SUPPLIES

Cardstock: (Forget-Me-Not, Pansy, Serenade, Wisteria) *Bazzill Basics Paper*

Patterned paper: (Lavender Pinstripe) *Susan Branch*

Paper accents: (Good, Luck laser cut words) *Sarah Heidt Photo Craft*

Dye ink: (Charcoal Gray) Nick Bantock, *Ranger Industries*

Color medium: (black pen)

Accent: (Mini Oval Ribbon Charm) *Making Memories*

Rub-ons: (Heidi white) Simply Stated Alphabets, *Making Memories*

Sticker: (Wish from Contemporary Words) Poem Stones, Sonnets, *Creative Imaginations*

Fibers: (purple gingham ribbon) *Offray*

Font: (Sleigh Ride) *www.twopeasinabucket.com*

Adhesive: double-sided tape

Tools: ruler, scissors

Finished size: 7" x 5"

FRONT

❶ Make card, using pattern. Ink edges.

❷ Cut Lavender Pinstripe paper to 5½" x 2½" and adhere to card.

❸ Cut Pansy cardstock to 4½" x 3½" and tear bottom. Adhere laser words and Wish sticker. Thread Charm on ribbon; wrap ribbon around piece and adhere ends in back. Adhere to card, overlapping striped paper.

INSIDE POCKET

❶ Cut Forget-Me-Not cardstock to 6½" x 4" for pocket. Adhere to card, leaving top open.

❷ Print sentiment on Wisteria cardstock. Cut to 5¼" x 3½" and tear along bottom edge. Adhere to pocket.

❸ Cut Pansy to 4½" x 1½" and tear along bottom edge. Rub on "Bye". Adhere to pocket.

TABBED NOTES

❶ Cut 3½" x 3¼" and 2¾" x 3½" pieces from Wisteria. Ink edges and write sentiments.

❷ Rub "notes" and "tips" on Forget-Me-Not. Trim into fold-over tabs and adhere.

Inside

CARD PATTERN   Enlarge 325%

Cut from Serenade

Each square = 1".
Cut on solid lines. Fold on dashed.

Butterfly Clock & Card

Designer: Alice Golden

SUPPLIES

All projects:

Patterned paper: (Friendship Word Plum, Moments in Time) Kelly Panacci Collection, *Sandylion*

Stamp: (Butterfly) Anna Griffin, All Night Media, *Plaid*

Dye ink: (Antique Linen) Distress, *Ranger Industries*

Accents: (Watch Parts) *7gypsies*

Adhesive:
  (Diamond Glaze) *JudiKins*
  double-sided tape

Tools: ruler, scissors

For card:

Cardstock: (Cream Serene Crepe) *Hanko Designs*

Font: (Elegant) www.dafont.com

Tools: computer and printer

For clock:

Frame kit: (Frame Basics) *Me & My Big Ideas*

Clock: (Hands, Movement) *Walnut Hollow*

Paint: (Pure Black) Artists' Pigments, FolkArt, *Plaid*

Accents:
  (Multicolor Hanging Rods) Life's Journey, *K&Company*

  (Antique Circle Jump Rings) *Making Memories*

  (½" Looking Glass frame) *Scrapworks*

Stickers: (Heritage, Time) Kelly Panacci Collection, *Sandylion*

Tools: anywhere hole punch, hammer, needlenose pliers, paintbrush, pushpin

Other: baby powder

Finished sizes:
  card 3¾" x 5"
  clock 6½" x 6½"

CARD

❶ Make card from cardstock.

❷ Cut Friendship Word Plum paper slightly smaller than card.

❸ Print sentiments on Moments in Time paper. Stamp with butterfly. Tear into strip and ink edges. Adhere strip to Friendship paper and adhere to card.

❹ Adhere watch parts with glaze.

CLOCK

❶ Paint clock hands, being careful not to bend them.

❷ Cover frame front and back with Friendship Word Plum paper, according to manufacturer's instructions.

❸ Cut Moments in Time paper to 5½" square and stamp butterflies. Apply clock face sticker to center and adhere to clock frame.

❹ To make hole for movement shaft, punch all layers through center of clock face. *Note: Start with small hole and enlarge gradually.*

❺ To neutralize adhesive on back of mini stickers, apply baby powder. Pierce hole in each tag top with pushpin and attach jump rings. Thread tags on metal bar and adhere bar ends to clock top, using glaze. Let dry.

❻ Attach support screw through frame back panel.

❼ Assemble frame according to manufacturer's instructions.

❽ Cover screw tops with Heritage button stickers.

❾ Place watch parts inside Looking Glass Frame and adhere to clock.

❿ Apply Time Flutters By sticker. Fold butterfly sticker wings to add dimension, apply powder to neutralize adhesive on wings, and adhere to frame.

⓫ Assemble clock mechanism according to manufacturer's instructions.

I DO, I DO LOVE YOU

CREATE A GIFT, WRAP, OR CARD FOR ANY WEDDING, FROM CLASSY AND ELEGANT TO FUN AND WHIMSICAL.

TOUCH OF GOLD MONOGRAMMED CARD

DESIGNER: LINDA BEESON

SUPPLIES

Gold metallic paper

White textured cardstock

½" circle punch

White eyelets: *Making Memories*

Initial sticker: *Mrs. Grossman's*

Gold photo corners: JoLee's By You, *EK Success*

Gold embroidery floss: *DMC*

½" circle punch

Finished size 5" square

INSTRUCTIONS

❶ Create card base from white textured cardstock.

❷ Attach initial sticker to white cardstock square. Apply photo corners and mat with gold paper. Adhere to card.

❸ Attach eyelet to back of card and knot embroidery floss through eyelet. Punch circle from gold paper and attach to card front with eyelet. Wrap floss around eyelet.

Clay & Natalie

Clay Norman & Natalie Larson
Are pleased to announce
Their decision to marry
On the 17th day of November 2004.
A reception will be held
In their honor that evening.
We invite you to
Celebrate this happy event with us.

Clay & Natalie

Clay Norman & Natalie Larson
Are pleased to announce
Their decision to marry
On the 17th day of November 2004.
A reception will be held
In their honor that evening.
We invite you to
Celebrate this happy event with us.

Clay & Natalie

Clay Norman & Natalie Larson
Are pleased to announce
Their decision to marry
On the 17th day of November 2004.
A reception will be held
In their honor that evening.
We invite you to
Celebrate this happy event with us.

UPSCALE DETAILS WEDDING INVITATIONS

DESIGNER: MARIA LARSON

Keep it simple or kick it up a notch, depending on your time and budget.

SUPPLIES

Textured cardstock: black, gray-blue, light blue, *Bazzill Basics Paper*

Silver flat eyelets: *Making Memories*

Silver mini flat eyelets: *Making Memories*

Buckle charm: *Making Memories*

Black fibers: *Pebbles in my Pocket*

Font: CK Elegant, "Fresh Fonts" CD, *Creating Keepsakes*

Finished size 5½" x 4¼"

Note: Invitations do not open.

EASY INVITATION

❶ Create invitation base from light blue cardstock.

❷ Print couple's names and information on gray-blue cardstock. Trim and adhere to invitation.

❸ Attach eyelets.

INTERMEDIATE INVITATION

❶ Create invitation base from light blue cardstock.

❷ Print names and information on gray-blue cardstock. Trim; tear edges (see photo). Adhere to invitation.

❸ Attach eyelets, and wrap black fiber around invitation.

ADVANCED INVITATION

❶ Create invitation base from black cardstock.

❷ Print names and information on light blue cardstock. Trim and mat with gray-blue cardstock. Tear edges of mat; adhere to invitation.

❸ Attach eyelets to invitation. Cut small cardstock strip, thread through buckle charm, and adhere to invitation.

INVITATION INSIGHTS

■ If you're going to make your own invitations, create a few different options so you can pick your favorite.

■ When you're deciding how simple—or advanced—you want to go, be sure to consider your time frame and the cost of the invitation, including postage and supplies.

■ Many scrapbook or craft stores will order charms or other embellishments in bulk if you need large quantities. Don't forget to check online.

WEDDING BANDS CARD

DESIGNER: JULIE HILLIER

SUPPLIES

White cardstock
Pink rose patterned paper: *Amscan*
"Congratulations!" stamp: *Anna Griffin*
Oval punch: *Marvy Uchida*
Pink chalk: *EK Success*
Pink satin ribbon: *Offray*
Gold metal rings
¼" hole punch

Finished size 4¼" x 5½"

INSTRUCTIONS

❶ Make card base from white cardstock. Cover front with rose patterned paper.

❷ Punch oval, stamp "Congratulations!" Punch hole in center and chalk edges.

❸ Tie two rings together with ribbon, and thread ribbon through hole in oval. Adhere ribbon ends to back of oval. Tie another piece of ribbon to top of rings and adhere to oval. Adhere oval to card.

PINK ROSE PETALS FLOWER CARD

DESIGNER: LAURA NICHOLAS

SUPPLIES

Cardstock: cream, pink, sage, *DMD Industries*
Pigment ink: Dune, *Clearsnap*
Pearl beads: *Westrim*
White organdy ribbon
Paper glaze: Aleene's, *Duncan*
Cotton swab

Finished size 5½" x 4¼"

INSTRUCTIONS

❶ Make card base from pink cardstock. Tear front edge of card; curl.

❷ Cut 2" cream cardstock square; mat with sage cardstock. Adhere to card.

❸ Tear two pink cardstock circles, one slightly larger than the other. Crumple circles; curl edges around cotton swab. Adhere smaller circle inside larger circle.

❹ Spread a circle of paper glaze in flower center; sprinkle with pearl beads. Press beads into glaze and let dry.

❺ Tear and curl cardstock leaves. Fold leaves in half to crease.

❻ Adhere leaves to flower; add three small loops of ribbon. Adhere flower to card.

❼ Lightly smudge edges of flower with ink, using a cotton swab.

A CIRCLE GUIDE

To create the flower, punch out two cardstock circles of different sizes. Trace the circles onto cardstock, then tear them out. This helps keep the circles proportioned and provides a guide to follow as you tear.

SUIT-YOUR-FANCY BRIDAL SHOWER CARDS

Make them simple or ornate depending on your budget and time.

DESIGNER: MARIA LARSON

SUPPLIES

Cardstock: light pink, pink, dark pink; Powder Room, *Chatterbox*

Floral Patterned Paper: Powder Room, *Chatterbox*

Narrow white ribbon: *Making Memories*

Pink eyelets: Dotlets, *doodlebug design*

White metal flower: Ting-a-lings, *Carolee's Creations*

Fonts:

Edwardian Script IT, *www.webaddress.com*

Garamond, Microsoft

½" square punch

Finished size 5½" x 4¼"

BASIC CARD

❶ Print "Bridal Shower" on pink card-stock and make card base.

❷ Cut thin strip of dark pink cardstock and adhere to left side of card.

❸ Punch light pink cardstock square, attach eyelet through flower, and adhere to card.

INTERMEDIATE CARD

❶ Create card base from pink cardstock.

❷ Print "Bridal Shower" on dark pink cardstock. Cut piece with "Bridal" to fit top half of card; adhere.

❸ Cut "Shower" strip and adhere to card. Attach eyelets to either side of strip.

❹ Cut thin strip of light pink cardstock and adhere to left side of card.

❺ Punch pink cardstock square, attach eyelet through flower, and adhere to card.

ADVANCED CARD

❶ Create card base from pink cardstock.

❷ Print "Bridal" on dark pink cardstock and "Shower" on pink cardstock. Cut piece with "Bridal" to fit top half of card; adhere.

❸ Cut floral patterned paper to fit (see photo). Tear bottom edge and curl up; adhere to bottom of card.

❹ Cut "Shower" strip, mat with light pink cardstock, attach eyelets, and add to card. Adhere ribbon over seam between cardstock and patterned paper.

❺ Cut thin strip of light pink cardstock and adhere to left side of card.

❻ Tear daisy from patterned paper; curl edges. Attach eyelet to daisy center and add to card.

A RECIPE FOR LOVE

COOK UP THE PERFECT INVITATIONS, GIFT LIST, AND
THANK-YOU CARDS FOR A SHOWER ANY BRIDE WOULD LOVE.

AN EVERLASTING MARRIAGE ADVICE BOOK

DESIGNER: WENDY JOHNSON

SUPPLIES

Cardstock: red, white

Composition book

Red gingham ribbon: *Offray*

Silver eyelets: Dotlets, *doodlebug design*

Font: Wednesday, "Journaling Genie Software" CD, *Chatterbox*

Mini wood rolling pin: *Lara's Crafts*

Red acrylic paint: *Delta*

Other: mini wire whisk, corner rounder punch, double-sided tape

Finished size 9¾" x 7½"

INSTRUCTIONS

❶ Cut two sheets red cardstock to fit composition book; round two corners using corner rounder. Adhere cardstock to covers with double-sided tape.

❷ Adhere ribbon along edge of composition book where cardstock and spine meet. Add bow.

❸ Print "Recipes for an Everlasting Marriage" on white cardstock. Trim, attach eyelets, and adhere to cover.

❹ Paint handles of rolling pin red; let dry. Adhere rolling pin and wire whisk.

RECIPE SHOWER INVITATION

DESIGNER: WENDY JOHNSON

SUPPLIES

Cardstock: red, white
Red Gingham Ribbon: *Offray*
Silver eyelets: Dotlets, *doodlebug design*
Font: Wednesday, "Journaling Genie Software" CD, *Chatterbox*
Mini wood rolling pin: *Lara's Crafts*
Red acrylic paint: *Delta*

Finished size 4¼" x 5½"

INSTRUCTIONS

❶ Print recipe invitation on white cardstock; mat with red cardstock.

❷ Cut two 1" strips of ribbon and adhere to invitation with eyelets.

❸ Paint handles of rolling pin red; let dry. Adhere to invitation.

THANKS FOR MIXING WITH US PARTY FAVORS

DESIGNER: WENDY JOHNSON

SUPPLIES

Cardstock: red, white
Ribbon: *Offray*
Eyelet: *Making Memories*
Font: Wednesday, "Journaling Genie Software" CD, *Chatterbox*
Wire whisk

INSTRUCTIONS

❶ Print "Thank You" or "Thanks for Mixing with Us" on white cardstock, and cut into tag shape. Mat with red cardstock.

❷ Set eyelet and tie tag to whisk with ribbon.

KIWI STRAWBERRY SPINACH SALAD

This delectable combination of ingredients will please both the eye and the palate of any bride-to-be!

WENDY JOHNSON

12 cups freshly torn spinach
2 pints fresh strawberries, halved
4 kiwi fruit, peeled and cut into ¼" slices
⅓ cup sugar
¼ cup olive oil
¼ cup raspberry vinegar
¼ tsp. paprika
¼ tsp. Worcestershire sauce
2 green onions, chopped
2 Tbsp. sesame seeds, toasted
1 Tbsp. poppy seeds

In a large salad bowl, combine the spinach, strawberries, and kiwi. In a blender or food processor, combine sugar, olive oil, vinegar, paprika, and Worcestershire sauce. Cover and process for 30 seconds. Add onions, sesame seeds, and poppy seeds. Pour over the salad and toss to coat. Serve immediately. Makes 12 servings.

Meaningful messages

Choose your favorite greeting card phrases

Marriage is the alliance of two people,
one of whom never remembers birthdays and
the other who never forgets.

— Ogden Nash

Marriage is not just spiritual communion;
it is also remembering to take out the trash.

— Dr. Joyce Brothers

Coming together is a beginning; keeping together is
progress; and working together is success.

— Henry Ford

Together is a wonderful place to be.

The best thing to hold onto in this world
is each other.

It doesn't matter where you go in life—
it's who you have beside you
that makes it worthwhile.

GLORIOUS GIFT WRAP

MAKE THE PACKAGE ALMOST
AS LOVELY AS THE GIFT.

WEDDING BLISS TAG

DESIGNER: KATHLEEN PANEITZ

SUPPLIES

Cardstock: black, white

French script background
stamp: *Stampin' Up!*

Black ink: *Printworks*

Bliss definition: *Making
Memories*

Silver floral sticker: *Magenta
Rubber Stamps*

Silver heart brads and Extreme
Eyelet: *Creative Imaginations*

Ivory tulle

Finished size 5" x 2¾"

INSTRUCTIONS

❶ Cut black cardstock tag.

❷ Stamp French script image
on white cardstock, and trim to fit half of
tag; adhere. Adhere Bliss definition to
side of tag.

❸ Adhere sticker to white cardstock,
tear edges, and mat with black cardstock. Adhere to tag.

❹ Attach brads to black section of tag.

❺ Ink edges of small cardstock square.
Adhere to top of tag and add eyelet.
Knot tulle through eyelet.

WEDDING CAKE
GIFT BAG

DESIGNER: KATHLEEN PANEITZ

SUPPLIES

White cardstock

White gift bag

Silver metallic paper: *Canford*

Wedding cake embossing template:
Lasting Impressions

Silver glitter: *Magic Scraps*

Pearl Strands: *Magic Scraps*

Clear jewels: *JewelCraft*

Concho: *Scrapworks*

Adhesive dots: All Night Media

Dimensional adhesive: Diamond Glaze,
JudiKins

Embossing stylus

Finished size 8¼" x 5¼"

INSTRUCTIONS

❶ Dry emboss cake on white cardstock.
Trim, and mat with silver metallic paper.
Decorate cake with silver glitter, using
dimensional adhesive. Adhere to bag.

❷ Emboss flowers for cake top; trim.
Adhere to bag with adhesive dots.
Adhere jewels to flower centers.

❸ Thread pearl strands through concho
and adhere to bag.

❹ Tear bottom edge of white cardstock
strip. Adhere thin strip of silver metallic
cardstock and strand of pearls. Adhere
to top of bag.

XOXO TAG

DESIGNER: MELANIE BAUER

SUPPLIES

All supplies by Chatterbox.
Cardstock: Light Rose, Rose; Solid Walls
Rose vellum: Powder Room Walls
Alphabet stickers: Scrapbook Address
Fastener: Rivets
Molding: Rosey
Other: white ribbon, sewing machine, white thread

Finished size 5" x 2½"

INSTRUCTIONS

❶ Cut tag from rose cardstock.

❷ Cut strip of vellum; adhere to tag, centered vertically.

❸ Cut strip of light rose cardstock, and add alphabet stickers to spell XOXO. Zigzag-stitch bottom and top edges of strip. Adhere to tag.

❹ Cut strip of molding, and adhere near top of tag.

❺ Punch hole in tag, and attach ribbon.

CONGRATS GIFT CARD HOLDER

DESIGNER: MELANIE BAUER

SUPPLIES

All supplies by Chatterbox.
Light rose cardstock: Solid Walls
Rose stripe patterned paper: Powder Room Walls
Rose vellum: Powder Room Walls
Heart accent: Powder Room Frame
Alphabet stickers: *Scrapbook Address*
Round, flower eyelets: Tacks
Molding: Rosey

Finished size: 5½" x 4"

INSTRUCTIONS

❶ Create card base from striped paper.

❷ Cut strip of cardstock, and adhere near top of card. Punch out heart image; adhere to left of strip. Spell "congrats" with alphabet stickers.

❸ Cut patterned vellum for gift card pocket; tear top edge. Apply adhesive along bottom and sides of vellum and adhere to card.

❹ Cut strip of molding, and adhere along bottom of patterned vellum. Set eyelets through molding holes, alternating between round and flowers.

WRAPPING UP MEMORIES ACCORDION ALBUMS

DESIGNER: SHANNON TIDWELL

SUPPLIES (for both albums)

Paper: Polka dot, *Artistic Scrapper*
  Definition paper, *7gypsies*
  Blox and Circles, *KI Memories*
Accordion albums: *K&Company*
Labels:
  Kiss the Bride, Follow Your Heart,
  me & my BIG ideas
  Eternal, Amore, *Pebbles Inc.*
Metal frame: *Scrapworks*
Metal edge protector: *7gypsies*
Banker's clip: *Staples*
Ribbon: *7gypsies*
Metal photo corners: Making Memories
Pink safety pin: *Li'l Davis Designs*
Decoupage adhesive: Podge, *Plaid*
Metal adhesive: *Li'l Davis Designs*
Other: metal clip, beaded chain, photos

Finished size 4½" x 3¾"

HIS ALBUM

1 Adhere patterned paper and photo to album cover with decoupage adhesive.

2 Adhere labels. Coat entire cover with decoupage adhesive.

3 Attach edge protector, clip, and frame with metal adhesive. Add chain.

4 Decorate inside pages as desired.

5 Close with banker's clip.

HER ALBUM

1 Adhere patterned papers to album with decoupage adhesive; let dry.

2 Pin safety pin to label. Adhere ribbon, photo, and label.

3 Secure metal photos corners with metal adhesive.

4 Decorate inside pages as desired.

A MAGNETIC LOVE

DESIGNER: KATHLEEN PANEITZ

SUPPLIES

¾" flat-bottomed marbles

¾" magnets: *Magnetic Specialty, Inc.*

¾" circle punch: *Marvy Uchida*

Bride and groom stickers: *Tracy Porter, Colorbok*

Floral photos cut from magazines

Fonts:
   Holiday MT, (church, bells, gift dingbats), *www.goblinville.com/fonts/dingbats.htm*

   Selfish, *www.fontshop.com*

Industrial-strength craft adhesive

INSTRUCTIONS

❶ Punch white cardstock circles and adhere to magnets. *Note: It is important to cover the magnets so that the black surface doesn't distort or show through your image.*

❷ Print and punch images to fit magnets. Adhere to lined magnets.

❸ Adhere marble.

ALL-OCCASION GIFTS

These magnets make fun gifts for any occasion. Package them in any empty metal box, such as a mint or cough drop box. You can decorate the box to fit the occasion. Personalize them with reduced copies of photos. Look for images on the Web and in magazines.

marble

image

white cardstock

magnet

LOVING FAVORS

PACKAGE TREATS FOR FRIENDS AND
GUESTS OF HONOR IN THESE FUN
FAVOR BOXES.

A TRIO OF BOXES

DESIGNER: LINDA BEESON

SUPPLIES

SILVER-STRIPED BOX:

Silver-striped paper: *Making Memories*

Alphabet stickers: *me & my BIG ideas*

White silk ribbon

RETRO RINGS BOX:

Pink cardstock

Patterned paper: *Memory Muse Designs*

Embroidery floss: black, gray, *DMC*

WHITE EMBOSSED BOX:

Embossed paper: *Paper Adventures*

Pink vellum: *Hot Off The Press*

"Love" rub-on: *Making Memories*

Silver ribbon: *JoAnn Stores*

Finished size 2¾" x 3¼" x 1¼"

INSTRUCTIONS

❶ Create box using pattern and paper.

❷ Add heart tag or gift card cut from paper and decorated with letter stickers or rub-on.

❸ Tie box with ribbon or floss.

SHARING JOY THANK-YOU CARD

DESIGNER: LINDA BEESON

SUPPLIES

Cardstock: cream, green

Pink floral patterned paper: Deja Views, *C-Thru Ruler Company*

Pink silk ribbon

Font: CK Nostalgia, "Creative Clips & Fonts by Becky Higgins" CD, *Creating Keepsakes*

Silver heart brad: *Impress Rubber Stamps*

Finished size 4¼" x 5½"

INSTRUCTIONS

❶ Make card base with cream cardstock. Cut floral patterned paper, mat with green cardstock, and adhere to card.

❷ Print greeting on white cardstock and mat with green cardstock. Adhere to card.

❸ Mat photo with green cardstock. Tie pink ribbon around photo, attach heart brad, and adhere to card.

SPECIAL DAY THANK-YOU CARD

DESIGNER: LINDA BEESON

SUPPLIES

Cardstock: black, white

Black/silver striped paper: *Pixie Press*

Embossed paper: cream, green, Paper Adventures

Font: 2 Peas Sophisticated, *www.twopeasinabucket.com*

Silver heart brad: *Impress Rubber Stamps*

Finished size 5½" x 4¼"

INSTRUCTIONS

❶ Make card base with black cardstock. Cut striped and green embossed paper rectangles to fit card front (see photo). Adhere. Adhere cream embossed paper strip (see photo).

❷ Print greeting on white cardstock. Add heart brad and mat with black cardstock. Adhere to card.

❸ Mat photo with black cardstock; adhere to card.

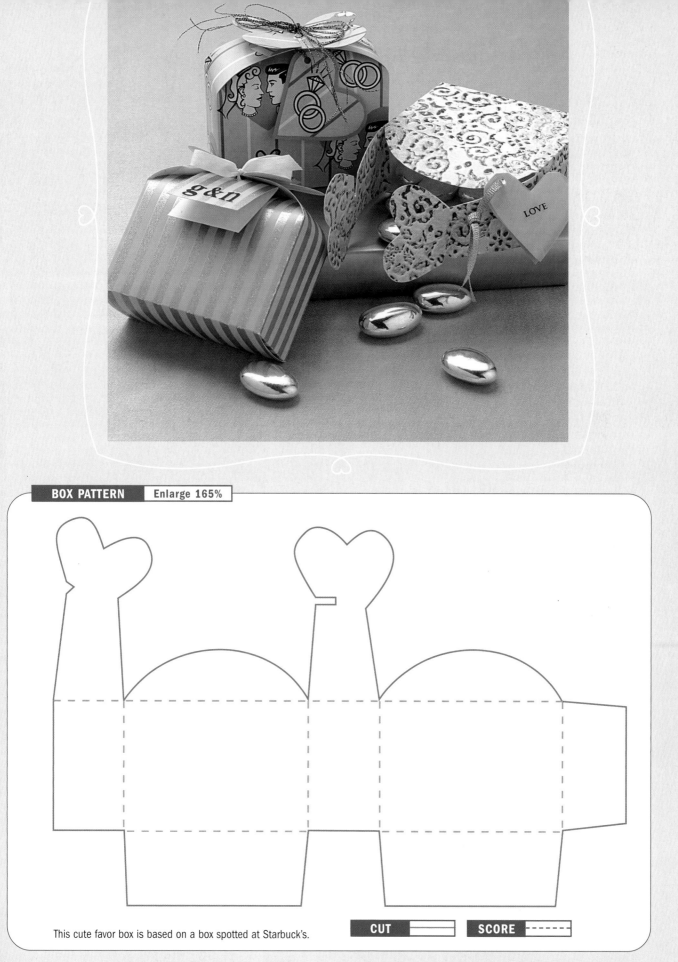

www.PaperCraftsMag.com **65**

JUST MARRIED PUNCH ART CARD

DESIGNER: TERA HODGES

SUPPLIES

Cardstock: black, peach, red embossed, white
1" circle punch: *Marvy Uchida*
1/16" circle punch: *Fiskars*
Scallop-edged scissors: *Fiskars*
Other: red satin ribbon, black pen

Finished size 5½" x 4¼"

INSTRUCTIONS

❶ Make card base from white cardstock; cut red cardstock and mat with card.

❷ Cut 2¾" black cardstock circle in half for car. Punch out taillights using the 1/16" circle punch. Cut two oval cardstock tires; adhere to card.

❸ Punch two 1" peach cardstock circles for bride and groom. Cut white cardstock oval for veil; trim bottom with scallop-edged scissors. Adhere pieces to card. Add ribbon.

❹ Cut white cardstock rectangle and write "Just Married"; adhere to card.

23 REASONS ANNIVERSARY CARD

DESIGNER: DARCY CHRISTENSEN

SUPPLIES

Cardstock: black, gray, red, sage
Font: CK Typewriter, "Fresh Fonts" CD, *Creating Keepsakes*
Other: gray thread, sewing machine

Finished size 6" x 5"

INSTRUCTIONS

❶ Create card base from sage cardstock.

❷ To make pocket, cut piece of black cardstock and zigzag-stitch to card around bottom and sides.

❸ Print date, title, and reasons why you love the recipient on gray cardstock.

❹ Tear out date, and cut out individual words of title. Adhere to card.

❺ Crumple piece of red cardstock, smooth out, and tear heart; adhere. Write "23" on gray cardstock, mat with sage cardstock, and adhere to heart.

❻ Cut reasons into strips, and place inside pocket.

CHAMPAGNE TOAST

DESIGNER: KATHLEEN PANEITZ

SUPPLIES

Rubber stamp: (The Toast) *Stampabilities*

Dye ink: (Coal Black) Designer Ink, *PrintWorks*

Pigment ink: (Petal Pink) VersaColor, *Tsukineko*

Cardstock: (white)

Patterned paper: (Pink Argyle, Pink Stripes) Floral Gathering, *Rusty Pickle*

Color medium: (pink chalk) Decorating Chalks, *Craf-T Products*

Accent: (Cotton Candy Bucklez) *Junkitz*

Fasteners: (silver mini brads) *Impress Rubber Stamps*

Fibers: (black gingham ribbon) *Offray*

Adhesive: dots, glue stick

Tools: scissors, chalk applicator

Finished size: 5⅛" x 4¼"

INSTRUCTIONS

❶ Make card from white cardstock.
❷ Trim Pink Stripes and Pink Argyle papers; adhere Pink Argyle slightly overlapping Pink Stripes.
❸ Adhere buckle to patterned papers.
❹ Thread ribbon through buckle and secure to paper with mini brads; adhere tails behind paper.
❺ Adhere embellished paper to card.
❻ Stamp champagne glasses on white with Coal Black; trim.
❼ Ink cardstock edges with Petal Pink; chalk heart bubbles. Adhere to card.

HAPPY HAPPY HAPPY ANNIVERSARY

DESIGNER: NICOLE KELLER

SUPPLIES

Rubber stamp: (Happy, Happy, Happy) *Hero Arts*

Pigment ink: (Graphite Black) Brilliance, *Tsukineko*

Cardstock: (pink)

Patterned paper: (Baby Girl Wash) Teri Martin, *Creative Imaginations*

Rub-ons: (Heidi) Simply Stated Alphabets, *Making Memories*

Fastener: (heart eyelet) Charmed Shapes, *Making Memories*

Fibers: (pink gingham ribbon) *Offray*

Adhesive

Tools: scissors, eyelet-setting tools, stylus

Finished size: 4¼" x 5½"

INSTRUCTIONS

❶ Make card from pink cardstock.

❷ Stamp Happy, Happy, Happy on Baby Girl Wash paper; trim and adhere to card.

❸ Adhere ribbon to card; trim.

❹ Spell "anniversary" with rub-ons on card.

❺ Set heart eyelet.

Oh, BABY!

Paper Crafts is thrilled to announce the arrival of darling baby announcements, cards, and gifts. You're cordially invited to share our joy!

Boy, Oh Boy!!!

After 9 months of construction our project is now complete!

Completion Date: August 2, 2003
Weight: 8 lb 1.5 oz
Length: 21 inches

Construction is Complete

Designer: Felice Clements

SUPPLIES

Cardstock:
    (metallic silver) *Making Memories*
    (black, blue, brown, green, red, yellow)

Textured cardstock: (Pinecone, Walnut) *Bazzill Basics Paper*

Vellum

Baby photo

Font: (Antique Type) www.scrapvillage.com

Adhesive:
    (foam tape) *3M*
    glue stick, vellum adhesive

Tools:
    (fine-tip scissors) PC Zision Scissors, *Provo Craft*
    ¼", ½" hole punches, ⅜" rectangle punch, ruler, scissors, computer and printer

Finished sizes:
    announcement 6" square
    tag 2½" x 4½"

TRUCKS

① Cut truck and/or backhoe pieces from desired colors of cardstock, following pattern.

② Punch ½" wheels from black. *Note: Cut six for cement truck and four each for dump truck and backhoe.* Adhere each pair of wheels together, slightly off center, with foam tape. Punch one ¼" hubcap for each pair of wheels from silver cardstock. Adhere.

③ Assemble vehicles, following pattern. *Note: Adhere some pieces with foam tape to add dimension.*

④ For dirt in dump truck, tear piece of brown cardstock and adhere torn side up in bed of truck.

ANNOUNCEMENT

① To make card, cut 6" x 12" piece of Walnut cardstock; score 5" and 6" from top.

② Print announcement details for inside and front of card on vellum with brown. Trim slightly smaller than card. Apply vellum adhesive to top of each piece and adhere. Score front vellum piece along lower fold of card so it opens easily.

③ Punch two rectangles through top of card. Cut ⅜" wide strip of Walnut and thread through holes (see Figure a). *Note: Substitute ribbon or fibers, if desired.*

④ Adhere cement and dump trucks to card.

⑤ Mat photo with Walnut and adhere inside card.

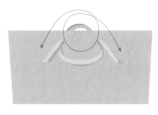

a THREAD PAPER STRIP

TAG

① Print "Boy, oh boy!!!" on Walnut cardstock and cut into tag.

② Cut ¾" x 1½" piece of green cardstock and mat with blue. Fold in half over top of tag and adhere. Punch ¼" hole through center and loop thin strip of Walnut cardstock through.

③ To create dirt, trim Pinecone cardstock to fit bottom of tag; tear top edge. Adhere dirt to tag. *Note: Don't apply adhesive to top edge.*

④ Adhere backhoe to tag, positioning top edge of dirt between tractor wheels.

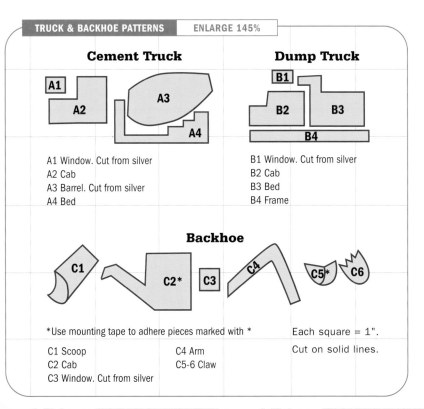

TRUCK & BACKHOE PATTERNS | **ENLARGE 145%**

Cement Truck

A1 Window. Cut from silver
A2 Cab
A3 Barrel. Cut from silver
A4 Bed

Dump Truck

B1 Window. Cut from silver
B2 Cab
B3 Bed
B4 Frame

Backhoe

*Use mounting tape to adhere pieces marked with *

C1 Scoop
C2 Cab
C3 Window. Cut from silver
C4 Arm
C5-6 Claw

Each square = 1".

Cut on solid lines.

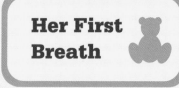

Her First Breath

Designer: Tania Willis

SUPPLIES

Cardstock: (Natural) *Bazzill Basics Paper*

Textured cardstock: (Aloe Vera, Baby Pink) *Bazzill Basics Paper*

Patterned paper: (Confetti) Groovy Gal Collection, *SEI*

Baby photo

Rubber stamps:
   (Antique Uppercase alphabet) *PSX*

   (Printer's Lowercase alphabet) *Hero Arts*

Dye ink: (Van Dyke Brown) Nick Bantock Collection, *Ranger Industries*

Paper accent: (round flower die cut) Groovy Gal Collection, *SEI*

Accent: (clear photo corners) *3L*

Fasteners: (pewter flower brads) *Making Memories*

Fiber: (brown gingham ribbon) *Michaels*

Adhesive

Tools:
   (corner rounder punch) *EK Success*

   (⅛" hole punch) *McGill*

   ruler, scissors

Finished size: 5½" x 4¼"

FRONT

❶ Make card from Aloe Vera cardstock.

❷ Cut Baby Pink cardstock slightly smaller than card. Lightly spray with water; crumple and flatten several times and let dry. Tear edges.

❸ Cut 3¼" x 2" piece of patterned paper; round corners.

❹ Stamp "Her first breath took mine away" on Natural cardstock, using random combination of upper and lowercase letters. Trim and ink edges.

❺ Adhere patterned piece, die cut, and stamped piece to Baby Pink piece. Add row of brads. Adhere to card.

Inside

INSIDE

❶ Stamp "Announcing our bundle of joy!" on Natural cardstock, using random combination of upper and lowercase letters. Trim, ink edges, and adhere inside card. Adhere bow.

❷ Secure photo inside card with photo corners. *Note: Be sure photo is removable so recipient can frame it, if desired.*

Simple Sentiments

So much has been said about babies! Add a quotation to your gift or card.

It is not a slight thing when they who are so fresh from God, love us.

—Charles Dickens

A babe in a house is a well-spring of pleasure.

—Martin Farquhar Tupper

Every child
born into the world is a
new thought of God,
an ever-fresh and
radiant possibility.

—Kate Douglas Wiggin
set in L Sarafina Light

If your baby is . . ."beautiful and perfect, never cries or fusses, sleeps on schedule and burps on demand, an angel all the time," you're the grandma.

—Theresa Bloomingdale

There are no seven wonders of the world in the eyes of a child. There are seven million.

—Walt Streightiff

Let him sleep . . .
for when he wakes,
he will move
mountains.

—Napoleon
set in Bodoni

We didn't give you
the gift of life.
Life gave us the gift of you.
-unknown

Gift of Life

Sentiment

We didn't give you the gift of life.
Life gave us the gift of you.

Designer: Melissa Deakin

SUPPLIES

Textured cardstock:
 (Petalsoft) *Bazzill Basics Paper*
 (Cream White) *The Paper Company*
Baby photo
Pigment ink: (Shell Pink) Anna Griffin, All Night Media, *Plaid*
Fibers: (pink satin ribbon)
Fonts:
 (Arial Narrow) *Microsoft*
 (Carpenter) *www.fonts.com*
Adhesive
Tools: ruler, scissors, computer and printer

Finished size: 5" square

INSTRUCTIONS

❶ Print birth information on smooth side of Petalsoft cardstock; trim and fold into card with textured side out.

❷ Print "Life" on Cream White cardstock with pink. Print sentiment over word with brown. Cut slightly smaller than card; ink edges and wrap with ribbon, tying ends into bow. Adhere to card.

❸ Mat photo with Petalsoft; ink edges and adhere to card.

Baby Girl

Designer: Deanna Hutchison

SUPPLIES

Textured cardstock: (June Berry, White) *Bazzill Basics Paper*

Patterned paper: (Burgundy gingham) *O'Scrap!*

Pigment ink: (Crimson) Anna Griffin, All Night Media, *Plaid*

Shrink plastic: (frosted) Ruff 'n Ready, *Shrinky Dinks*

Rub-ons: (Lab Coat alphabet) Small Alphawear, *Creative Imaginations*

Accents: (white wire) *Toner Plastics*

Fibers: (white organdy ribbon) *Offray*

Adhesive: adhesive dots, glue stick

Tools: ruler, scissors, needlenose pliers, tweezers, heat tool, baking sheet

Finished size: 5" x 4"

INSTRUCTIONS

❶ Make card from June Berry cardstock. Cut White cardstock slightly smaller than card and adhere.

❷ Cut patterned paper slightly smaller than White piece. Tear bottom edge and adhere to card.

❸ Cut eight 2½" squares of shrink plastic. Apply ink to frosted side of squares.

❹ Place squares on baking sheet and, holding each square with tweezers, shrink with heat tool. Apply letters to squares to spell "Baby girl."

❺ Cut two 9" lengths of wire and shape with pliers. Adhere to card with adhesive dots. *Note: Place adhesive dots where letter squares will cover them. Adhere letter squares over wire with adhesive dots.*

❻ Tie bow and adhere to top corner.

TAG

1 Remove hole reinforcer from shipping tag.

2 Punch 15 squares from patterned and handmade papers and Rye cardstock; ink edges. Adhere squares to tag. Trim top corners of tag.

3 Machine-stitch tag edges. Attach hanger to top of tag with eyelet; add ribbon.

4 Stitch floss through button and knot ends on top. Adhere to square on tag.

5 Paint heart brad; let dry and lightly sand. Attach to square on tag.

6 Stamp "Baby" on squares (see photo).

CARD

1 Make card from Light Sky cardstock. Cut White cardstock slightly smaller than card and adhere; zigzag-stitch edges. Apply chalk to stitching.

2 Attach photo turns to corners of card with blue brads; lightly sand brads.

3 Adhere tag to card.

4 Print "It's a boy" with label maker. *Note: Add apostrophe with paint.* Lightly sand label and attach to card with silver brads.

5 Punch baby photo into 1" circle; adhere inside bottle cap with foam tape. Adhere bottle cap to card.

Bottle Cap Baby

Designer: Karen Robinson

SUPPLIES

Cardstock: (Rye) *Bazzill Basics Paper*

Textured cardstock:
(White) *Bazzill Basics Paper*
(Light Sky) *Chatterbox*

Patterned paper:
(tan/blue stripe, blue check) *Sweetwater*
(Raindrop Plaid, Raindrop Ribbon, Light Blue Linen) *Keeping Memories Alive*

Specialty paper: (white handmade)

Baby photo: (approx. 1")

Rubber stamps: (Sampler Alphabet) Brenda Walton, All Night Media, *Plaid*

Dye ink: (Prussian Blue) Nick Bantock, *Ranger Industries*

Paint: (Wicker White acrylic) FolkArt, *Plaid*

Color medium: (blue chalk) *Craf-T Products*

Paper accent: (shipping tag) *Avery Dennison*

Accents:
(silver hanger) *Jest Charming*
(white button) *Making Memories*
(silver photo turns) *7gypsies*
(bottle cap) *Frugal Cropper*
(blue label tape) *Dymo*

Fasteners: (blue, silver, silver heart brads, silver eyelet) *Making Memories*

Fibers:
(blue floss) *DMC*
(light blue thread) *Coats & Clark*
(light blue striped ribbon)

Adhesive: double-sided tape, foam tape

Tools:
(label maker) *Dymo*
(1" circle, ¾" square punches) *Family Treasures*
(¼" hole punch) *McGill*
ruler, scissors, sewing machine, eyelet-setting tools, paintbrush

Other: sandpaper

Finished size: 5" x 4"

Welcome, Little One

Designer: Jenny Grothe

SUPPLIES

Rubber stamps: (welcome, little one from Fun Phrases set; yeah, baby onesie from A Little Love set) *Stampin' Up!*; (Adore, Celebrate, Happiness, Laughter, Love from Express It set) Magnetic Date Stamp, *Making Memories*

Chalk ink: (Malted Mauve, Midnight Black) VersaMagic, *Tsukineko*

Textured cardstock: (Bazzill White) *Bazzill Basics Paper*

Cardstock: (white)

Patterned paper: (Baby Pink Mini Gingham, Baby Pink Faded Dots, Baby Pink Plaid) *Pebbles Inc.*

Color medium: (pink chalk)

Accent: (Perfect Pink safety pin) *Making Memories*

Adhesive

Tools: scissors, chalk applicator

Finished size: 4" x 8½"

INSTRUCTIONS

① Cut 4" x 8½" piece of Baby Pink Plaid paper for card base.

② Trim Baby Pink Faded Dots paper; chalk edges.

③ Randomly stamp sentiments on Baby Pink Faded Dots with Malted Mauve. *Note: Stamp some words partially off paper. Adhere to card.*

④ Stamp sentiment on Bazzill White cardstock with Midnight Black; trim. Adhere to card.

⑤ Trim square from white cardstock.

⑥ Stamp onesie on square with Midnight Black; chalk edges. Mat with Baby Pink Mini Gingham paper; chalk edges.

⑦ Secure safety pin to embellished square; adhere to card.

ONESIE STAMP SOURCE

The A Little Love set by Stampin' Up! was only available to stamp party hostesses as part of a 2004 promotion.

- Check out online auction sites such as www.ebay.com to purchase the set.

- Use a different baby stamp such as Baby Onesie (#3158B) **Delta Rubber Stampede**, 800/423-4135, *deltacrafts.com/RubberStampede* or try an accent such as Baby Girl Outfit, Jolee's Boutique, **EK Success**, 800/767-2963, *www.eksuccess.com*.

Little Pink Buggy

Designer: Kathleen Paneitz

SUPPLIES

Rubber stamp: (Buggy Boogie) *Stampabilities*

Dye ink: (Coal Black) Designer Ink, *PrintWorks*

Pigment ink: (Petal Pink) VersaColor, *Tsukineko*

Cardstock: (white)

Patterned paper: (Unit 21) Art Warehouse, *Creative Imaginations*

Color medium: (pink chalk) Decorating Chalks, *Craf-T Products*

Accent: (pink mesh) *GottaMesh*

Fasteners: (pink eyelets) *Impress Rubber Stamps*

Fibers: (pink gingham ribbon) *Offray*

Adhesive

Tools: scissors, eyelet-setting tools, chalk applicator

Finished size: 4⅜" square

INSTRUCTIONS

① Make card from white cardstock.

② Trim Unit 21 paper to fit card front; adhere.

③ Trim pink mesh; adhere to card.

④ Stamp buggy on white cardstock with Coal Black; trim.

⑤ Ink stamped cardstock edges with Petal Pink; chalk buggy bonnet.

⑥ Set eyelets; adhere embellished piece to card.

⑦ Tie ribbon in bow; adhere to card.

Baby Memorabilia Box

Designer: Layle Koncar

SUPPLIES

Patterned paper: (Lot 22) Art Warehouse, *Creative Imaginations*
Frame box: (white) All Night Media, *Plaid*
Baby photo
Dye ink: (Van Dyke Brown) Nick Bantock Collection, *Ranger Industries*
Stickers: (White Flea Market alphabet) Sonnets, *Creative Imaginations*
Paint: (gray acrylic) Ceramcoat, *Delta*
Rub-ons:
   (date Impress-ons) Art Warehouse, *Creative Imaginations*
   (Heidi alphabet) Simply Stated, *Making Memories*
Accents: (black photo corners)
Fibers: (blue polka dot ribbon) Li'l Davis Designs
Adhesive:
   (Scrappers' Spray) *Creative Imaginations*
   (adhesive dots) *Glue Dots International*
Tools: ruler, scissors, craft knife
Other: baby memorabilia

Finished size: 5½" x 6¾" x 1¾"

INSTRUCTIONS

❶ Cut two 12" lengths of ribbon. Adhere end of one length to front edge of lid; adhere end of other length to bottom of box with adhesive dots.

❷ Measure and cut patterned paper to fit all sides of box and underneath lid, allowing ⅛" margins for each piece. *Note: Cut frame window in front piece with craft knife. Ink edges.*

❸ Adhere paper pieces to box with spray adhesive. *Note: Lid and bottom pieces should cover ribbon ends.*

❹ Cut piece of cardstock ½" smaller than frame window; stamp baby's foot or hand with acrylic paint. Let dry and mat with patterned paper, cut ¼" larger than window. Place matted piece behind window.

❺ Spell "baby" with alphabet stickers on side of lid; accent stickers with ink.

❻ Attach baby photo underneath lid with photo corners. Spell baby's name and birth date with rub-ons.

❼ Place memorabilia in box and tie closed with ribbon.

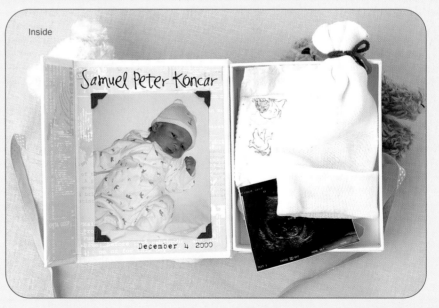

Inside

Samuel Peter Koncar

December 4 2000

Baby Journal

Designer: Camille Gregersen

SUPPLIES

Textured cardstock: (Baby Pink, Lemonade) *Bazzill Basics Paper*

Patterned paper: (Unit 21) Art Warehouse, *Creative Imaginations*

Mini composition book

Magnetic stamp: (Remember from Express It set) *Making Memories*

Rubber stamps: (Antique Type alphabet) *Hero Arts*

Pigment ink: (Black) VersaColor, *Tsukineko*

Accent: (handprint pewter plaque) *Making Memories*

Fasteners: (pink, yellow brads) *Making Memories*

Fibers:
   (pink grosgrain ribbon) *Michaels*
   (white twill ribbon) *Wrights*

Adhesive: glue stick, metal adhesive

Tools: scissors

Finished size: 3¼" x 4½"

INSTRUCTIONS

1 Cut patterned paper to fit front and back covers of composition book. *Note: Do not adhere yet.*

2 Adhere plaque to torn piece of Lemonade cardstock, using metal adhesive. Mat with Baby Pink cardstock. Adhere to front paper piece.

3 Stamp "Baby journal" on twill ribbon; trim and adhere to front piece. Add brad to each end.

4 Adhere front piece to book cover.

5 Stamp "Remember" along 8" length of pink grosgrain ribbon; adhere one end of ribbon to top edge of back cover. Adhere back paper piece to cover.

DESIGNER TIP

When you give the Baby Journal away, you might remind the recipient that although it isn't large enough for a standard baby book, it's a handy size for jotting down all those baby milestones—first words, funny stories, etc.—before they're forgotten.

Adoption is when a child grows in its Mommy's heart instead of her tummy.

Adoption

Designer: Melissa Deakin

SUPPLIES

Textured cardstock:
(Vanilla) *Bazzill Basics Paper*
(Cream White) *The Paper Company*

Patterned paper: (Peony Sanded Floral) *Me & My Big Ideas*

Vellum: *Stampin' Up!*

Pigment ink: (Shell Pink) Anna Griffin, All Night Media, *Plaid*

Accents: (Cream Hydrangea Blossoms, pink button) *Making Memories*

Fasteners: (antique brass brads) *Making Memories*

Fibers:
(cream/pink trim) Just Write! *Me and My Big Ideas*
(pink satin) *Offray*
(white thread)

Fonts:
(Songwriter) *Autumn Leaves*
(Satisfaction) *www.myfonts.com*

Adhesive

Tools: ½", ¼" hole punches, ruler, scissors, needle, computer and printer

Finished size: 6" square

INSTRUCTIONS

❶ Make card from Vanilla cardstock; ink edges.

❷ Trim patterned paper slightly smaller than card; ink edges and adhere.

❸ Cut vellum pocket and attach to card with brads.

❹ Stitch button to flowers and adhere to pocket.

❺ Print "Heart" and "Congratulations" on Cream White cardstock with pink. Print sentiment over "Heart" with brown. Cut into tags and ink edges. Punch ½" circles from patterned paper and adhere to tops of tags; punch ¼" holes through center of circles, tie tags together with ribbon, and trim.

Sentiment

Adoption is when a child grows in its Mommy's heart instead of her tummy.

Bonus Idea

Add a special touch to a thank-you card for a baby gift: take a photo of your baby with the gift and add it to the card. Contributing Editor Valerie Pingree created this card for one of her friends.

Designer: Linda Beeson

SUPPLIES

Textured cardstock: black, light blue, medium blue, light pink, medium pink, white; *Bazzill Basics Paper*

Black laser die cuts: buggy, rattle, *Deluxe Cuts*

Woven labels: "so girly", "Oh, boy!"; threads, *me & my BIG ideas*

Black polka dot ribbon: *Michaels*

Rhinestones: *Cousin Corporation*

Other: hole punch

Finished size 5" square

INSTRUCTIONS

❶ Adhere laser die cut to 3½" white cardstock square. Punch two holes in bottom right corner. Thread ribbon through holes.

❷ Adhere rhinestones to rattle bow or buggy wheels.

❸ Mat with medium pink or blue cardstock. Mat with light pink or light blue cardstock, adhering woven tag between layers.

❹ Adhere to black card base.

Girl Buggy & Boy Rattle

3-D Announcement

Designer: Felice Clements

SUPPLIES

Textured cardstock: dark blue, light blue, *Bazzill Basics Paper*

Vellum

Fonts

Wednesday (for baby's name), Journaling Genie Software, *Chatterbox*

CK Journaling, "Creative Lettering Vol. 2" CD, *Creating Keepsakes*

Other: small hole punch, 2 baby photos (approx. 2½" x 3½"), bone folder or scoring tool

Finished size
   4" x 5½" closed;
   6" x 5½" opened

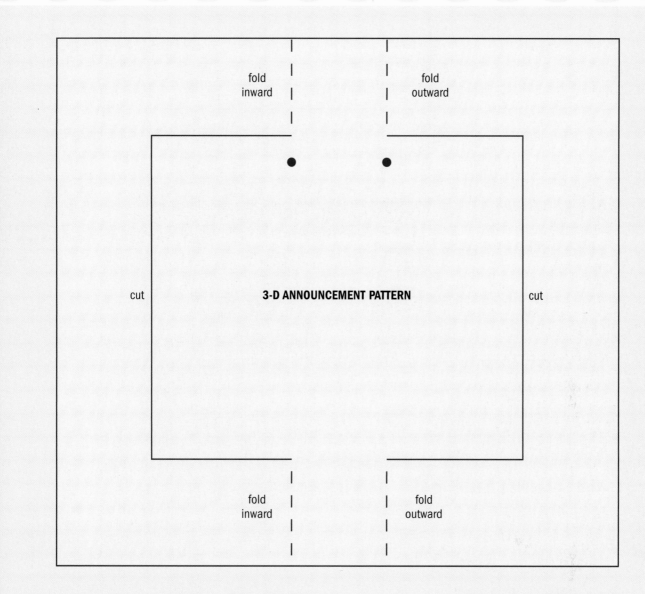

fold inward

fold outward

cut

3-D ANNOUNCEMENT PATTERN

cut

fold inward

fold outward

INSTRUCTIONS

❶ Cut card base from light blue cardstock, using pattern. Cut and fold as indicated, using bone folder or scoring tool (see figure a).

❷ Mat each photo with a 3¼" x 3¾" piece of dark blue cardstock, approx. ½" from top.

❸ Adhere a photo block to each side of card center.

❹ Print announcement on vellum. Trim to 3" x 3⅝".

❺ Place vellum piece over one photo block. Punch two holes where indicated, going through all layers.

❻ Cut a long ⅛" wide strip of light blue cardstock. Thread through holes to attach vellum piece (see figure b). *Note: Substitute ribbon or fiber, if desired.*

a

b

Sweet Girl Frame

Designer: Linda Beeson

SUPPLIES

Wood frame: *Provo Craft*

Patterned paper: pink gingham, pink/blue floral, *Daisy D's*

Pink lace trim: *JoAnn Fabrics*

Font: Miss Brooks, *www.themeworld.com*

"sweet" metal word: *Making Memories*

Metal label holder: *Two Peas in a Bucket*

Pink brads: *Family Treasures*

Watermark ink: VersaMark, *Tsukineko*

Other: pink acrylic paint, fine sandpaper, white embossing powder, jewelry adhesive, heat embossing tool.

Finished size 8" square

FRAME

❶ Paint outside and inside edges of frame.

❷ Trace frame shape on patterned papers. Cut out.

❸ Adhere papers and trim to frame, referring to photo for placement (see "Adhere Paper Smoothly").

METAL PIECES

❶ Lightly sand metal word and label holder.

❷ Apply watermark ink to front of each piece, and sprinkle with embossing powder. Emboss to create white finish.

❸ Lightly sand edges of metal pieces, if desired.

❹ Attach brads to label holder. Adhere metal pieces to frame with jewelry adhesive.

ADHERE PAPER SMOOTHLY

To adhere paper to a picture frame, notebook, or bucket, use one of the following types of adhesive to keep the paper smooth:

Adhesive sheets

Decoupage adhesive

Glue stick

Spray adhesive

Baby Animals Frame

Designer: Emily Cannon

SUPPLIES

Wood frame: *Provo Craft*

White acrylic paint: *Delta*

Decoupage adhesive: *Delta*

Paper animal accents: elephant, giraffe, *Westrim Crafts*

Blue buttons: *Westrim Crafts*

Other: blue organza ribbon

Finished size: 11" x 7"

INSTRUCTIONS

1 Paint frame.

2 Decoupage animal accents to frame, following manufacturer's instructions.

3 Adhere buttons and bow to frame with decoupage adhesive.

BONUS IDEAS

Things to display in the top frame opening:

- Baby's hospital bracelet

- A string of alphabet beads that spell baby's name

- Baby's name in stickers, die cuts, or dimensional letters

- A lock of baby's hair

- Baby's footprints

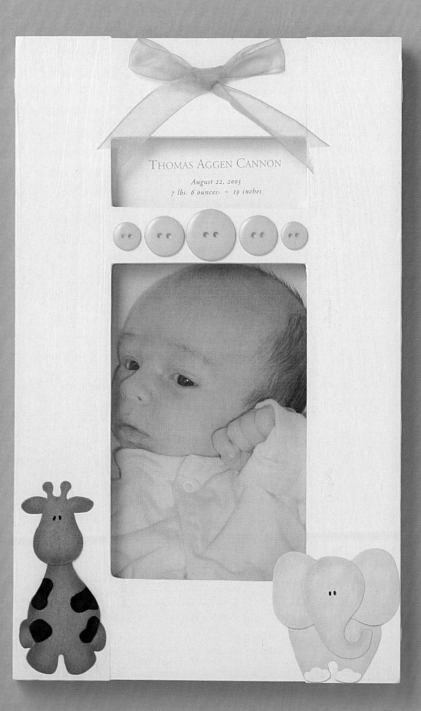

THOMAS AGGEN CANNON

August 22, 2003
7 lbs. 6 ounces · 19 inches

a kit just for you!

the new mom's survival kit

hershey hugs and kisses -
for you and baby both because you both deserve them

clock-
to remind you that time will pass by too quickly, enjoy every moment

mirror -
to remind you that you are important, too

marbles -
to replace the ones that you will lose

rubberband -
to remind you that flexibility is the key

lifesavers -
to save you from one of those days

tissue -
to dry those tears the baby's and yours

lollipop -
to lick all your problems

eraser -
to remind you that every mom makes mistakes

puzzle piece -
because you are an important piece in your child's journey through life

New Mom's Survival Kit Tag

Designer: Teri Anderson

SUPPLIES

Cardstock: white, yellow gingham, *Georgia-Pacific*

Light blue polka dot paper: *O'Scrap!*

Die cuts: rattle, 2 stars; *O'Scrap!*

Font: 2Peas Fairy Princess, *www.twopeasinabucket.com*

White organza ribbon: *Close to My Heart*

Other: light blue brads, hole punches (½", ⅛")

Finished size: 11" x 6"

INSTRUCTIONS

1 Make tag with yellow gingham cardstock.

2 Print Survival Kit text on white cardstock. Cut into rectangle; mat with light blue cardstock. Attach brads to corners.

3 Adhere to tag.

4 Adhere light blue strip to tag bottom. Adhere die cuts.

5 Punch ½" circle from light blue cardstock. Adhere to top of tag. Punch ⅛" hole through center.

6 Thread ribbon through hole.

SURVIVAL KIT

Put the survival kit items in a gift bag or box, and tie the tag to the top.

Little Book of Baby Advice

Designer: Nicole Keller

SUPPLIES

Notebook: Paper Reflections, *DMD Industries*

Yellow patterned papers: polka dot, gingham, *Current*

Mint green patterned paper: *Provo Craft*

Safety pin die cuts: Paper Bliss, *Westrim Crafts*

Yellow buttons: *Dress it Up*

Green embroidery floss: *DMC*

Font: Glitter Girl, *www.twopeasinabucket.com*

Other: ¼" hole punch

Finished size 5½" x 5"

COVER

1. Gently pry coils from notebook and remove cover.

2. Trace notebook cover, including holes, on yellow patterned paper. Cut out; punch holes.

3. Adhere paper to notebook cover; replace coils.

TITLE BLOCK

1. Print "The Little Book of Baby Advice for the New Mom" on polka dot paper. Cut into 2¾" square and mat with green patterned paper.

2. Stitch buttons to corners. Adhere square to cover.

3. Add safety pin die cuts.

BABY SHOWER IDEA

A book of baby advice is a gift any new mom will cherish. Pass the book around at a baby shower so guests can write their best wishes for the new baby and words of advice to the new mom.

TAG BASE

1. Cut tag shape from patterned paper. Mat with white cardstock.

2. Sponge tag edges with blue or pink ink.

3. Cut ¾" x 1¾" rectangle from white cardstock. Ink edges. Fold over top of tag and adhere. Set eyelet through center.

4. Thread ribbon through eyelet and safety pin. Knot at top of tag. Adhere safety pin to tag.

GIRL TAG

1. Tear two strips of embossed flower paper. Adhere to card.

2. Adhere acrylic letters to pink textured cardstock. Cut into rectangle; sponge edges with white ink.

3. Punch two ⅟₁₆" holes in each side. Thread floss through holes.

4. Adhere to tag, wrapping floss ends in back and securing with tape.

5. Ink edges of mini tag. Tie string through hole. Adhere to large tag.

6. Add rattle sticker, bow, brads, and brad stickers as shown in photo.

BOY TAG

1. Print "Congratulations" on white cardstock. Cut out; chalk edges. Adhere to tag.

2. Tear edges of child definition; adhere to tag.

3. Ink edges of mini tag. Tie string through hole. Adhere to large tag.

4. Add rattle sticker, brads, and brad stickers as shown in photo.

Congratulations Tags

Designer: Kathleen Paneitz

SUPPLIES

FOR BOY TAG:

Blue patterned paper: *7gypsies*

Child definition: *Daisy D's*

Gold heart brad: *Creative Imaginations*

Blue gingham ribbon: *Offray*

Blue ink: Versacolor, *Tsukineko*

Font (for "Congratulations"): Mistral, *www.myfonts.com*

FOR GIRL TAG:

Pink textured cardstock

Pink embossed flower paper

Pink patterned paper (background): *KI Memories*

"baby" clear acrylic letters: *KI Memories*

Pink organza ribbon: *Michaels*

White embroidery floss: *DMC*

Pink ink: Versacolor, *Tsukineko*

Other: white ink, pink bow, ⅟₁₆" hole punch, tape

FOR BOTH

White cardstock

Mini tag: *Avery*

Round gold brads: *Creative Imaginations*

Alphabet brad stickers: Bradwear Impress-ons, *Creative Imaginations*

Rattle dimensional sticker: Jolee's By You, *EK Success*

Adhesive: *Therm O Web*

Other: white string, silver eyelet, large gold safety pin, sponge, ½" hole punch

Finished size: 5" x 3"

Diaper Place Cards

Designer: Jacque Jensen

SUPPLIES

White paper

Gingham patterned paper: *Frances Meyer*

Matching eyelets: *Cut-It-Up*

Metal flowers: *Carolee's Creations*

Font: Amazone BT, *www.myfonts.com*

Other: white organza ribbon, 2" safety pin

Finished size: 2½" x 4"

INSTRUCTIONS

1. Cut and loosely fold diaper.
2. Set eyelets through front and side panels of diaper.
3. Thread ribbon through eyelets.
4. Thread metal flowers on ribbon ends and knot.
5. Tie bow and attach safety pin.
6. Adhere name to front.
7. Fill with candy, nuts, or other favors.

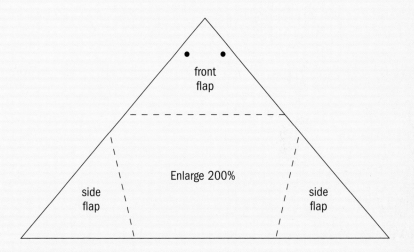

front flap

side flap

Enlarge 200%

side flap

Because

she taught you

not to run with

scissors.

Repay Mom's words of wisdom with gifts of gratitude—
made while sitting still with scissors!

EAU DE
COLOGNE

Extra-Surfine

MOM

cherished memories

Mother's Day Book Bag

Designer: Sande Krieger

SUPPLIES

Cardstock: (Light Olive) Great Room Collection, *Chatterbox*

Patterned paper:
(Butter Bloom) Great Room Collection, *Chatterbox*

(green striped)

Accents: (decorative antique copper round, silver brads, heart Mini Plaque) *Making Memories*

Fasteners:
(Silver Locks) *7gypsies*

(hook and loop tape) *Velcro*

Fibers: (green ribbon) *May Arts*

Adhesive: double-sided tape

Tools: awl, ruler, scissors

Finished size: 5" x 6½" x 1¾"

INSTRUCTIONS

❶ Cut out bag, using pattern.

❷ Adhere body pieces, wrong sides together. Fold according to pattern.

❸ Fold sides according to pattern. Adhere one long tab inside bag back.

❹ Pierce holes for silver brads through front tab, using awl. Adhere to bag front, re-pierce holes and attach brads.

❺ Adhere latch to back with adhesive. Attach decorative brads to front flap of latch. Adhere hook and loop tape to latch and bag for closure.

❻ Make handle from ribbon and silver locks. Attach to bag sides.

❼ Adhere plaque to front.

Bonus Ideas

- Place a gift book in the bag, or include a gift card from your mom's favorite bookstore.
- Make a charming bookmark from matching cardstock and embellishments.

BOOK BAG PATTERN — Enlarge 285%

BOOK BAG BODY
Cut from Butter Bloom and Green Striped.

LATCH
Cut from Light Olive

SIDES
Cut 2 from Light Olive

Each square = 1". Cut on solid lines. Score on dashed lines.

Magnets For Mom

Designer: Amber Crosby

SUPPLIES

Cardstock: (cream)

Textured cardstock: (pink)

Patterned paper:
(Script Large) *7gypsies*
(Pink ABC Blocks) *Anna Griffin*
(pink swirl)

Photos

Rubber stamps: (Antique Uppercase, Antique Lowercase alphabet) PSX, *Duncan*

Dye ink: (black)

Paper accents:
(Slash Pockets) *Lil' Davis Designs*
(Tags) *Chantilly Lace*

Accent: (label holder) *Making Memories*

Rub-on: ("M" Monogram) *Me & My Big Ideas*

Fasteners:
(magnet strips) *Crafts, Etc.*
(mini brads) *All My Memories*

Fibers: (cream, pink gingham ribbons)

Font: (Times New Roman) *Microsoft*

Adhesive: double-sided tape

Tools: computer and printer, ruler, scissors

Finished size: 3" x 3¾"

DIAMOND MAGNET

❶ Cover pocket outside with Pink ABC Block paper. Line pocket inside with Script Large paper.

❷ Rub "M" on cream cardstock. Stamp "Mom". Trim cardstock into square and adhere to pocket. Adhere gingham ribbon around square.

❸ Adhere magnets to pocket back.

SWIRL MAGNET

❶ Cover pocket with pink swirl paper. Line pocket inside with Script.

❷ Print sentiment in pink on cream cardstock; trim and ink edges. Attach to pocket with brads.

❸ Stamp "Mom" on pink cardstock, adhere behind label holder and trim excess.

❹ Thread cream ribbon through label holder. Adhere label holder and ribbon to pocket.

❺ Adhere magnets to pocket back.

TAGS

❶ Embellish with ribbons, patterned papers, and photos.

Mom's Memories Box

Designer: Heather Erickson

SUPPLIES

Cardstock: (white)

Patterned paper: (Butter Bloom/Butter Ticking plaid, Scarlet Bloom) *Chatterbox*

Box with clear lid: *Xpedx*

Photo

Fasteners: (brads)

Fibers:
(Celery ribbon) *Making Memories*
(brown, olive ribbon) *Offray*

Font: (Monument)

Adhesive: double-sided tape

Tools: awl, computer and printer, ruler, scissors

Finished size: 11½" x 9" x 2"

LID

❶ Cut white cardstock to fit inside lid. Cover with Scarlet Bloom paper.

❷ Print "Mother" on Butter Bloom plaid paper, cut to 3½" x 9", and adhere to left side.

❸ Cut ¾" strip of Butter Ticking plaid paper and adhere where papers meet.

❹ Tie three olive ribbons to Celery ribbon. Attach Celery ribbon to plaid strip with brads.

❺ Adhere brown ribbon left of plaid strip.

❻ Mat photo with Butter Ticking plaid. Adhere photo to piece.

❼ Pierce six small holes in lid and attach piece, using brads (see photo).

BOX

❶ Cover box with Butter Ticking plaid.

❷ Adhere green ribbon around box sides and embellish with brads.

❸ Fill box with mementos, such as photos and drawings.

Influential Women Tag Booklet

Designer: Alisa Bangerter

SUPPLIES

ALL PROJECTS:

Tags: (large Almond, Sky, Tan) Toe Tags, *The Stamp Doctor*

Binder ring

Fibers: (lace, ribbon)

Tools: computer and printer, paintbrush, ruler, scissors

Other: wedge sponge

COVER TAG:

Paper: (white)

Patterned paper: (TeaDye Script) *Design Originals*

Color medium: (light brown chalk) *Craf-T Products*

Paint: (pink) Ceramcoat, *Delta*

Accents:
   (Metal frame from Beyond Postmarks) *K&Company*
   (brown, cream buttons)

Font: (CK Opa's Hand) "Heritage, Vintage and Retro Collection" CD, *Creating Keepsakes*

Adhesive

PHOTO TAGS:

Patterned paper:
   (Green, Blue) *Hot Off The Press*
   (Shorthand) *Design Originals*

Specialty paper: (Sky Blue Mesh) Maruyama, *Magenta*

Color medium: (light brown chalk) *Craf-T Products*

Paint: (coral, green, pink, white) Ceramcoat, *Delta*

Paper accents: (small Almond, Sky, Tan Toe Tags) *The Stamp Doctor*

Accents:
   (metal frames, photo corners) *K&Company*
   (buttons, charms, safety pins)

Stickers: (assorted)

Fibers: (floss, rickrack)

Fonts: (CK Opa's Hand) "Heritage, Vintage and Retro Collection" CD; (CK Newsprint) "Fresh Fonts" CD, *Creating Keepsakes*

Adhesive

Other: memorabilia

Finished size: 2⅝" x 5"

COVER TAG

❶ Cut patterned paper to 2⅝" x 3¼" and adhere to tag bottom.

❷ Drybrush paint on tag and frame edges.

❸ Print sentiment on white paper; crumple, chalk, and adhere behind frame.

❹ Adhere frame to tag.

❺ Embellish with ribbon, buttons, and lace.

PHOTO TAGS

Each tag represents one influential woman (mother, grandmother, etc.)

❶ Decorate and embellish one tag to represent each person, using patterned papers, paint, chalk, accents, fibers, and fonts.

❷ Measure back of tag and print out information such as name, birth/death dates, spouse, and synopsis of person's life and interests. Trim and adhere to tag back.

❸ Assemble finished tags on ring.

❹ Tie ribbon assortment on ring.

DESIGNER TIP

Photocopy original photos, especially if they are one of a kind.

Bonus Ideas

- Make tags to represent girlfriends, sisters, aunts, children, or heroines.

- Print personal information in story form or make a list.

- To store additional memorabilia, adhere a small envelope to the back of each tag.

love you,

mom!

She's saved your crayon drawings all these years.
Now, make her a card that she'll treasure just as much.

Flowers & butterflies

Give her a card
as beautiful
as a mother's love.

Retro Flowers

Designer: Alisa Bangerter

SUPPLIES

Light green textured cardstock

Vellum

"mom" embellishment: *Meri Meri*

Pink chalk: Craft-T Products

Adhesive foam squares:
Therm O Web

Other: sewing machine, white thread

Finished size 5" x 7"

INSTRUCTIONS

❶ Make light green card base.

❷ Tear 4½" x 6½" piece of vellum.
Chalk edges.

❸ Machine-stitch vellum to card along
edges.

❹ Adhere embellishment with adhesive
foam squares.

Monarch Beauty

Designer: Kathleen Paneitz

SUPPLIES

Cardstock:
   Mandarin, Natural, *Bazzill Basics Paper*
   Ivory floral embossed paper: *K&Company*
   Butterfly Wallpaper patterned paper: *PSX*

Font: Rage Italic, *www.myfonts.com*

Watermark ink: Versamark, *Tsukineko*

Copper embossing powder: *Stampin' Up!*

Copper mini brads: *Magic Scraps*

Mini adhesive dots: *Glue Dots International*

Other: black wire, long nose pliers, heat embossing tool

Finished size: 5" x 4"

INSTRUCTIONS

❶ Make Mandarin card base.

❷ Print "Happy Mother's Day" on Natural cardstock and cut out. Apply ink and embossing powder to edges and heat emboss.

❸ Cut a 4½" x 3¾" piece of floral embossed paper. Attach greeting with mini brads and adhere to card base.

❹ Cut a butterfly from patterned paper.

❺ Cut two 2" lengths of wire. Curl one end of each with pliers. Adhere straight ends to back of paper butterfly (see photo).

❻ Adhere butterfly to card with mini adhesive dots. *Note: Adhere only body to card. Wings should be free, creating a 3-dimensional effect.*

Butterflies & Ribbons

Designer: Kathleen Paneitz

SUPPLIES

Cardstock: Black, Sand, *PSX*

Butterfly patterned paper: *PSX*

Acetate sheet (transparency): *3M*

Pewter butterfly sticker: *Magenta*

Black gingham ribbon: *Offray*

Metal alphabet charms: *Making Memories*

Font: Scriptina, *www.documentsanddesigns.com*

Finished size 3½" x 8"

INSTRUCTIONS

❶ Make Sand card base.

❷ Cut a 3⅜" x 7⅞" piece of butterfly paper and mat with card base.

❸ Cut a 1¾" x 2⅝" piece of Sand cardstock and adhere to upper left corner.

❹ Print "Happy" and "Mother's Day" on transparency (see photo for placement). Cut same size as butterfly paper.

❺ Place transparency over card.

❻ Mat butterfly sticker with Black cardstock. Adhere to transparency over Sand rectangle. Adhere transparency to card.

❼ Wrap ribbon around card front and tie with bow.

❽ Adhere alphabet charms to spell "MOM".

Folding Photo Card

Designer: Nancy Church

SUPPLIES

White cardstock

Patterned paper: Flora Bella Dots Flat, Garden Party Large Roses Flat, *K&Company*

Lightweight cardboard or foam core

Rose stickers: *K&Company*

Vellum tag: Making Memories

30" length sheer, wire-edged white ribbon

Fray check: *Dritz*

Pink eyelet: *Making Memories*

Black pen (for writing on vellum): Slick Writer, *American Crafts*

Other: calligraphy pen (for journaling,) eyelet setter, clear beads, twine, bone folder

Finished size 4½" square

INSIDE

❶ Trim three pieces of 8½" x 11" cardstock to make three 8½" squares.

❷ Follow figures a, b, and c to create folded interior of book, using a strong adhesive. *Note: The top and bottom of the middle diamond should fold backward, while the top and bottom of the side diamonds should fold forward to collapse the entire unit into a square.*

❸ Cut pictures or patterned paper into 4" squares and adhere as desired. For folded squares, cut paper or pictures in half diagonally before adhering so that book will close easily. Add stickers and journaling.

COVER

❶ Cut two 4½" squares of cardboard or foam core. Cover with two 5½" squares patterned paper, mitering corners.

❷ Lay ribbon horizontally across inside back cover and adhere with fabric glue.

❸ Adhere back of last photo page to inside of back cover.

❹ Adhere back of first photo page to inside of front cover. Fold card closed.

❺ Set eyelet in vellum tag. Add beads to twine and tie tag to ribbon. Tie ribbon around book. Apply Fray Check to ribbon ends.

DESIGNER TIP

To make a larger 6" square book, use 12" x 12" paper. Any size will work as long as it's square. Want to put more or fewer pictures in the book? You can vary the number of cardstock squares inside as long as you use an odd number of squares.

a Fold each diagonally, crease, then flip over.

b Fold each piece in half, crease and open, then fold the other way.

fold up   fold down   fold up

c Overlap and adhere with strong adhesive. Be sure that folds face as shown.

The Meaning of Mother

Designer: Renee Senchyna

SUPPLIES

Cardstock: beige, rust
Patterned paper: *Carolee's Creations*
Font: CK Twiggy, "Creative Clips & Fonts" CD, *Creating Keepsakes*
Eyelet letters: *Making Memories*
Chalks: *Craf-T Products*
Other: raffia

Finished size 7⅜" x 5⅜"

INSTRUCTIONS

❶ Make card base from patterned paper.

❷ Print poem on beige cardstock, leaving enough space between lines to attach eyelet letters. Crop to 6½" x 4½" rectangle and chalk edges.

❸ Attach eyelet letters to spell "mother".

❹ Mat with rust cardstock and adhere to card base.

❺ Adhere raffia bow.

DESIGNER TIP

To make chalk go on smoothly, apply it with a cotton ball.

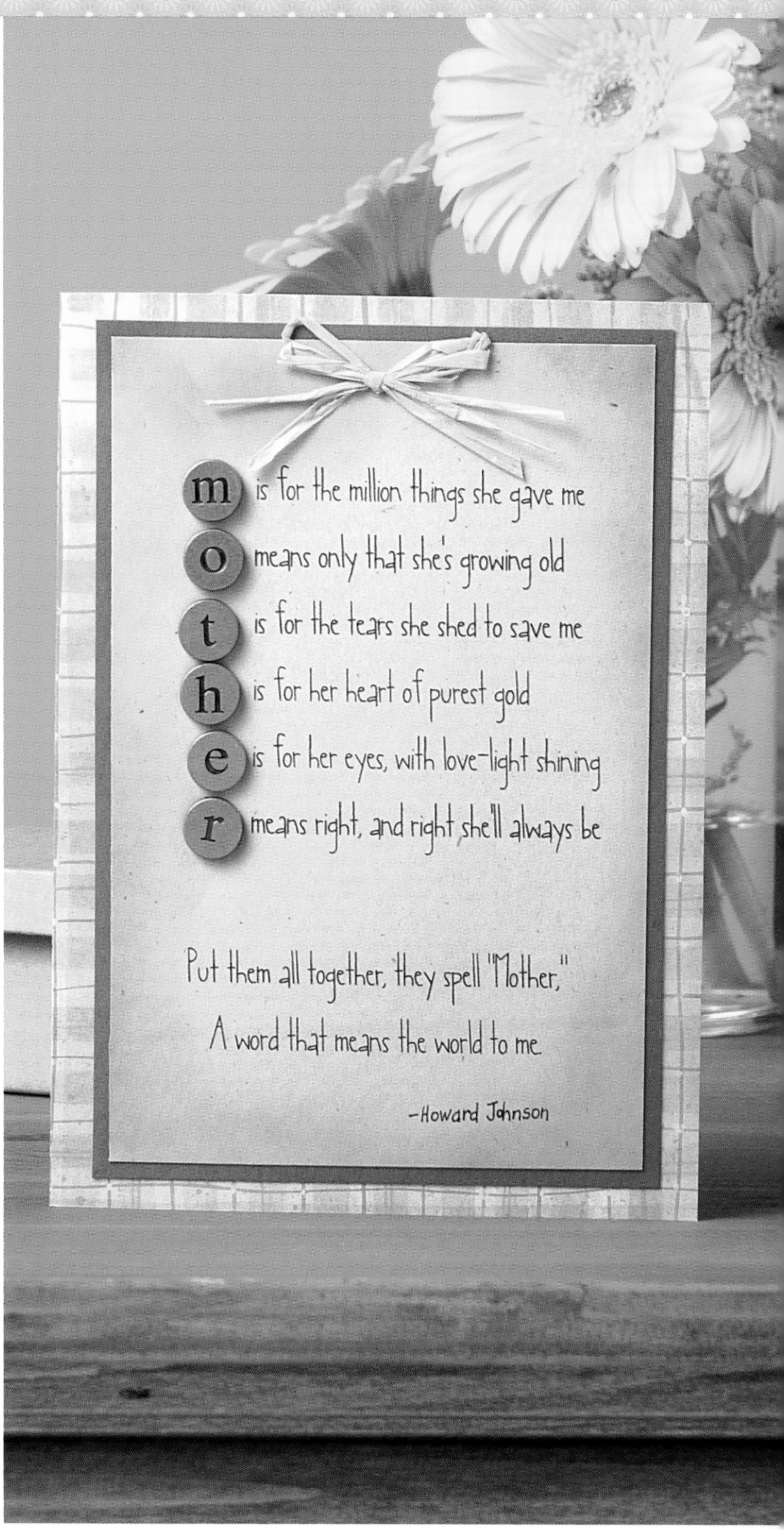

m is for the million things she gave me

o means only that she's growing old

t is for the tears she shed to save me

h is for her heart of purest gold

e is for her eyes, with love-light shining

r means right, and right she'll always be

Put them all together, they spell "Mother,"
A word that means the world to me.

—Howard Johnson

Like a Quilt

Designer: Valerie Pingree

SUPPLIES

Cardstock: (light green)

Textured cardstock: (white)

Accents:
(Raspberry mini buttons) *Lasting Impressions for Paper*
(fabric swatches) *P&B Textiles*

Rub-ons: (stitches) *Autumn Leaves*

Font: (CK Letter Home) "Creative Clips & Fonts by Becky Higgins" CD, *Creating Keepsakes*

Adhesive: (HeatnBond Ultra iron-on) *Therm O Web*

Tools: ruler, scissors, iron, computer and printer, craft knife

Other: pencil

Finished size: 6" square

INSTRUCTIONS

❶ Make 5¼" square card from white cardstock.

❷ Cut quilt pieces from iron-on adhesive, following pattern. Iron pieces to reverse side of fabric, following manufacturer's instructions; trim. Iron fabric pieces to front of card.

❸ Add rub-on stitches between fabric pieces. Adhere buttons to bottom.

❹ Print sentiment on light green cardstock and trim to 6" square. To make sleeve, cut slits above and below sentiment. Place quilt card in sleeve.

Bonus Ideas

- Print the following sentiment inside the card: "Thanks for keeping me warm through the years. Happy Mother's Day."

- Make an anniversary card that says, "I'm crazy about you."

- In lieu of fabric, use patterned paper or color copies of fabric.

SENTIMENT

A good mother is like a quilt; she keeps her children warm and doesn't smother them.

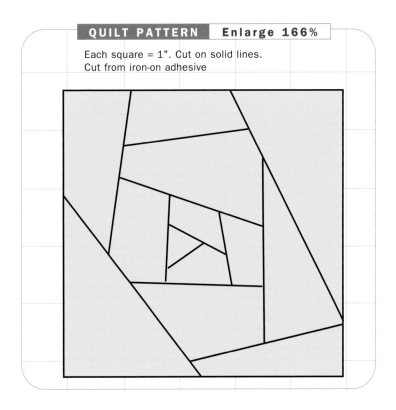

QUILT PATTERN   Enlarge 166%

Each square = 1". Cut on solid lines.
Cut from iron-on adhesive

Still a Child

Designer: Amber Crosby

SUPPLIES

Textured cardstock: (Rosey) *Bazzill Basics Paper*

Patterned paper: (Brianna Text & Botanicals) *K&Company*

Dye ink: (Espresso) Adirondack, *Ranger Industries*

Paper accents: (cardstock tags) Plain Jane Tags to Go, *FoofaLa*

Rub-ons: (Monograms alphabet) *Me & My Big Ideas*

Sticker: (child quote from Mother of Mine) Twill Sayings, *All My Memories*

Fasteners: (Bronze brads) *All My Memories*

Fibers: (red gingham ribbon) *Offray*

Adhesive: (Terrifically Tacky Tape) Art Accentz, *Provo Craft*

Tools: ruler, scissors

Finished size: 7" x 5"

INSTRUCTIONS

1. Make card from cardstock. Trim patterned paper to fit bottom of card; apply double-sided tape along bottom and side edges and adhere to card to create pocket.

2. Adhere ribbon to top of pocket.

3. Ink edges of tags; apply rub-on letters to spell "Mom." Insert brads through top holes. Tuck tags in pocket and adhere in place.

4. Add sticker.

Simple Sentiments

Select a heartwarming phrase to express your love for Mom or Grandma.

There was never a great man who had not a great mother.

—Olive Schreiner
set in Linoscript

I REMEMBER MY MOTHER'S PRAYERS AND THEY HAVE ALWAYS FOLLOWED ME. THEY HAVE CLUNG TO ME ALL MY LIFE.

—Abraham Lincoln
set in Minion RegularSC

A mother's arms are made of tenderness and children sleep soundly in them.

—Victor Hugo

*You may have tangible wealth untold;
Caskets of jewels and coffers of gold.
Richer than I you can never be—
I had a mother who read to me.*

—Strickland Gillilan

A mother is a person who, seeing there are only four pieces of pie for five people, promptly announces she never did care for pie.

—Tenneva Jordan

That best academy, a mother's knee.

—James Russell Lowell

Biology is the least of what makes someone a mother.

—Oprah Winfrey
set in Versailles Bold

Who ran to help me when I fell, and would some pretty story tell, or kiss the place to make it well? My mother.

—Ann Taylor

Through my grandmother's eyes, I can see more clearly the way things used to be, the way things ought to be, and most important of all, the way things really are.

—Ed Cunningham

Between the earth and sky above, nothing can match a grandmother's love.

set in B VAG Rounded Bold

Like a Mother to Me

Designer: Deanna Hutchison

SUPPLIES

Textured cardstock: (Bottle Glass, Lobster Bisque) *Bazzill Basics Paper*

Patterned paper: (Paisley Medium) Romantiques, *Beary Patch*

Accent: (gold dragonfly charm)

Fibers: (green organdy ribbon)

Font: (Andy) *www.fonts.com*

Adhesive:
  (foam tape) *3M*
  glue stick

Tools: ruler, scissors, computer and printer

Finished size: 4¼" x 5½"

INSTRUCTIONS

❶ Make card from Bottle Glass cardstock.

❷ Trim patterned paper slightly smaller than card; mat with Lobster Bisque cardstock. Adhere torn piece of Lobster Bisque to bottom corner of matted piece. Wrap ribbon around top. Adhere piece to card.

❸ Print "You're like a mother to me" on Bottle Glass. Cut into three strips and adhere to card with foam tape. Adhere dragonfly with foam tape.

Grandma, I Love You

Designer: Kathleen Paneitz

SUPPLIES

Cardstock: (black)

Textured cardstock: (Dawn) *Bazzill Basics Paper*

Patterned paper: (Somerset Bouquet) *K&Company*

Cardstock Photo Mat: (Black) *Westrim Crafts*

Photo

Accents:
   (silver label holder) *Two Peas in a Bucket*
   (grandma woven label from Grandmother) Threads, *Me & My Big Ideas*

Fasteners:
   (Pewter Country Heart brad) *Creative Impressions*
   (purple brads) *Magic Scraps*

Fibers: (black printed ribbon from Emotions) *Making Memories*

Adhesive

Tools:
   (1¾" square punch) *Marvy Uchida*
   ruler, scissors

Finished size: 5¾" x 4"

INSTRUCTIONS

❶ Make card from black cardstock.

❷ Trim patterned paper slightly smaller than photo mat; tear approx. 2½ " from right edge. Adhere woven label to piece. Attach label holder over label with purple brads. Adhere piece to photo mat.

❸ Wrap ribbon around left side of photo mat through window (see photo). Adhere in place and add heart brad.

❹ Punch square from Dawn cardstock and adhere photo behind opening. Trim cardstock and adhere behind photo mat.

❺ Adhere photo mat to card.

An Aunt is Everything

Designer: Brandi Barnes

SUPPLIES

Textured cardstock: (sage green)

Patterned paper: (Old Blue Roses) *Anna Griffin*

Card: (Kraft) Paper Reflections, *DMD, Inc.*

Photo

Rubber stamp: (By Definition Background) *Stampin' Up!*

Pigment ink: (Bamboo) VersaColor, *Tsukineko*

Paint: (Antique White acrylic) FolkArt, *Plaid*

Sticker: (Pewter photo corner from Eight Corners) *Magenta Rubber Stamps*

Fastener: (Pewter decorative brad) *Making Memories*

Fibers: (green printed ribbon from Emotions) *Making Memories*

Font: (Vladimir Script) www.myfonts.com

Adhesive

Tools: foam paintbrush, ruler, scissors, computer and printer

Other: paper towel

Finished size: 5" x 7"

INSTRUCTIONS

❶ Paint brad and photo corner sticker; rub paint from raised areas with paper towel. Let dry.

❷ Stamp background on cardstock; trim. Adhere photo and photo corner. Attach ribbon to edge with brad and adhesive. Adhere piece to card.

❸ Print "Only an aunt . . ." on patterned paper. Trim to fit bottom of card and tear top edge. Adhere to card.

❹ Print sentiment on cardstock, trim and adhere inside card.

Sentiment

Can give hugs like a mother . . .

Can keep secrets like a sister . . .

And share love like a friend.

Learn, Live, Love

Designer: Lisa Schmitt

SUPPLIES

Cardstock: peach textured, yellow, *Bazzill Basics Paper*

Parchment patterned paper: pink, yellow, Sonnets, *Creative Imaginations*

Vellum: *Creative Imaginations*

Script stamp: *Stampa Rosa*

Stickers: "learn," "live," "love"; *Wordsworth*

Stickers: square border, heart, "Mom", Sonnets, *Creative Imaginations*

Ink: mustard, sepia, *Ranger Industries*

Pink trim: *EK Success*

Card template: 5-C, *Deluxe Cuts*

Other: pewter heart charm, pewter safety pin, silver eyelet, silver flower eyelet, silver split ring, orange ribbon, yellow organdy ribbon

Finished size 5¼" square

CARD

Use card template and photo as placement guides.

1 Make yellow card base.

2 Cut 5" square peach cardstock and mat with card base.

3 Adhere square border sticker to left side of card.

4 Cut center strip from pink patterned paper. Adhere "learn," "live," and "love" stickers.

5 Wrap strip with trim and orange ribbon. Tie bow. Attach heart charm to ribbon with safety pin. Adhere strip to card.

6 Cut 2" yellow cardstock square and 2" x 2½" vellum rectangle. Stamp both with script, using mustard ink. Age edges of square with scissors. Color edges of cardstock with sepia ink. Adhere pieces to card.

7 Adhere heart, and "Mom" stickers (see photo).

A Card for Grandma

Designer: Lori Bergman

SUPPLIES

White cardstock

Light pink paper

Photo transfer fabric: *June Tailor*

Other: child's artwork, colored chalk, paper piercing tool, white thread, embroidery needle

Finished size 7" x 5"

INSTRUCTIONS

1 Make white card base.

2 Scan and print child's artwork on transfer fabric following manufacturer's instructions. Cut 6" x 4" piece around it. Pull out threads to fray edges. Mat with white cardstock.

3 Punch holes every ¼" around edge. Sew with running stitch.

Running Stitch
Up at odd, down at even numbers.

All I Am or Hope to Be…

Designer: Darcy Christensen

SUPPLIES

Kraft cardstock

Collage patterned paper: *The Paper Company*

Oval tag: *The Paper Company*

Silver eyelet: *Making Memories*

Font: Courier New, *Microsoft*

Adhesive foam squares: *Therm O Web*

Other: cream lace, white string, buttons, 3½" square photo, sewing machine, white thread

Finished size 7" x 4½"

INSTRUCTIONS

❶ Make kraft card base. Cut 2" x 3¼" window in top of card. Adhere photo to inside of card.

❷ Cut a 4" square of patterned paper. Tear bottom edge. Adhere to card. Machine stitch paper edges.

❸ Stitch lace below window.

❹ Thread string through button holes and tie in front. Adhere buttons with adhesive foam squares.

❺ Print quotation on tag (see photo). Set eyelet. Tie tag to one button with string. Adhere tag to card with adhesive foam squares.

ENVELOPE

❶ Make envelope from peach cardstock following pattern.

❷ Add flower eyelet to front flap. Thread yellow ribbon through.

❸ Make two small tags from yellow parchment. Adhere, back to back, with eyelet. Add heart sticker.

❹ Attach tag to ribbon with split ring. Tie ribbon into bow.

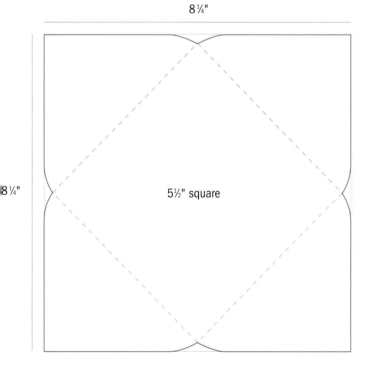

8¼"

8¼"

5½" square

Enlarge 250%   Score and fold on dashed lines.

Spring Lilac Frame

Designer: Kathleen Paneitz

SUPPLIES

12" x 12" lavender script patterned paper: *Mustard Moon*

Dimensional stickers: dragonfly, flower, lilacs; Grand Adhesions, *K&Company*

Fibers: *EK Success*

Foam core: *Michaels*

⅛" hole punch: *McGill*

Other: 4" x 6" photo, scoring tool, craft knife, double-sided tape, spray adhesive, chipboard, lavender organza ribbon

Finished size 8½" x 10½"

FRAME

❶ Cut 8½" x 10½" frame from foam core. Cut 4" x 6" opening.

❷ Wrap frame with patterned paper (see "How to Wrap a Frame").

❸ Wrap fibers around frame, knotting and taping in back to secure (see Figure a).

❹ Tie ribbon into bow; adhere to frame. Add dimensional stickers as desired.

a

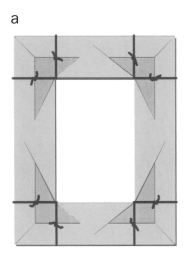

BACKING

❶ To make backing, cut chipboard slightly smaller than frame. Adhere photo to center with repositionable adhesive.

❷ To create opening in back for photo removal, cut chipboard around three sides of photo; score fourth side.

❸ Punch two holes, approx. 4" apart, in top of chipboard. Insert ribbon through holes for hanging; adhere ends in front.

❹ Adhere front of backing to frame, using double-sided tape.

BONUS IDEAS

■ Create frames in various styles, using different papers and embellishments. Make a frame for Father's Day, a wedding, or a baby's nursery.

■ To display the frame on a table, simply cut a foam core triangle, cover it with patterned paper, and attach it to the back of the frame. Or, purchase a miniature easel.

A Mother's Love Frame

SUPPLIES

Pink cardstock

White paper

Pink patterned paper: *Provo Craft*

Wood frame: *Ikea*

Ceramic flowers: *Oriental Trading Co.*

Font: Caslon 540 Italic and Swashes, *Microsoft*

Other: 4" x 6" photo, scoring blade, craft knife, spray adhesive, double-sided tape

Finished size 5" x 7"

INSTRUCTIONS

❶ Wrap frame.

❷ Print, cut out, and mat "A Mother's Love" title. Adhere.

HOW TO WRAP A FRAME

❶ Coat back of patterned paper with spray adhesive. Place paper, adhesive side up, on flat surface. Place frame face down on center of paper (see Figure a).

❷ Score paper along frame edges; wrap paper back over edges as though wrapping a present (see Figures b and c). Adhere with double-sided tape. Note: If frame is too large for paper to entirely cover each side, see "For Larger Frames."

❸ Cut an X through paper covering frame opening. Fold paper back and adhere behind frame (see Figures d and e).

FOR LARGER FRAMES

❶ Cover front of frame, and as much of the sides as possible.

❷ Cut two strips from matching paper to fit top and bottom sides of frame, adding ½" to length and width.

❸ Adhere strips to bottom and top sides, flush with front of frame, wrapping ¼" around each corner. Cut slits in corners; wrap excess paper behind frame.

❹ Cut strips for right and left sides, adding ½" to the width only. Adhere to frame, wrapping excess behind frame.

a b c

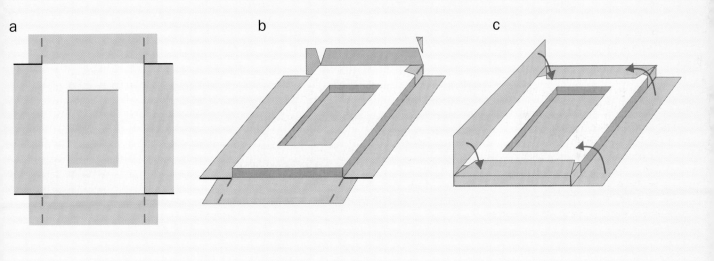

d e

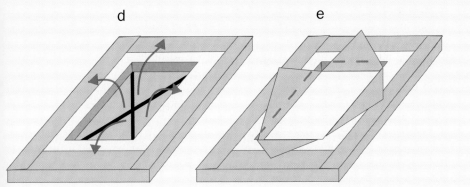

Grandma's Album

Designer: Linda Beeson

SUPPLIES

12" x 12" black textured cardstock: *Bazzill Basics Paper*

Patterned paper: burgundy floral, cream rose, *Daisy D's*

Mini 3-ring binder

"Grandma" metal word: *Making Memories*

1" x 2" cardboard dominos: *Sunday International*

Cranberry Wine acrylic paint: *DecoArt*

Dimensional lacquer: *Sakura Hobby Craft*

Other: gold ink, crinkled burgundy ribbon, gold heart nail head, 4 photos to fit dominos, fine sandpaper, decoupage or spray adhesive

Finished size 6½" x 6"

ALBUM

1. Remove pages from binder.

2. Wrap front cover with rose patterned paper, adhering paper with decoupage or spray adhesive. *Note: Fold paper edges under as though wrapping a gift.*

3. Tear edge of burgundy patterned paper. Apply gold ink along torn edge. Wrap paper over left side of front cover (see photo).

4. Tear one edge of black textured cardstock; wrap remainder of cover, positioning torn edge over burgundy paper.

5. Cut two pieces of desired patterned paper the same size as album pages. Adhere inside covers to hide raw edges. Insert album pages.

EMBELLISHMENTS

1. Trace domino on photos. Cut out and adhere to dominos. Adhere to cover.

2. Lightly sand metal word. Paint with Cranberry Wine; let dry. Coat with dimensional lacquer. Adhere to cover.

3. Wrap ribbon around cover; tie in front. Adhere gold heart.

Simple Sentiments

Select a heartwarming phrase to express your love for Mom or Grandma.

The only thing better than having you for my mother is my children having you for a grandmother.

You put the "grand" in grandma!

It was from you that I first learned to think, to feel, to imagine, to believe
—John Sterling

Book of Mom-isms

Designer: Darcy Christensen

SUPPLIES

Cardstock: brown textured, dark tan, light tan, rust

12" x 12" cardstock: cream, oatmeal

Patterned paper: antique script, brown leather, cream crackle, *Karen Foster*

Rust diamond patterned paper: Over the Moon Press, *EK Success*

Rusty Hardware stickers: *Sticker Studio*

Alphabet tag stickers: *Sticker Studio*

Fonts:

CK Typewriter, "Fresh Fonts" CD, *Creating Keepsakes*

Courier New, *Microsoft*

Copper eyelet: *Making Memories*

Other: 2 coordinating beads, jute, cream fibers, thread (tan, white), sewing machine

Finished size 4⅝" x 5½"

BOOK

❶ Cut 4⅝" x 11" piece of light tan cardstock for book cover. Cut three 4¼" x 10¼" pieces of cream cardstock for pages.

❷ Fold all pieces in half widthwise; place cream pieces over cover piece. Machine-stitch along fold with tan thread.

❸ Cut two holes through book spine. Thread jute through holes; knot on outside of book. Add bead to each end.

FRONT COVER

❶ Cut brown leather paper piece slightly smaller than book cover; adhere to cover. Adhere torn antique script paper to bottom corner. Zigzag-stitch paper edges with white thread.

❷ Spell "mom" with tag stickers. Print the following letters each on different paper or cardstock: "i, s, m, s." Cut out and adhere below tag stickers.

❸ Print the following message, with 1–3 words each on different paper or cardstock.

"those annoying things your mom used to say and do that now you find quite useful."

❹ Cut out message and adhere to bottom of cover. Add stickers as desired.

PAGES

❶ Cut piece of paper or cardstock slightly smaller than each page; adhere to page.

❷ Print message for each page, using fonts in different styles and sizes to make pages fun and easy to read (see "Page Ideas").

❸ Embellish pages with torn patterned paper, stickers, and tags as desired.

PAGE IDEAS

❶ Inside cover: Print a short message about how you benefited from your mother's advice.

❷ First page: Print your mother's name, followed by "Mom-isms" (see photo).

❸ On each remaining page, list one piece of advice you received from your mother, followed by some related memories. Here are some examples from designer Darcy Christensen:

- **If you quit now, you'll regret it later.**

  (Piano lessons, sports, or school projects—we learned to stick with it and never give up.)

- **Work before play.** (Farm work, homework, or housework—she always wanted our jobs done first. I have found this to be invaluable advice.)

- **Always send a thank-you note.** (I remember writing thank-you notes on Christmas, since Mom said we couldn't use a present until we'd written a thank-you.)

- **Always wear a slip.** (Even if we thought it wasn't necessary, we still put on a slip, just in case. Yes, I still wear a slip . . . just in case.)

- **Homemade is always better.** (Whether it was bread, Christmas cards, or prom dresses, Mom always wanted us to learn to make it ourselves.)

❹ Last page: "You'll know what I mean when you're a mom."

Bonus Idea

This book fits neatly inside a CD case. Tie ribbon or fibers around the case for attractive gift packaging.

THANKS FOR BEING my

FROM COVER TO COVER

Making—and reading—a book has never been so much fun!

D-A-D SPELLS LOVE

Designer: Wendy Johnson

SUPPLIES

Cardstock: light blue, cream, beige, *SEI*

Olive plaid patterned paper: Cabin Collection, *Chatterbox*

Jump ring, spiral clip, black eyelets: *Making Memories*

Gold Brads: Impress *Rubber Stamps*

Star button: *Dress It Up*

Black ink: *Close To My Heart*

"for you" rubber stamp: *Savvy Stamps*

Chalk: *Craft-T Products*

Font: CK Stenography, "Fresh Fonts" CD, *Creating Keepsakes*

Other: jute, twill tape, paper raffia, cream floss, needle, blue button, sandpaper

Finished size
5½" square closed,
5½" x 18½" open

ACCORDION CARD BASE

❶ Cut blue cardstock 5½" square. Attach jute loop with brad (see photo).

❷ Cut 3 cream cardstock pieces 4½" x 9". Score and fold in half.

❸ Adhere 3 cream pieces together alternating folds for accordion (see Figure a).

❹ Adhere last cream panel to blue cardstock center, covering points of brad (see Figure a).

COVER

❶ Cut 4½" square of patterned paper. Sew button to center right side. Adhere square to cream cardstock front panel.

❷ Cut twill tape and adhere to square (see photo).

❸ Stamp "for you" on cream cardstock. Cut into mini tag shape, punch hole and sand edges. *Note: If you do not have sandpaper, use a nail buffer.*

❹ Put jump ring through mini tag and hook through twill tape.

D-A-D PANELS

❶ Print "D-a-d" on three colors of cardstock, using 200 point font.

❷ Trim and mat as desired. Adhere to panels.

❸ Embellish with stamps, torn paper, eyelets, buttons, brads, spiral clip, and chalk as desired.

PHOTO PANEL

❶ Cut 2½" x 3" patterned paper pocket for last page of book. Stitch floss around pocket edge. Adhere three edges to page, leaving top of pocket open.

❷ Adhere photo to pocket front.

❸ Make gift tag and mat with coordinating blue cardstock. Add personal message to tag. Embellish with eyelet and paper raffia.

LET KIDS ADD LOVE

Children can add their own personal touches by:

- Signing or drawing on the tag.
- Inserting love or chore coupons in the pocket.
- Putting a note to Dad in the pocket.

Honor your dad, stepdad, uncle, brother, or father figure with a made-with-love remembrance.

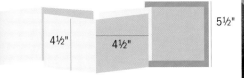

4½"   4½"   5½"

a

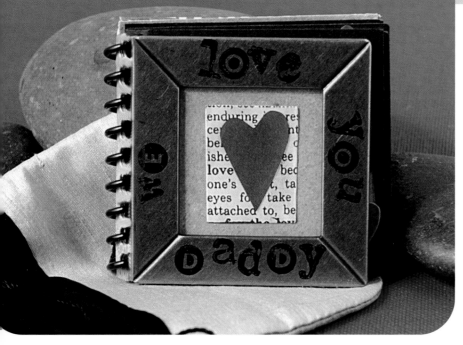

WE LOVE YOU DADDY MiNi ALBUM

Designer: Tracy Miller

SUPPLIES

Cardstock: black, kraft, red

Patterned paper: Love, *Lil' Davis*

Cardboard

Metal frame: Details, *Making Memories*

Rubber stamps:
Round letters, *PSX*
Typewriter font, *Rubber Stampede*

Solvent ink: black; StazOn, *Tsukineko*

Dye ink:
Black, *PSX*
Van Dyke Brown; Nick Bantock, *Ranger Industries*

Heart punch: Paper Shapers, *EK Success*

Love tidbits stickers: Real Life, *Pebbles Inc.*

Metal adhesive: Li'l Davis

Decoupage adhesive: Mod Podge, *Plaid*

Temporary adhesive: Mono Adhesive Tape, *Tombow*

Other: foam brush, rubber brayer, photos

Finished size 2¼" x 2½"

COVERS

❶ Cut two 2¼" x 2½" cardboard pieces.

❷ Cut two 2¾" x 3" patterned paper pieces.

❸ Decoupage patterned paper to cardboard, using brayer to smooth. Let dry.

❹ Apply thin line of adhesive to cardboard edges. Fold paper over edges. *Note: For neat appearance, fold over corners first, then the sides.*

❺ Cut two 2¼" x 2½" patterned paper pieces to line covers. Adhere with decoupage adhesive and smooth with brayer.

❻ Seal covers with dcoupage adhesive. Let dry.

❼ Stamp message on metal frame with black solvent ink. Adhere to front cover with metal adhesive. Place stickers in center.

PAGES

❶ Cut black cardstock to 2¼" x 2½" for inner pages.

❷ Cut 2⅛" x 4" red cardstock pieces; score and fold in half. Adhere to pages. Embellish as desired with photos, children's drawings, stickers, and stamps (see photo).

❸ Bind at local copy shop.

DESIGNER TIPS

- Paper is easier to fold neatly if you score it first.

- To age paper edges, press them into a brown dye-based ink.

BIG IDEAS FOR A MINI ALBUM

This cute little book can inspire endless ideas. Try making:

- A friendship autograph book for the graduate.

- A teacher gift filled with student photos, artwork or autographs.

- A baby brag book for a new dad or grandparents.

- A pet brag book for an animal lover.

- A thoughtful gift for a traveler. The small size fits easily into luggage.

- A mini wedding album as a thank-you gift for bridal party members.

FATHER'S DAY ACCORDION ALBUM

Designer: Kari Barrera

SUPPLIES

6 sheets dark blue 12" cardstock: *Chantilly Lace*

Patterned paper: Dark Blue Circles, Large Plaid; Den, Chatterbox Plaid; Sitting Room, *Chatterbox*

Chipboard

Photos or Poems

Alphabet stickers: denim SI alpha stickers, *Chatterbox*

Cream sandstone textured paint: *DecoArt*

Silver bookplate

Brown grosgrain ribbon

Other: decoupage adhesive, sewing machine, brown thread, needle, loose-weave burlap, double-sided tape, hot glue, sandpaper

Finished size
  6" x 6" x ¾" closed,
  6" x 72" open

COVER

❶ Cut two 6" square pieces chipboard.

❷ Cut two 6½" square pieces Sitting Room Plaid paper.

❸ Coat back of paper with decoupage adhesive. Place chipboard centered on paper.

❹ Trim corners off paper. Fold over the edges. *Note: Trimming corners makes it easier to fold and create a smooth finished corner.* Repeat for other piece of chipboard.

❺ Tear edges of cover photo.

❻ Paint edges of photo with textured paint. Let dry. *Note: To create texture, start from the outside edges and pull the paintbrush inward.*

❼ Secure photo to burlap with double-sided tape. Stitch in place with brown thread. *Note: This technique looks better the less precise it is. Simply sew around the focal point and trim excess thread away.* Trim and fray edges. Set aside.

❽ Paint thin coat of textured paint over bookplate; let dry. Sand lightly to give an aged effect.

❾ Cut patterned paper to fit inside bookplate frame. Spell book title with alphabet stickers. Set aside.

❿ Wrap ribbon around book covers. Adhere in center of front album cover only (see photo).

⓫ Adhere photo over ribbon with thin line of hot glue.

⓬ Center bookplate and title below photo. Adhere with hot glue.

INSIDE PAGES

❶ Cut dark blue cardstock into eleven 6" x 12" strips. Fold strips in half to make 6" squares.

❷ Adhere strips together, alternating folds, to create long accordion (see Figure a on p. 105).

❸ Adhere completed accordion inside covers with decoupage adhesive. Let dry.

PAGE DECORATION

❶ Cut 5½" squares of patterned paper. Adhere to pages.

❷ Decorate with pictures, poems, stories, or letters to your father.

❸ Tie book closed with ribbon.

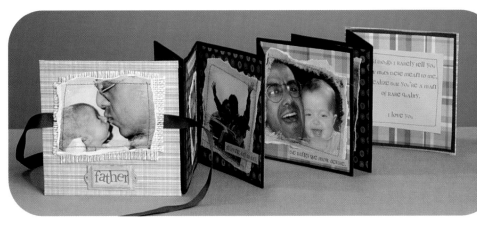

WE LOVE YOU TAG BOOKLET

Designer: Melanie Maughan

SUPPLIES

Large shipping tags

Photos

Gingham fabric: *JoAnn Stores*

Mini brads: American Pin and Fastener

Heart punch: Paper Shapers, *EK Success*

Heart snap, star charm: *Making Memories*

Silver wire: *Artistic Wire*

Nailheads: *JewelCraft*

Other: ribbon, button, safety pin, alphabet stamps

Finished size 5" x 2"

INSTRUCTIONS

❶ Score tags 1⅛" from top.

❷ Print words with alphabet stamps or a favorite font.

❸ Adhere photos and embellish as desired.

❹ Tie together with ribbon.

DADDY LOVES ME

Designer: Janelle Clark

SUPPLIES

Cardstock: brown, tan

Frame die cut: *My Mind's Eye*

Photo

Alphabet stamps: *Close To My Heart*

Red ink: Brilliance, *Tsukineko*

Embossing powder: silver ultra thick, *Ranger Industries*

Pewter metallic rub-on finish: *Craf-T Products*

Brass bookplate

Black mini brads

Other: watermark ink, heat tool

Finished size 5¾" square

INSTRUCTIONS

❶ Cut card from brown cardstock.

❷ Cut apart frame die cut at each corner. Reassemble to 5" square frame. Trim excess.

❸ Place 3½" square photo behind frame and mat with tan cardstock. Adhere to card.

❹ Rub brass bookplate with watermark ink. Sprinkle with silver embossing powder and heat with heat tool. While still hot, repeat embossing process until bookplate is fully covered.

❺ Rub bookplate randomly with pewter rub-on finish.

❻ Stamp "daddy loves me" on tan cardstock with red ink. Trim and place in bookplate.

❼ Fasten bookplate to card with brads.

DESIGNER TIPS

- Use long tweezers to hold the bookplate while heating, or hold it down with a chopstick or skewer on a heat-resistant surface.

- Work over a craft tray or shoebox lid to capture messy embossing powder.

- You don't have to stamp each letter of your greeting individually. Use unmounted stamps to assemble the entire phrase on a block, then stamp once.

SiMPLY, DAD

Designer: Amber Crosby

SUPPLIES

Cardstock: blue textured, brown textured, green, *Bazzill Basics Paper*

Barnwood Tan paper: Real Life Printed Paper, *Pebbles Inc.*

Hands photo sticker: Real Life Sticker Snapshot, *Pebbles Inc.*

Brown gingham ribbon: *Impress Rubber Stamps*

Antique white label holder: *Making Memories*

Alphabet stickers: *PSX*

Silver mini brads: *Stampin' Up!*

Mini adhesive dots

Finished size 7" x 5"

INSTRUCTIONS

❶ Make green card base.

❷ Adhere thin strip of patterned paper to top of card.

❸ Adhere ribbon over strip. Embellish with mini brads.

❹ Mat photo sticker with brown cardstock. Adhere to card center.

❺ Adhere larger strip of patterned paper near bottom.

❻ Spell "DAD" on blue cardstock with alphabet stickers and place in label holder.

❼ Thread ribbon through label holder holes and adhere label holder and ribbon to large strip with mini adhesive dots.

I'LL ALWAYS LOOK UP TO YOU, DAD

Designer: Shanna Burkholder

SUPPLIES

Cardstock: aqua, fuchsia, white, *Creative Memories*

Striped paper: *Bo Bunny Press*

Photo

Fasteners: Rivets, *Chatterbox*

Watch crystals: *Scrappin' Extras*

White plastic measuring tape

Font: CK Journaling, "The Art of Creative Lettering Combo" CD, *Creating Keepsakes*

Other: fuchsia chalk, adhesive dots, adhesive pop-up dots, ¼" hole punch, 1" circle punch, glue pen

Finished size 4⅝" x 6½"

INSTRUCTIONS

❶ Create card base from aqua cardstock.

❷ Mount striped paper on white cardstock. Punch ¼" holes in corners and attach fasteners.

❸ Mount striped piece on card base.

❹ Cut piece of measuring tape, chalk, and adhere at an angle.

❺ Print "No matter how tall I grow, I will always look up to you, Dad" on white cardstock. Print "D-A-D" and punch out letters with 1" circle punch.

❻ Mat quote block with fuchsia cardstock and adhere to card front.

❼ Trim and mat photo with aqua cardstock and adhere as shown in photo.

❽ Cut strip of fuchsia cardstock and adhere above quote block. Attach circle letters to strip with adhesive pop-up dots.

❾ To adhere watch covers, apply thin layer of glue to rims with glue pen and place carefully over letters. *Note: Letters should almost touch dome of covers.*

SHANNA'S DESIGNER TIPS

▪ Chalk shows up more brilliantly on a white plastic measuring tape than on a yellow one or one made of fabric.

▪ Vary the colors of your paper to match the clothing or background in the photo. Or, simply pick more traditional colors such as navy and red.

DAD'S LOVE iS MAGNETiC

Designer: Linda Beeson

SUPPLIES

Patterned paper: blue circle, green plaid, *Chatterbox*

White paper

Metal bulletin board: *Target*

½" x ⅞" rectangular page pebbles: *Making Memories*

Ink: black, blue, *Making Memories*

Alphabet stamps: Pixie Antique, *PSX*

White acrylic paint: Apple Barrel, *Plaid*

Adhesive-backed magnet sheets: Magnetic Specialty, Inc., *Michaels*

½" oil board stencils: Duro, *Dick Blick*

Other: sandpaper, stencil brush

Finished size 7" x 5¼"

BOARD

❶ Cut blue circle paper to size of metal board and adhere.

❷ Lightly sand edges.

D-A-D MAGNETS

❶ Brush white paint over stencils.

❷ When dry, sweep blue stamp pad across stencils.

❸ Adhere white paper behind stencils to highlight letters.

❹ Adhere magnet to back. Trim to fit.

WORD MAGNETS

❶ Stamp words on green plaid paper.

❷ Cut out to match page pebbles shapes.

❸ Adhere pebbles to paper. Back with magnet sheet. Trim to fit.

PHOTOS

❶ Hold photos or other memorabilia against board with word magnets, or back photos with magnet sheet.

MORE MAGNETIC IDEAS

■ Create a girl's gift to her father. Include magnet words such as daughter, her name, and words that fit her personality.

■ Change paper and designs to personalize the board. Use paper that reflects a hobby, interest, or school colors.

■ Make a magnet board for a birthday, Mother's Day, wedding, teacher, or Grandparents Day gift.

WHERE TO BUY

Looking for other metal bulletin boards, magnets, and magnet frames? Three By Three Seattle has a great selection and will spark more ideas. 206/784-5839, *www.threebythree.com.*

LOVE YOU DADDY

Designer: Linda Beeson

SUPPLIES

Rubber stamps: *Hero Arts* (alphabet, little squares background); *PSX* (alphabet); *Penny Black* (All Over Mural background); *Post-modern Design* (Tape Measure)

Screw eyelets: *Making Memories*

Other: ink (black, mustard, red, brown), cardstock (rust, ivory, yellow-gold), black heart eyelet, photos, scissors, adhesive, eyelet-setting tools, sandpaper

finished size: 5½" x 4½"

INSTRUCTIONS

❶ Make rust card.

❷ Stamp images on background with various ink as desired.

❸ Age edges of photos with sandpaper. Trim and adhere photos to card.

❹ Stamp children's initials with black on yellow gold cardstock. Trim and adhere to photos.

❺ Stamp "Love you Daddy" on ivory cardstock with black. Ink background and trim into strip.

❻ Attach strip to card with screw eyelets. Attach heart eyelet in corner.

DAD GRAFFITI

Designer: Linda Beeson

SUPPLIES

Rubber stamps: *Stampa Barbara* (alphabet); *PSX* (alphabet); *Hero Arts* (alphabet, little square background); *Art Impressions* (large square background)

Tag template: *Deluxe Cuts*

Eyelet: *Creative Imaginations*

Textured cardstock: blue, *Bazzill Basics Paper*

Texture patterned paper: Studio Nightfall Canvas, *Making Memories*

Other: ink (black, blue, watermark), embossing powder (black, silver), circle punch, adhesive, scissors, embossing heat tool, eyelet-setting tools

Finished size: 5½" x 4¼"

INSTRUCTIONS

❶ Make blue card.

❷ Stamp large square background on texture patterned paper. Ink with blue. Tear one edge; adhere to card.

❸ Punch circle from blue cardstock. Ink with watermark and emboss with silver; stamp "D" in embossing powder with black while still warm. Adhere to card.

❹ Create blue tag and cover half with texture patterned paper with one edge torn.

❺ Stamp little squares background on tag; ink tag with blue. Stamp words on paper and directly on tag with black; emboss with black. Cut out stamped letters and adhere to tag as desired.

❻ Set eyelet in tag; add fibers. Adhere to card.

IMAGINE MONEY CLIP

Designer: Marla Bird

SUPPLIES

Cream cardstock

12" x 12" patterned paper: Soft Sage, *Rusty Pickle*

Ink jet printable canvas: *OfficeMax*

Photo money clip: *Memory Maker*

Photos: 2 small for clip, 3 for copying on canvas

Walnut ink: *7gypsies*

Font: Typewriter Rough, *www.clipart.com*

Accents:
    Bark wire: *7gypsies*
    Pressed flower: *Nature's Pressed*

Other: ruler, scoring tool, double-sided tape, craft glue, ink jet color printer, foam paintbrush

Finished size 3" square

INSTRUCTIONS

❶ Cut 12" x 6" piece of patterned paper. Score and fold in half widthwise to form 12" x 3" strip. Seal with double-sided tape.

❷ Score strip every 3"; fold accordion-style to make card.

❸ Print photos on canvas, following manufacturer's instructions. Cut slits in edges of canvas and tear out photos.

❹ Adhere photos inside card with double-sided tape.

❺ Print words and sentiment on cream cardstock. Trim and tear edges. Daub with diluted walnut ink, using foam paintbrush. Let dry and adhere to card. Add dried flower to front of card.

❻ Close card and tie with bark wire. Place photos in money clip and slip over wire.

Bonus Idea

Wrap the card with ribbon, fibers, or beaded wire in place of bark wire.

A TIP FROM MARLA

I purchased an inexpensive paper cutter and replaced the cutting blade with a scoring blade. I use this paper cutter exclusively for scoring. It's my ultimate time saver!

LET'S PLAY BALL

Designer: Linda Beeson

SUPPLIES

Cardstock: black, brown textured

Crackle patterned paper: *Sticker Studio*

Baseball patterned paper: *Wubie Prints*

Alphabet stickers: *Sticker Studio* (for "Father's")

Black ink pad: *Making Memories*

⅜" alphabet tiles: Jolee's Boutique, *EK Success*

Finished size 4¼" x 5½"

INSTRUCTIONS

❶ Make card base from 8½" x 5½" piece of brown textured cardstock.

❷ Cut crackle paper and mat with black cardstock. Tear baseball paper; rub torn edge with black inkpad; layer over crackle paper. Adhere layers to card front.

❸ Spell "Happy Father's Day" with stickers and alphabet tiles.

VINTAGE TRAVELS

Designer: Lisa Schmitt

SUPPLIES

Cardstock: cream, patterned gray, tan

Metallic cardstock: brown, gold, *Bazzill Basics Paper*

Card: *DMD Industries*

Rubber stamps: Journeys Collage stamp, Voyage Ticket Stamp Set, Sundial stamp from Weather Stamp Set, *Club Scrap*

Postage stamp punch: *Marvy Uchida*

Pigment ink: white, Brilliance, *Tsukineko*

Dye ink: Van Dyke Brown; Nick Bantock, *Ranger Industries*

Alphabet stamps: *PSX*

Other: black ink, deckle-edge scissors, twine, hole punch

Finished size 7" x 5"

INSTRUCTIONS

❶ Drag brown inkpad over card front (see photo).

❷ Stamp sundial in top right corner with Van Dyke Brown ink.

❸ Attach torn strip of patterned gray cardstock near card bottom.

❹ Stamp ticket image in black ink on gold metallic cardstock. Cut into rectangle; round corners. Punch hole in corner.

❺ Stamp Journeys Collage with Van Dyke Brown on cream cardstock. Trim with deckle-edge scissors; mat with tan cardstock.

❻ Wrap twine around collage and tie on ticket. Attach to card front.

❼ Punch brown metallic cardstock with postage stamp punch. Stamp "D-A-D" and attach near card bottom.

Age card with inkpad.

GOLF BAG

Designer: Susan Neal

SUPPLIES

Rubber stamps: *My Sentiments Exactly* (Happy Father's Day sentiment); *PSX* (Golf set)

Chalk ink: Dark Moss, ColorBox, *Clearsnap*

Cardstock: *Bazzill Basics Paper* (navy, buff)

Patterned paper: *Chatterbox* (Dark Den Circles, Big Den Stripe)

Corner punch: Simplicity, Corner Adorner, *EK Success*

Other: adhesive, scissors

Finished size: 3¾" x 9"

INSTRUCTIONS

❶ Make navy card.

❷ Stamp golf bag and sentiment with Dark Moss on buff cardstock; cut out.

❸ Corner punch opposite corners on navy cardstock. Insert corner of stamped image and adhere; trim excess.

❹ Mat golf bag with Big Den Stripe and buff; trim to fit card and adhere.

❺ Mat sentiment with Dark Den Circles and buff; trim to fit card and adhere.

OLD MODEL T

Designer: Nichole Heady

SUPPLIES

Rubber stamps: *Stampin' Up!* (By Definition background, Airplane set, Classic alphabet set)

Dye ink: *Stampin' Up!* (Garden Green, Basic Black)

Solvent ink: Forest Green, StazOn, *Tsukineko*

Cardstock: *Stampin' Up!* (Garden Green, Naturals Ivory, Basic Black)

Transparent shrink plastic: *PolyShrink*

Silver paint pen: Painty Pen, ZIG, *EK Success*

Other: green fibers, hole punch, sand paper, sponge, adhesive, scissors, embossing heat tool or oven

Finished size: 4" square

INSTRUCTIONS

❶ Make Natural Ivory card.

❷ Sand shrink plastic. *Note: Sand vertically and horizontally to create* cross hatch pattern.

❸ Stamp truck with Forest Green on shrink plastic. Add accents with silver paint pen; place in oven or use heat tool to shrink.

❹ Stamp By Definition background with Garden Green on Naturals Ivory cardstock. Circle kinship with silver paint pen; trim excess. Mat on Basic Black cardstock and ink edges.

❺ Cut tag from Garden Green cardstock, punch hole at end. Crumple paper; secure fibers and adhere truck accent.

❻ Adhere stamped image and truck accent to card.

❼ Stamp "Father" on card with Basic Black.

Pay Tribute to a Teacher

Start the new school year—or commemorate a previous one—
with a thank-you gift for Teacher. You're sure to earn some extra credit!

Class Picture Wall Hanging

Designer: Wendy Johnson

SUPPLIES

Cardstock: blue, red

White paper

Foam core board

Class photo

Alphabet stamps (for frame): Antique UC, *PSX*

Alphabet stamps (for "Class of 2004"): *Making Memories*

Watermark ink: VersaMark, *Tsukineko*

Dye ink: Black Beauty, *The Angel Company*

Cork sheet: *Magic Scraps*

Red eyelets: *Making Memories*

Blue gingham ribbon: *Offray*

Red apple charm: *Doodlebug Design*

Fonts:
   CK Primary: "Art of Creative Lettering" CD, *Creating Keepsakes*

   PC Type: "For Font's Sake" CD; PC Crafter, *Provo Craft*

Drill and ¼" bit

Finished size 8½" x 10"

ASSEMBLE

❶ Cover foam core board with blue cardstock. Stamp alphabet border, using watermark ink.

❷ Cut cork sheet to 7" x 8½". Set eyelets in top corners. Adhere to board.

❸ Drill holes in center of eyelets, through entire board.

❹ To make hanger, thread ribbon through eyelets and knot ends.

ACCENT

❶ Stamp class year on bottom of cork sheet, using black ink.

❷ Print names of teacher and school or grade on white paper, using assorted fonts. Cut out and mat with cardstock. Adhere to cork sheet.

❸ Adhere class photo to cork sheet.

❹ Tie ribbon through apple charm; adhere next to photo.

Bonus Ideas

Make a matching card and tag for Teacher.

Teacher Note Cards

Designer: Jennifer Miller

SUPPLIES

Cardstock: white, yellow textured, *Bazzill Basics Paper*

Wood schoolhouse embellishment: *Provo Craft*

Transparent stationery box: *Impress Rubber Stamps*

Fonts:
Marydale, *www.typequarry.com*

2Ps Just Plain Little, 2Ps Dreams, *www.twopeasinabucket.com*

Red ribbon

Finished size 5" x 4"

INSTRUCTIONS

① Make card base with white cardstock. Print "From the desk of [teacher's name]" on bottom.

② Print quotation around the border of a square on white paper:

The important thing is not so much

that every child should be taught

as that every child should be given

the wish to learn. —John Lubbock

③ Trim quote; mat with textured cardstock, and adhere to card. Add schoolhouse embellishment.

Bonus Ideas

- Create cards using different colors and school-themed embellishments.

- Make a matching tag and tie it to the stationery box with ribbon.

- Make note cards for different seasons or holidays.

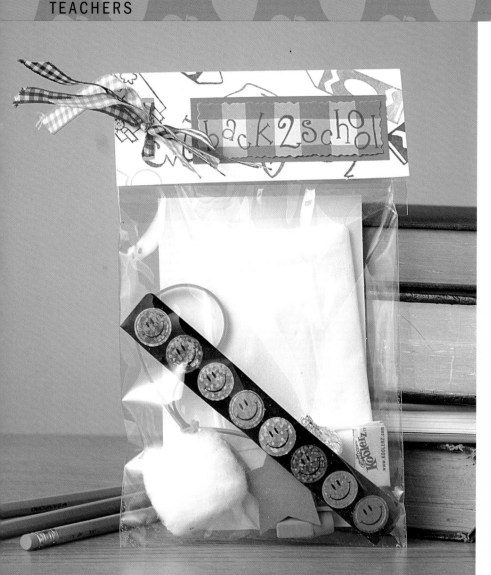

KIT

1 Adhere stamps to acrylic handle to spell "back 2 school". Stamp image on gingham paper with Star Spangled Blue ink. Trim with deckle-edge scissors. Mat with red cardstock.

2 Place kit contents and Survival Kit sheet (see "School Survival Kit") in plastic bag.

3 Cut a 5¼" x 4" piece of white cardstock and randomly stamp with school images in all ink colors. Fold in half and adhere over top of plastic bag.

4 Punch two holes in side of bag topper and add ribbons.

SURVIVAL KIT SHEET

Print the following text on a sheet of white paper, using your favorite fonts:

SCHOOL SURVIVAL KIT

Cotton ball—to remind you that this room is full of kind words and warm feelings.

Chocolate kiss—to comfort you when you are feeling sad.

Tissue—to remind you to help dry someone's tears.

Happy face stickers—to remind you that a smile is so important.

Star—to remind you to shine and always try your best.

Rubber band—to remind you to stretch yourself to learn.

Penny—to remind you that you are valuable and special.

Toothpick—to remind you to pick out the good qualities in your classmates.

Bandage—to heal hurt feelings in your friends and in yourself.

Eraser—to remind you that we all make mistakes, and that is okay.

Gum—to remind you to stick with it!

HAVE A GREAT YEAR!

Back 2 School Survival Kit

The perfect remedy for first-day-of-school jitters.

Designer: Kelly Lautenbach

SUPPLIES

All supplies from Close To My Heart unless otherwise noted.

Cardstock: red, white

Papers:
   Star Spangled Blue gingham patterned
   White

Gingham ribbon: blue, green, red, yellow

Rubber stamp set: School Days

Self-adhesive stamp sets: Playful lower-case alphabet and numbers

Acrylic handle (for stamps)

Ink: Holiday Red, Kentucky Green, Star Spangled Blue, Sunny Yellow

Deckle-edge scissors

Hole punch

Adhesive: Mono, *Tombow*

Resealable plastic bag

Contents for kit: cotton ball, chocolate kiss, tissue, happy face stickers, paper star, rubber band, penny, toothpick, bandage, eraser, gum

Finished size 8" x 5"

- Self-adhesive alphabet stamps make it easy to stamp multiple kits!

- Angle the letter placement for a whimsical look. It will also look less obvious if you don't stamp straight.

- Be sure the items in the bag are appropriate for the age of the child receiving it.

Bonus Ideas

- Come up with some other fun kit supplies to help the first day of school go smoothly.

- Create similar survival kits for going to college, having a baby, getting married, or moving into a new home.

Simple Sentiments

Express your gratitude to a teacher with an uplifting message:

One good teacher outweighs a ton of books.

—Chinese proverb
Set in AmerType Bd BT

A teacher affects eternity;
he can never tell where
his influence stops.

—Henry Brooks Adams

A teacher takes a hand, opens a mind, and touches a heart.

Teachers plant seeds of knowledge that will grow forever.

Pencil Tag

Designer: Patty Lennon

SUPPLIES

Cardstock: black, burgundy

Notebook patterned paper: *Karen Foster Design*

Apple die cut: Embossible Designs, *We R Memory Keepers*

Stickers: A+, pencil, *Creative Imaginations*

Silver square eyelet: *Creative Imaginations*

Font: CK Plain Jane, "Creative Clips & Fonts by Becky Higgins" CD, *Creating Keepsakes*

Black gingham ribbon

⅛" hole punch

Finished size 4¼" x 3"

INSTRUCTIONS

1. Cut tag from black cardstock. Adhere piece of burgundy cardstock to front.

2. Print quotation on notebook patterned paper.

3. Trim quotation and punch holes in margin. Adhere at slight angle to tag. Adhere apple die cut and stickers.

4. Add eyelet and ribbon.

Class Memories Album

Designer: Candace Leonard

SUPPLIES

White cardstock

Black mini album: *Kolo*

Blue ribbon: gingham, variegated, *Offray*

Alphabet rubber stamps: Artistic lower-case, Pastel Pop, Printer's Type Alphabet, *Hero Arts*

Dye ink: black, blue; Memories, *Stewart Superior*

Font: Blissful, 2Ps *www.twopeasinabucket.com*

Metal-rimmed tag: *Avery*

White tags

White rickrack

Apple button: Dress It Up, *Jesse James & Co.*

Student photos

Other: adhesive dots, button shank remover

Finished size 7" x 7¾"

INSTRUCTIONS

❶ Replace ribbon on album with blue gingham ribbon.

❷ Print album title (to show through cover window) and dedication page (for front page) on white cardstock. Trim and adhere to album.

❸ Adhere each student's photo to a page. Stamp student's name on tag with blue ink. Add variegated ribbon and adhere next to photo.

❹ Stamp school year on metal-rimmed tag, using black ink. Add rickrack and adhere to album cover.

Inside

Thank You, Teacher

Designer: Melissa Caligiuri

SUPPLIES

Cardstock: kraft, red, *Bazzill Basics Paper*

Aged typewriter alphabet stickers: Nostalgiques, Rebecca Sower, *EK Success*

Aged typewriter alphabet stickers: Nostalgiques, Rebecca Sower, *EK Success*

Finished size 4" x 5½"

INSTRUCTIONS

1 Make kraft card base.

2 Cut one 1½" and two ¼" wide bands of red cardstock. Adhere to card base.

3 Add pencil and alphabet stickers as shown in photo.

DEDICATION PAGE TEXT

A school is more than books and desks

And learning two plus two.

It's people who share their skills and care,

And try their best in all they do.

Please accept our heartfelt appreciation.

Our school's a better place

Because of your dedication.

A TIP FROM CANDACE

Practice stamping with alphabet stamps on a scrap of paper. This will help you determine how hard to press the stamp to create a clear image. *Note: Avoid rocking the stamp as you press it on the paper—this can cause the image to smear.*

Bonus Ideas

- Have the students hand-write their names on the tags, instead of stamping them.

- Include handwritten messages or drawings from the students next to their photos.

Teen Scene

Cruise your way into any teenager's heart with fun gifts, funky décor, and fabulous ways to entertain friends.

Inside

Parisian Photo Purse

Designer: Lori Bergmann

SUPPLIES

Cardstock: (pink)

Specialty paper: (Pink Eiffel Tower, Ooh La Dot fabric from Paris Group) *Michael Miller Memories*

Photo pockets: (2½" x 3½" adhesive-backed Singles) Qwikit, *Provo Craft*

Color medium: (Black, Flamingo Painty pens) ZIG, *EK Success*

Accents:
    (pink crystal beads) *Crafts, Etc.*
    (black bugle beads) *JewelCraft*
    (rose wire) *Artistic Wire*

Fasteners:
    (Floral Snap-Charm) *Prym-Dritz*
    (black eyelets)

Fibers: (black waxed linen thread) *Sulyn Industries*

Adhesive: (510 machine) *Xyron*

Tools:
    (Purse template) Coluzzle Stampendous, *Provo Craft*
    (corner rounder punch) *Marvy Uchida*
    (bent chain nose pliers, round nose pliers) *NSI Innovations*
    (Snap-Charm Applicator Tool) *Prym-Dritz*
    wire cutters, eyelet-setting tools, heavy-duty needle, ruler, scissors

Finished size: 4" x 3"

PURSE

❶ Cut one purse shape from each fabric paper, using purchased template. *Note: Don't cut handle.* Adhere shapes together, right sides out.

❷ Place template on purse again and cut slits to hold down flap. *Note: Slide template up ¼" before cutting top slit to allow room for snap.*

❸ Cut two 3⅝" x 5⅝" rectangles from pink cardstock. Fold in half to create four pages. Adhere photo pocket to both sides of each page, making sure openings face same direction. Burnish pockets to adhere securely and remove bubbles. Round page corners with punch.

❹ Fold purse, following template manufacturer's instructions, and gently crease bottom fold. Stitch pages in place along fold with waxed thread.

❺ Set eyelet in each corner of purse.

HANDLE & CLOSURE

❶ Thread end of 8" wire length through one eyelet, fold wire ½" from end and twist around wire length, using pliers.

❷ String beads on wire.

❸ Repeat step 1 to attach other end of handle to eyelet on same side of purse.

❹ Repeat steps 1–3 to create opposite handle.

❺ Set snap between purse slits, following manufacturer's instructions. Color flower with paint pens. Touch up back of snap and eyelets with Black pen to match fabric.

Latest & Greatest

A WHOLE NEW SIDE OF FABRIC

Paper crafting has a softer side. Fabric with adhesive or paper backing is now available from several manufacturers and comes in a wide variety of colors and patterns. You can punch, die-cut, sew, and tear it, even journal or print on it! Check for fabrics to suit your cards and other crafts from the following manufacturers:

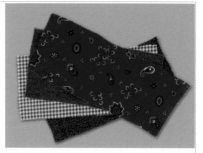

Delta (800/423-4135, *www.deltacrafts.com*)

Making Memories (801/294-0430, *www.makingmemories.com*)

Me & My Big Ideas (949/583-2065, *www.meandmybigideas.com*)

Michael Miller Memories (646/230-8862, *www.michaelmillermemories.com*)

Shortcuts Crafts (866/329-9800, *www.shortcutscrafts.com*)

Teen Contact Cards

Designer: Candace Leonard

SUPPLIES

All supplies from KI Memories unless otherwise noted.

Cardstock: (Piñata from Summer set) Collection IV

Patterned paper: (Summer Chic Stripe from Summer set) Collection IV

Paper accent: (flower die cut from My Girl Mod Blox & Tags sheet) Collection IV

Fonts: (Airplanes, Tasklist) *www.twopeasinabucket.com*

Adhesive: (dots) no source

Tools: (paper trimmer, computer and printer) no source

Finished size: 3½" x 2"

INSTRUCTIONS

❶ Print Teen's name and contact information on cardstock. Cut to finished size.

❷ Adhere strip of patterned paper to left side.

❸ Adhere die cut with adhesive dot.

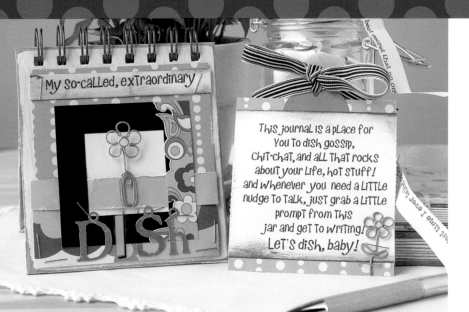

Let's Dish Journal

Designer: Teri Anderson

SUPPLIES

Cardstock: (White) *Provo Craft*

Patterned cardstock: (Farout Flowers, Love Beads/Dreamy Pink) Hippie Chick, *SEI*

Paper: (white)

Journal: Junk It Up!, *K&Company*

Jar: *Provo Craft*

Chalk ink: (Charcoal) ColorBox, *Clearsnap*

Paint: (White) Apple Barrel, *Plaid*

Paper accent: (Pink circle tag) Hippie Chick, *SEI*

Accents:
   (flower clips) Eco-Africa, *Provo Craft*
   (Eyelet Letters Classic) *Making Memories*
   (staples) *Swingline*

Stickers: (Hippie Alphabet, frame from Frames, Tags and Labels sheet) Hippie Chick, *SEI*

Fibers: (black and cream ribbon) Hippie Chick, *SEI*

Fonts:
   (Hairbrained) "15 Fonts: Playful" CD, *Autumn Leaves*
   (CK Stenography) "Fresh Fonts" CD, *Creating Keepsakes*

Adhesive: double-sided tape, metal

Tools: stapler, paintbrush, computer and printer, ruler, scissors

Other: sandpaper

Finished sizes:
   journal 4½" x 4¾"
   tag 3½" x 3¾"

JOURNAL

❶ Paint journal cover White; let dry. Sand edges.

❷ Cut 4" square of Love Beads cardstock; adhere strip of Farout Flowers cardstock to bottom. Adhere 1¾" square of White to center. Cut strip of Dreamy Pink cardstock; distress edges with scissors. Place flower clip on center and adhere across white square where patterned cardstock pieces meet. Adhere frame sticker over square.

❸ Print "My so-called, extraordinary" on White cardstock; trim, ink edges, and adhere to top of piece.

❹ Spell "Dish" with eyelet letters and alphabet sticker.

❺ Embellish piece with staples and adhere to journal.

TAG

❶ Cut tag from Love Beads cardstock. Tie ribbon through circle tag and adhere to top.

❷ Print journal instructions on White cardstock; trim, ink edges, and adhere to tag.

❸ Staple flower clip to bottom.

JOURNAL INSTRUCTIONS

This journal is a place for you to dish gossip, chit-chat, and all that rocks about your life, hot stuff! And whenever you need a little nudge to talk, just grab a little prompt from this jar and get to writing! Let's dish, baby!

JAR

Think up 25–50 questions for a teen to answer in her journal. Include questions about her school, life, family, and aspirations (see "Let's Dish Questions" for ideas). Print questions on white paper and cut into strips; fold and place in jar.

LET'S DISH QUESTIONS

What is the best thing about being a teenager?

If you had a $100 gift certificate to the mall, what would you buy?

What do you wish your yearbook said about you?

If you could have any formal dress, what would it look like?

What is the best thing your mom/dad ever told you?

Who are your favorite actors and actresses? Why?

Where would you live if you could live anywhere in the world?

How much allowance do you receive? How much *should* you receive?

Who is the cutest guy in school?

What is your favorite way to spend a Friday night?

Bonus Ideas

■ Design the journal and questions for an adult—a sister or girl-friend would love receiving this as a gift!

■ Use a basket to present the journal and jar to your favorite teen. Include a bag of candy, a CD from her favorite band, and a set of pens.

"Let's Talk" Locker Magnet

Designer: Kathleen Paneitz

SUPPLIES

Patterned paper: (Citrus Stripe) *KI Memories*

Wood shape: (Retro Girl) Playwood Punchouts, *Plaid*

Magnets

Rub-ons: (forever friends) *Wordsworth*

Stickers: (let's talk from Friendship 1) Jelly Labels, *Making Memories*

Accents: (Friendship Washer Word, Green Hydrangea Blossom) *Making Memories*

Fastener: (orange brad) *Karen Foster Design*

Adhesive:
   (industrial-strength) E-6000, *Eclectic Products*
   spray

Tools: craft knife, scissors

Finished size: 3" wide

INSTRUCTIONS

❶ Adhere paper to wood shape with spray adhesive. Trim paper with craft knife.

❷ Apply rub-on and adhere sticker. Attach washer to flower with brad; adhere to wood shape.

❸ Adhere magnets with industrial-strength adhesive.

Bonus Idea

Use other wood shapes, paint, paper and embellishments to create magnets to suit your favorite teen's taste.

Simple Sentiments

Add memorable words of wisdom to your teen's gift.

Remember that as a teenager you are at the last stage of your life when you will be happy to hear that the phone is for you.
    —Fran Lebowitz

Cherish your dreams.
Follow your passions.
They are the guiding hands
of your heart.
    —Flavia
    set in Bembo, Adobe

Delight in your youth.
    —Pearl Jam
    set in Giddyup, Adobe

Figuring out who you are is the whole point of the human experience.
    —Anna Quindlen

I love to see a young girl go out and grab the world by the lapels.
    —Maya Angelou

Girlfriends Forever!

She's been there through diets and chocolate binges, breakups and promotions, and can always make you laugh. Send her a card to celebrate your sisterhood.

Friends Are Flowers

Designer: Toni Armstrong

SUPPLIES

Cardstock: (white)

Patterned paper: (Bubblegum Cupcake Bloomers) *Doodlebug Design*

Specialty paper: (inkjet vellum)

Rubber Stamp: (Skipping Flowers) *Penny Black*

Dye ink: (Black) Memories, *Stewart Superior Corp.*

Color medium: (watercolor pencils) *Prismacolor*

Accents: (Crystal Stickles Glitter Glue) *Ranger Industries*

Fasteners: (pink eyelets) *Doodlebug Design*

Font: (Rock Star) *www.twopeasinabucket.com*

Adhesive: double-sided tape

Tools:
(blender pen) *Dove Brushes*
computer and printer, eyelet-setting tools, scissors, ruler

Finished size: 4¼" x 5½"

INSTRUCTIONS

❶ Make card from cardstock; set aside.

❷ Stamp design on cardstock and trim to 3½" square. Color design using watercolor pencils and blender pen. Add glitter glue for dimension.

❸ Cut patterned paper slightly smaller than card and attach stamped piece with eyelets.

❹ Print greeting on vellum, trim and attach below stamped piece with eyelets. Attach finished piece to card.

DESIGNER TIPS

- Stamp the image with dye ink so it won't smear when you use the blender pen.

- Allow 4–6 hours for the glitter to dry. A little of this product goes a long way.

- Use inkjet vellum to keep the printed sentiment from smearing.

Stand A Little Taller Card

Designer: Melissa Deakin

SUPPLIES

Cardstock: (black)

Textured cardstock:
  (Bazzill White, Petunia) *Bazzill Basics Paper*
  (Buttered Corn Ribbed Paper) *Mrs. Grossman's*

Patterned paper: (Simple Stripes) Colorful, (Green Tea Linen, Lipstick Flower) Birthday, (Splash Linen) Water, (Green Tea Flower) Camouflage, *KI Memories*

Pigment ink: (Black) Colorbox, *Clearsnap*

Accent: (pink rhinestone)

Punch: (Retro Flower) Whale Of A Punch, *EK Success*

Font: (Stop Sign) www.twopeasinbucket.com

Adhesive: double-sided tape

Tools: computer and printer, scissors, ruler

Finished size: 6" square

INSTRUCTION

❶ Make card from Bazzill White cardstock.

❷ Cover card front with strips of patterned paper and textured cardstock.

❸ Cut shoe and strap, using pattern; adhere to card.

❹ Punch flower from Bazzill White and adhere to shoe. Adhere rhinestone to flower center.

❺ Print sentiment on Green Tea Linen paper, ink edges and adhere to card.

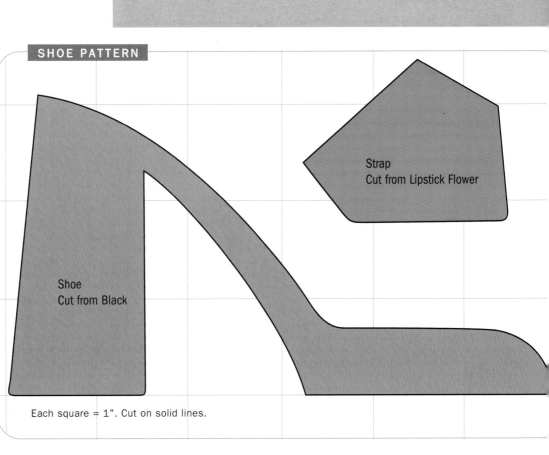

SHOE PATTERN

Strap
Cut from Lipstick Flower

Shoe
Cut from Black

Each square = 1". Cut on solid lines.

Flip Flop Friendship Album and Box

Designer: Anne Heyen

SUPPLIES

For flip-flop:

Paper maché box: (flip-flop) *Nicole*

Acrylic paints: (Asphalt, Espresso, Strawberries & Cream) Scrapbook Colors Kits, *Making Memories*

Paper accents: (oval tag, for you die-cuts) My Girl Frames & Labels, *KI Memories*

Accents:
   (bead chain, eyelet) *Making Memories*
   (flower charm) Lipstick Icicles, *KI Memories*

Adhesive: (Mod Podge) *Plaid*

Tools: eyelet-setting tools, paintbrush

For mini album:

Cardstock: (brown) *Close To My Heart*

Patterned paper: (My Girl Wisdom) *KI Memories*

Photos

Color medium: (black pen) *American Crafts*

Paper accents:
   (Letter Circles) *Scrapworks*
   (Frames & Labels, Mod Blox & Tags) My Girl, *KI Memories*
   (Family Twist Ties) *Pebbles Inc.*

Accents:
   (blossom, metal flowers, page pebbles) *Making Memories*
   (silver frame) *Diecuts with a View*

Stickers: (clear epoxy shapes) *Creative Imaginations*

Fasteners: (brads, eyelets) *Making Memories*

Fibers: (pink, olive ribbon) *Making Memories*

Adhesive: adhesive dots

Tools: eyelet-setting tools, scissors

Finished sizes:
   box 2" x 4" x 1¾"
   album 1¾" x 3¾"

BOX

① Mix equal amounts Asphalt and Espresso to create dark brown. Paint sole dark brown and strap Strawberries & Cream. Paint Strawberries & Cream dots along lid using wooden end of brush; let dry. Brush a finish coat of decoupage adhesive over painted areas. *Note: A satin water-based varnish may be used instead of the decoupage adhesive.*

② Adhere For You die cut to oval die cut and set eyelet. Loop on bead chain with flower charm, and attach to strap.

MINI ALBUM

① Accordion-fold cardstock in 1¾" intervals; keep folded. Cut out album, using pattern.

② Decorate album, using photos and embellishments.

③ Place album in box.

Bonus Ideas

DIFFERENT SHAPES, DIFFERENT SEASONS

Adapt this idea to the many shapes and sizes of boxes you find in the craft store.

■ Make an Easter traditions mini album to place inside a small oval paper maché box.

■ Heart-shaped boxes are wonderful for Valentine's Day, Mother's Day, or any occasion for the expression of love.

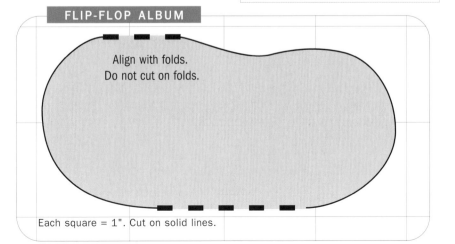

FLIP-FLOP ALBUM

Align with folds.
Do not cut on folds.

Each square = 1". Cut on solid lines.

Bikini Diet Card

Designer: Alice Golden

SUPPLIES

Textured Paper: (Sun Yellow Watercolor Ribbed) *The Robin's Nest*

Card: (Bliss Pink) Box O' Cards, *Diecuts With A View*

Rubber stamps: (Circles and Hearts Fancy Notes set) *Hero Arts*

Pigment ink: (Sunflower) ColorBox, *Clearsnap*

Accent: (Bikini charm) Glitter Beach Babe Color, Lil' Charms, *American Traditional Designs*

Fastener: (Ruby Red mini brad) *Limited Edition Rubberstamps*

Font: (Dreams) *www.twopeasinabucket.com*

Adhesive: double-sided tape

Tools:
   (word processing software) Word, *Microsoft*

   computer and printer, paper trimmer

Finished size: 4¼" x 5½"

INSTRUCTIONS

❶ Trim card to finished size.

❷ Print "Good luck with your diet!" on inside of card.

❸ Print half circle text on Sun Yellow paper (see "Create Circular Text"). Trim slightly smaller than card.

❹ Stamp large circle centered under text. Randomly stamp large and small circles.

❺ Attach charm with brad; adhere piece to card.

CREATE CIRCULAR TEXT

❶ Open a new document in Microsoft Word. *Note: Be sure drawing toolbar is displayed.*

❷ Select WordArt button (tilted blue "A" on the drawing toolbar).

❸ Select the WordArt style you want, then type your text in the box as desired.

❹ To select the text formation, click on the "ABC" button on the WordArt toolbar. Click and drag the squares around the shape to alter it as desired.

she wore an itsy bitsy, teeny weeny-

DESIGNER TIPS

■ Start with a pre-made card to save time. Trim it down to the size needed.

■ Print your text first on a piece of copy paper. Use repositionable tape to adhere a small piece of paper or cardstock over the text and run it through the printer again. This will allow you to print on small pieces of paper and have your text positioned exactly where you want it.

Inside card

Good luck with your diet!

Shop 'Til You Drop Card

Designer: Kathleen Paneitz

SUPPLIES

Cardstock: (white)

Patterned Paper: (Pink Argyle) *Rusty Pickle*

Color medium: (Black pen) ZIG Writer, *EK Success*

Paper accents:
   (white jewelry tags) *Avery*
   (Pink & Black Purse Accents) *Meri Meri*

Rub-ons:
   (Black) Color Rubs, *Scrapworks*
   (Expressions), *Doodlebug Design*
   (Pastel) Jenni Bowlin, *Li'l Davis Designs*
   (Black Graphic Icons) *KI Memories*

Fibers: (violet thread)

Adhesive: adhesive dots, double-sided tape

Tools: paper trimmer

Finished size: 5½" x 4¾"

INSTRUCTIONS

1 Make card from white cardstock.

2 Cover front of card with Pink Argyle paper.

3 Adhere purse accents.

4 Rub on Graphic rectangle.

5 Spell "Shop til you drop" on card with rub-ons.

6 Spell "save," "50," and "sale" on tags with rub-ons. Write "% off" with pen. Tie tags to purse handles and adhere.

7 Rub on scratch lines above and below purses.

Purseonally Card

Designer: Jennifer Miller

SUPPLIES

Cardstock: (white)

Textured cardstock: (pink, light green) *Bazzill Basics Paper*

Patterned papers: (Chic Plaid, Chic Stripe, Green Tea Bitty Blossom, Simple Stripe) *KI Memories*

Rubber stamps: (Purse from Good Times set, purseonally from A Little Love set) *Stampin' Up!*

Dye ink: (black) *Ranger Industries*

Accent: (circle tag) *Avery*

Fibers: (light green two-toned ribbon) *May Arts*

Adhesive: double-sided tape

Punches:
   (circle) *EK Success*
   (corner rounder) *Creative Memories*

Tools: scissors, craft knife, ruler

Finished size: 4" x 5½"

INSTRUCTIONS

1 Make card from pink cardstock.

2 Trim green cardstock slightly smaller than card and round corners.

3 Trim white cardstock to four ¾" squares and adhere to green cardstock.

4 Stamp purses on patterned papers and cut out. Mount on white squares.

5 Stamp "purseonally" on pink cardstock, punch with circle punch, and adhere to tag. Punch hole in tag top, tie ribbon through tag, and adhere ends to back of green cardstock.

6 Adhere completed piece to card.

DESIGNER TIPS

■ Use a craft knife on a self-healing mat to cut away the inside of the purse handle.

■ A Xyron machine is useful to apply adhesive to the purse cut-outs because the handles are so delicate.

Bonus Ideas

■ Create a cute, quick gift tag with the same materials.

■ Adapt this card for your favorite shoe addict by changing the stamp to a shoe, and using the title Sole Mates.

Call Me! Address Book

Designer: Linda Beeson

SUPPLIES

Textured cardstock: (Pinecone) *Bazzill Basics Paper*

Patterned paper: (Apron/Table Ticking, Debossed Daisy, Paper Bag Daisy, Robin Egg) Granny's Kitchen, *SEI*

Address book

Rubber stamps:
    (Conversation Dots Set) *Hero Arts*
    (Lady In Feather Hat) *Victorine Originals*

Dye ink: (Black) Memories, *Stewart Superior Corp.*

Chalk ink: (Chestnut Roan) ColorBox, *Clearsnap*

Rub-ons:
    (black alphabet) Alpha, *Chatterbox*
    (Providence alphabet) *Making Memories*

Accent: (telephone charm) *Impress Rubber Stamps*

Fibers: (brown ribbon)

Adhesive: double-sided tape

Tools:
    (circle punches) Paper Shapers, *EK Success*
    (circle punches) *Marvy Uchida*
    (Oval Shapemaker) *AccuCut*
    scissors, ruler

Finished size: 4" x 6"

INSTRUCTIONS

Age all oval and circle edges with Chestnut Roan ink.

❶ Wrap address book cover with Debossed Daisy and Paper Bag Daisy paper. Adhere 1" strip of dotted side of Apron paper.

❷ Cut 2¾" x 3⅝" oval from solid side of Paper Bag Daisy.

❸ Cut 2½" x 3⅜" oval from solid side of Robin Egg paper. Stamp lady with Black. Mat with larger oval.

❹ Stamp solid side of Robin Egg with Friends sentiment, using Black; punch out, and mat with Pinecone cardstock.

❺ Stamp solid side Paper Bag Daisy with Cherish sentiment and Chestnut Roan; punch out and double-mat with Robin Egg and Pinecone cardstock.

❻ Adhere matted oval and circles to cover.

❼ Rub on "Friends" and "Call me".

❽ Tie charm with ribbon; trim, and adhere to cover.

Bonus Idea

ALWAYS WEAR RED MEMO BOOK

Make an outrageous red memo book to keep all your important information.

Blue in the Hair

Designer: Allison Strine

SUPPLIES

Cardstock: blue, glossy white

Patterned paper: light blue, peach, *Creative Imaginations*

Metal-rimmed vellum tag: *Making Memories*

Light blue ribbon: *Making Memories*

Rubber stamps: Girlfriends, Blue in the Hair, *River City Rubber Works*

Ink:

    Black pigment; ColorBox, *Clearsnap*

    Embossing, *Ranger Industries*

Embossing powder: Denim; Adirondack, *Ranger Industries*

Heart punch: Paper Shapers, *EK Success*

Adhesive dots: *Glue Dots International*

Colored pencils

Heat tool

Finished size 5½" x 4"

INSTRUCTIONS

❶ Make card base with blue cardstock.

❷ Cut light blue patterned paper slightly smaller than card. Stamp and emboss "Blue in the hair" sentiment on bottom. Mat with peach patterned paper. Adhere to card with adhesive dots. Adhere ribbon around edges, mitering corners.

❸ Stamp girlfriends image on glossy white cardstock with black ink. Color with pencils and cut to fit metal-rimmed tag. Adhere to tag.

❹ Punch heart from peach patterned paper; adhere next to sentiment.

Simple Sentiments

There's something beautiful about finding one's innermost thoughts in another.

—Oliver Schreiner

Friends are those rare people who ask how we are and then wait to hear the answer.

—Ed Cunningham

Grab Your Hat Card

Designer: Julie Medeiros

SUPPLIES

Cardstock: (black, white)

Patterned paper: (Leopard Lady)
The Hat Collection, *Reminisce*

Accents: (white alphabet brads)
Bradletz, *Provo Craft*

Rub-ons: (Trademark white)
Simply Stated Alphabets, *Making Memories*

Sticker: (hat from The Hat Collection Sticker Sheet)
Reminisce

Adhesive: double-sided tape

Tool: paper trimmer

Finished size: 4½" x 6¼"

INSTRUCTIONS

❶ Make card from white cardstock. Adhere patterned paper to front.

❷ Trim right side at angle.

❸ Cut trapezoid shape approx. 3" x 1¾" from black cardstock. Mat with white cardstock. Adhere to card.

❹ Rub-on "Grab your". Spell "Hat" with brads.

❺ Adhere hat sticker.

Simple Sentiments

One loyal friend is worth
ten thousand relatives.

—Euripides, Greek playwright

Ah, how good it feels . . .
the hand of an old friend.

—Mary Engelbreit

For My Friend Card

Designer: Sara Horton

SUPPLIES

Cardstock: (black, cream)

Patterned paper: (Vintage French from Altered Book Pack) *Limited Edition Rubberstamps*

Photo transparency sheet: (Broadway Ladies) Transparencies, *Limited Edition Rubberstamps*

Rubber stamp: (Guerin-Boutron trade card) *Rubber Baby Buggy Bumpers*

Dye ink: (Coal Black) Ancient Page, *Clearsnap*

Fluid Chalk ink: (Chestnut Roan) Colorbox, *Clearsnap*

Accents:
(black tassel) *Limited Edition Rubberstamps*

(gold metallic heart button) Favorite Findings, *Blumenthal Lansing*

Font: (P22 Monet Regular) *www.myfonts.com*

Adhesive: double-sided tape, craft glue

Tools: computer and printer, wedge sponge, scissors, wire cutters, ruler

Finished size: 4" x 5½"

INSTRUCTIONS

Note: Age all cut and torn edges with Chestnut Roan ink.

❶ Make card from cream cardstock.

❷ Tear Vintage French paper into strips; layer and adhere to card.

❸ Cut two transparencies and two cream cardstock pieces the same size. Adhere transparencies to cardstock; adhere pieces to card.

❹ Stamp Guerin-Boutron on cream cardstock using Coal Black, trim, and tear image in half lengthwise. Adhere stamped pieces at an angle over transparencies.

❺ Print "for my friend..." on cream cardstock. Trim, mat with black cardstock, and adhere to card.

❻ Adhere tassel to card with craft glue.

❼ Cut off button shank with wire cutters and adhere button to card.

Hinge Of Friendship Card

Designer: Melanie Maughan

SUPPLIES

Cardstock: (kraft)

Textured cardstock: (Dark Scarlet) *Bazzill Basics Paper*

Patterned paper: (Chocolate Pinstripe, Scarlet Bloom) *Chatterbox*

Dye ink: (Vintage Photo) Distress, *Ranger Industries*

Accent: (Hinge Brad) *Frost Creek Charms*

Fibers: (brown ribbon) *Michaels*

Font: (AL Age Old Love) "Vintage Fonts" CD, *Autumn Leaves*

Adhesive: adhesive dots

Tools: computer and printer, scissors, ruler

Other: wedge sponge

Finished size: 3¾" x 8½"

INSTRUCTIONS

Ink all paper and cardstock edges.

1 Make card from kraft cardstock.

2 Cut Scarlet Bloom paper to 3¾" x 3¼" and fold upper right corner. Adhere to card. Attach hinge.

3 Adhere Chocolate Pinstripe paper to card bottom and trim to fit.

4 Print sentiment on kraft and trim to fit, leaving space for ribbon; adhere ribbon. Mat with Dark Scarlet cardstock and adhere to card.

5 Adhere ribbon where papers meet and trim to fit.

Simple Sentiments

Add a friendship phrase to your card.

Friends are always worth the trouble.
—Kellian Kennedy

True friendship is felt, not said.
—Mariecris Madayag
set in Triplex Light, Emigre

Shared joy is double joy, and shared sorrow is half-sorrow.
—Swedish proverb

If we're friends much longer, we'll start to look alike.

Friendship is born at that moment when one person says to another:
"What! You, too?
Thought I was the only one."
—C. S. Lewis
set in Bembo Bold, Adobe

I've discovered a way to stay friends forever—
There's really nothing to it.
I simply tell you what to do
And you do it!

—Shel Silverstein

The world would be so lonely, in sunny hours or gray,
Without the gift of friendship, to help us every day.

—Hilda Brett Farr

Gathering of Girlfriends

Designer: Amber Crosby

SUPPLIES

Cardstock: (Natural, Paper Bag) *Bazzill Basics Paper*

Patterned paper: (Red Sanded Floral, Red Ticking) *Daisy D's*

Paint can: *The Container Store*

Library pocket and card: *Autumn Leaves*

Rub-ons: (alphabet) Simply Stated, *Making Memories*

Accents:
(fabric pockets) Grace, (White Daisy Blossoms, metal photo corners) *Making Memories*

(Friendship woven label from Best Friends, You're Invited woven label from Invitation) Just Write! Threads, *Me & My Big Ideas*

Fasteners: (antique copper brads) *All My Memories*

Fibers:
(cream ribbon) *7gypsies*

(red/white striped ribbon) *Impress Rubber Stamps*

Finished sizes:
   invitation 4½" x 7½"
   favor can 4¼" x 5"

INVITATION

❶ Cover library card with Red Ticking paper. Adhere 1½" wide strip of Red Sanded Floral paper to bottom. Adhere friendship label to bottom.

❷ Print party details on Natural cardstock; trim and adhere to card. Attach photo corners with metal adhesive.

❸ Punch hole through top of card and add ribbon.

❹ Cover front of library pocket with Red Sanded Floral. Adhere 1¾" wide strip of Red Ticking to bottom. Spell "Girlfriends" on bottom of pocket with rub-ons (see photo).

❺ Join two flowers together with brad; adhere to fabric pocket. Adhere pocket to library card with double-sided tape. Print "Girls' night out" on Natural; trim and adhere inside fabric pocket. Adhere You're Invited label next to pocket.

❻ Place card in library pocket.

FAVOR CAN

❶ Cover paint can with Red Sanded Floral paper. Adhere 1¾" wide strip of Red Ticking paper around bottom.

❷ Cut 2¾" square of Paper Bag cardstock; punch two holes through right side and tie with ribbon.

❸ Spell "Girlfriends" on top of square with rub-ons. Place brad through center of flower and adhere to fabric pocket; adhere pocket to square. Adhere square to can.

❹ Fill can with candy or other favors.

Inside invitation

You are invited to a Girls' Night Out Party! Please join us for shopping, food, and fun.

Date: March 17, 2004
Place: 123 Party Lane
Time: 5:00 p.m.

RSVP

friendship

Bonus Ideas

■ Fill the can with body care products, cosmetic samples, note cards, or bonbons!

■ Create coordinating invitations and favor cans for a baby or bridal shower, graduation party, or luncheon.

Fonts:
   (Lindsay Black Dress) *Lettering Delights*
   (Antique Type) *www.scrapvillage.com*

Adhesive: double-sided tape, glue stick, metal adhesive

Tools: ruler, scissors, hole punch, eyelet-setting tools, computer and printer

Other: favors to fill can

Just the Girls

Designer: Gretchen Schmidt

SUPPLIES

Cardstock: (Oatmeal) *Making Memories*

Textured cardstock: (Brown) *Making Memories*

Notebook paper

Recycled office paper

Tabbed index card

Dye ink: (Old Paper) Distress Ink, *Ranger Industries*

Accents:
 (black label tape) *Dymo*
 (paper clips)

Fasteners: (staples, gold brad)

Font: (1722 Roman) *www.p22.com*

Adhesive

Tools:
 (label maker) *Dymo*
 stapler, pencil, computer and printer, water in spray bottle, wedge sponge

Finished size: 4¼" x 5½"

INSTRUCTIONS

❶ Cut Oatmeal cardstock to 8½" x 5½". Fold in half; open. Align tabbed side of index card along fold at top of front; trace. On back of card, align index card with tab away from fold; trace. Cut top of card along traced lines. Ink edges.

❷ Create "Girls night" and "Out" labels and adhere to front and back tabs of card (see photo).

❸ Cut recycled office paper slightly smaller than card. To create aged look, sponge with ink and spray with water; let dry. Adhere, slightly angled, to card front and staple corners.

❹ Print party details for front and inside of card on notebook paper; tear and ink edges. Adhere to slightly larger pieces of torn brown cardstock. Add brad and paper clips and adhere to card.

❺ Create "Just the girls" label and adhere to front of card.

Bonus Ideas

- Use dictionary or script patterned paper instead of recycled office paper.

- Use decorative brads and paper clips from Making Memories or other craft supply manufacturers.

Inside

Sweet Feet Pedicure Kit

Designer: Brooke Lindquist

SUPPLIES

Cardstock:
(Blossom, Limeade) *Bazzill Basics Paper*
(white)

Vellum

Gift bag: (White) *Close to My Heart*

Rubber stamp: (Flower Power) *Close to My Heart*

Dye ink: (Baby Pink, Sweet Leaf) *Close to My Heart*

Stickers: (Pretty Petals tag, square, border) Snip Its, *Pebbles Inc.*

Fasteners: (white eyelets) *Close to My Heart*

Fibers: (Olive Waxy Flax) *Scrapworks*

Font: (Goofball) *www.twopeasinabucket.com*

Adhesive:
(pop-up dots) *Close to My Heart*
glue stick

Tools:
(stipple paintbrush) *Close to My Heart*
ruler, scissors, eyelet-setting tools, computer and printer

Other: tissue paper; foot wash scrub, pumice stone, lotion, nail file, cuticle oil, nail polish

Finished sizes:
bag 5¼" x 8½"
tag 5" x 2½"

BAG

❶ Stamp flower repeatedly on Blossom cardstock with Baby Pink. Trim and adhere to top of bag. Brush with Baby Pink, using stipple brush.

❷ Trim Limeade cardstock to fit bottom of bag; brush with Sweet Leaf, and adhere.

❸ Adhere border sticker to white cardstock and trim cardstock into wavy border. Set eyelets and adhere to bag.

❹ Adhere square flower sticker to white cardstock; adhere to slightly larger white square with pop-up dots. Adhere to bag.

TAG

❶ Adhere tag sticker to white cardstock.

❷ Print "Sweet feet pedicure kit" and contents of kit on vellum; trim slightly narrower than tag.

❸ Attach vellum piece to tag with eyelet.

❹ Tie tag to bag handle with flax.

DESIGNER TIP

I used the stipple brush and ink to add texture to the cardstock, and to match the shading on the die cuts. This method will add depth and texture to any project.

Bonus Ideas

■ Make the evening of pampering more relaxing. Include the following note on the invitation: "Pajamas, bathrobes, and bedroom slippers only!"

■ Make a kit for a new mom (filled with baby lotion, shampoo, a brush, and nail clippers) or someone who's ill (filled with cough drops, facial tissues, and a favorite movie).

❷ Cut cardstock to 2½" x 3½" for pocket and cover with mesh. Adhere to card at sides and bottom, using mounting tape.

❸ Print invitation on white shipping tag and insert in pocket. Adhere silver disc to top.

❹ Trim wine glass sticker to fit silver tag and adhere.

❺ Adhere silver bookplate sticker to white paper and trim excess paper. Stamp "New Year" with black ink inside bookplate.

❻ Attach brads to bookplate and tag stickers.

❼ Tie floss around silver tag.

❽ Adhere silver tag and bookplate to pocket with adhesive dots.

❾ Emboss sides and bottom of card and set with heat tool.

PARTY SET
A complete ensemble begins the New Year with a shine. Create a gift bag, resolutions book, and place cards with the same papers, stickers, and embellishments.

Shiny New Year Invitation

Designer: Michelle Tardie

SUPPLIES

Black cardstock: Dark Black, *Bazzill Basics Paper*

White paper

Swirls patterned paper: Metallic Collection, *Creative Imaginations*

White shipping tag

Alphabet stamps: Antique Upper Case, *PSX*

Black pigment ink: ColorBox, *Clearsnap*

Embossing ink: *Ranger Industries*

Silver embossing powder: *PSX*

Font: Bookman Old Style, *Microsoft*

Accents:

Silver mesh: *Magic Mesh*

Wine glass sticker: Wedding; Snapshots, *Pebbles Inc.*

Embossed silver stickers: bookplate, tag, disc; Metallic Collection, *Creative Imaginations*

Black brads: *Karen Foster Design*

Silver embroidery floss: *DMC*

Adhesive dots: Mini Glue Dots, *Glue Dots International*

Mounting tape: Scotch, *3M*

Other: computer and printer, heat tool

Finished size 5¾" x 3¾"

INSTRUCTIONS

❶ Make card base from cardstock. Cut swirl paper slightly smaller than card base and adhere.

Simple Sentiments

Ring in the New Year with words of wisdom:

And now let us welcome the New Year full of things that have never been.

—Rainer Maria Rilke
Set in Futura Light from Adobe Systems, Inc.

Live it up on New Year's Eve! You've got a whole year to live it down.

My fondest memories
of the past year
are the ones that include you.

—Bill Vaughan
Set in Futura Light from Adobe Systems, Inc.

My New Year's resolution is to stop feeling guilty about not keeping last year's resolution.

Set in Rockwell ExtraBold

An optimist stays up until midnight to see the new year in. A pessimist stays up to make sure the old year leaves.

—Bill Vaughan
Set in MrsEavesBold

Good tidings for the year,
health, prosperity,
joy, and cheer.
Time's up!
Live like there's no tomorrow!

Set in Memphis Light

Youth is when
you're allowed to stay up late on New Year's Eve.
Middle age is when you're forced to.

—Bill Vaughn

Counting down to midnight . . .

The Gift That Keeps on Giving

Remind your loved ones that you're thinking of them all year long with a handmade calendar.

As the year draws to a close, everyone starts looking for a new calendar—so a personalized calendar is the ideal gift for your loved one. It's especially meaningful when it includes photos, significant quotes, and reminders of memorable occasions. Add birthdays, anniversaries, and special reminders, and each page will send your love every day of the year.

Calendar Cover

Designer: Wendy Sue Anderson
All calendar tops are 8" square.

SUPPLIES

Cardstock: green, white; *Chatterbox*

Paper: dark green, light green, maroon, orange, peach, pink, purple, *Chatterbox*

Sand pigment ink: Memories, *Stewart Superior*

Assorted buttons

Cream embroidery floss: Stitches, *Making Memories*

Font: CK Newsprint, "Fresh Fonts" CD, *Creating Keepsakes*

Other: foam dots, sewing machine, white thread

INSTRUCTIONS

❶ Cut calendar top from green cardstock.

❷ Cut squares from pink, orange, light green, and maroon paper. Wet and curl edges. Machine-stitch after squares dry. Mount on calendar top.

❸ Cut flower, flip flops, pumpkin, and holly leaves from cardstock, using patterns. Ink edges and add buttons. Adhere to cardstock squares.

❹ Print year and quote on white cardstock; trim, and ink edges. Mat with green cardstock and machine-stitch around edges. Adhere to calendar cover, using foam dots.

Online Bonus Project

MASTER CALENDAR PAGE

Visit *www.PaperCraftsMag.com/ projects* to download this Master Calendar to your computer. Print each month on cardstock. Adhere upside down to back of calendar tops in order (i.e., attach January page to back of February calendar top, February page to back of March top, etc.) so when calendar hangs from wall both sides hang appropriately.

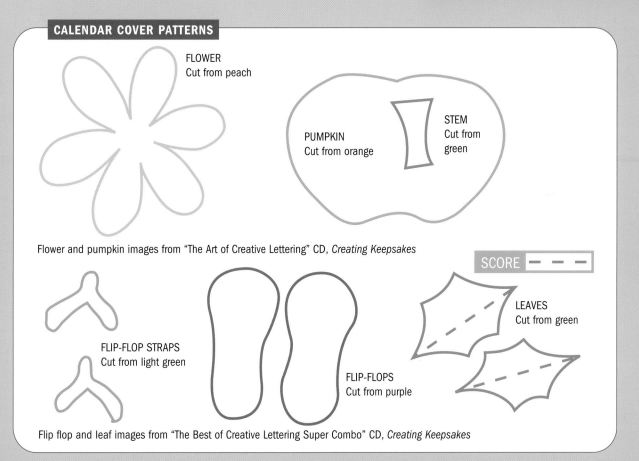

CALENDAR COVER PATTERNS

FLOWER
Cut from peach

PUMPKIN
Cut from orange

STEM
Cut from green

Flower and pumpkin images from "The Art of Creative Lettering" CD, *Creating Keepsakes*

SCORE

FLIP-FLOP STRAPS
Cut from light green

FLIP-FLOPS
Cut from purple

LEAVES
Cut from green

Flip flop and leaf images from "The Best of Creative Lettering Super Combo" CD, *Creating Keepsakes*

let it snow!

Snow Cream

1-3 Cups of Snow (make sure it's clean!)
1/2 Cup Whipping Cream
1 T. Sugar
2-3 drops Vanilla flavoring

In a separate bowl, mix cream, sugar
and vanilla. Slowly add snow to desired
consistency. Eat and enjoy!

February

Designer: Heather Erickson

SUPPLIES

Cardstock: pink, red, sage green

Photos

Accents:
    Red button: *Making Memories*
    Metal grommet: *Making Memories*
    Mini clothespins: *Joann Stores*

String

Font: CK Stenography, "Fresh Fonts" CD, *Creating Keepsakes*

Brown pigment ink pad: *Marvy Uchida*

Other: eyelet-setting tools, foam dots, sandpaper

January

Designer: Nancy Church

SUPPLIES

White cardstock

Purple speckled paper: *Making Memories*

Accents:
    White eyelets: *Making Memories*
    White brads: Snaps, *Making Memories*
    Alphabet stickers: Just My Type, *Doodlebug Design*

Snowflake clip art images: "Creative Clips & Fonts for Everyday Celebrations" CD, *Creating Keepsakes*

Font: CK Typeset, "Creative Clips & Fonts by Becky Higgins" CD, *Creating Keepsakes*

Snow Cream recipe: www.huntsville.about.com/cs/food/a/snowcream.htm

Eyelet setting tools

INSTRUCTIONS

❶ Cut calendar top from white cardstock and use to mat smaller square of purple speckled paper.

❷ Print recipe on white cardstock and tear edges. Adhere to calendar.

❸ Print snowflakes on white cardstock; trim. *Note: Snowflake squares have colored backgrounds. Attach to calendar with eyelets and brads.*

❹ Spell "let it snow" using alphabet stickers.

Each day I love you more...
today, more than yesterday...
and less than tomorrow.

Rosemonde Gerard

INSTRUCTIONS

1 Cut 8" square of red cardstock for backing. Cut 8" square frame with 6" square opening from red cardstock. Cut eight 1" x 8" strips of red cardstock. Shade frame and strips with ink.

2 Attach grommet to frame, using eyelet-setting tool. Adhere strips, with a slight overlap, to back of frame, using foam dots for dimension; work from bottom to top.

3 Cut heart and leaves, using patterns. Shade with ink and sand lightly. Adhere leaves to heart; add red button. Hang heart from grommet with string; secure to calendar with foam dot.

4 Print quote on pink cardstock; trim. Mat photos with pink. Shade mats with ink and sand edges lightly. Attach photos and quote to strips with clothespins.

5 Adhere calendar to backing square to reinforce.

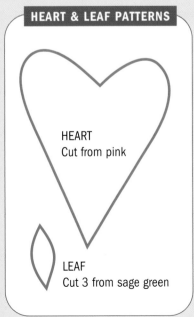

HEART & LEAF PATTERNS

HEART
Cut from pink

LEAF
Cut 3 from sage green

March

Designer: Nancy Church

SUPPLIES

Cardstock: green, navy, yellow, white

Green gingham paper: *Pebbles Inc.*

Photo

Accents:
   Pot of gold image: "Creative Clip Art for Boys" CD, *Creating Keepsakes*

   Buttons: Button Box, *Making Memories*

   Black eyelets: *Making Memories*

   Wire

Tag punch: *EK Success*

Font: CK Tall Type, "Creative Clips & Fonts by Becky Higgins" CD, *Creating Keepsakes*

Yellow chalk: Chalklets, *EK Success*

Sponge

Eyelet-setting tools

INSTRUCTIONS

1 Cut calendar top from green cardstock. Cover with gingham paper.

2 Mat photo with navy cardstock; adhere to calendar.

3 Print text on white cardstock, punch tag shapes, and sponge with chalk. Wrap wire around tags, adhere to calendar, and add buttons.

4 Print pot of gold on white cardstock. Double mat with green and yellow cardstock. Accent with black eyelets, wire handles, and buttons. *Note: Place wire and buttons directly over images to add dimension. Adhere to calendar.*

April

Designer: Wendy Sue Anderson

SUPPLIES

Textured cardstock: light yellow, sage green, terra cotta

Plaid patterned paper: Cottage Plaid, *Chatterbox*

Photo

Accents:
　Buttons
　Hemp

Leaf punch: *EK Success*

Dye ink: Sand; Memories, *Stewart Superior*

Font: CK Letter Home, "Creative Clips & Fonts by Becky Higgins" CD, *Creating Keepsakes*

Other: ¹⁄₁₆" hole punch, sewing machine, thread

INSTRUCTIONS

❶ Print text on green cardstock and trim to create calendar top.

❷ Cut pot and flower pieces using patterns. Rub edges with ink. Punch green leaves and cut stems, then rub with ink. Adhere to calendar top.

❸ Adhere buttons for flower centers. Punch holes on sides of pot, thread hemp through, and tie.

❹ Cut plaid paper strip, wet, and roll edges. Adhere to calendar top.

❺ Mat photo with terra cotta; machine-stitch edges and adhere to calendar top.

May

Designer: Heather Erickson

SUPPLIES

Ivory cardstock

Floral patterned paper: Laura Ashley, *EK Success*

Photo

Metal label holder and grommet: *Making Memories*

Ribbon: cranberry, maroon, sage; *Offray*

Brown chalk: *Craf-T Products*

Eyelet-setting tools

POT AND LIP
Cut from terra cotta

FLOWER
Cut 3 from light yellow

"Walk a little slower Daddy,"
said a child so small,
"I'm following in your footsteps
and I don't want to fall.

Sometimes your steps are very fast,
Sometimes they're hard to see;
So walk a little slower, Daddy,
For you are leading me.

Someday when I'm all grown up,
You're what I want to be;
Then I will have a little child
Who'll want to follow me.

And I would want to lead just right,
And know that I was true,
So walk a little slower, Daddy,
For I must follow you."

INSTRUCTIONS

❶ Cut calendar top from ivory cardstock.

❷ Adhere two pieces of coordinating floral patterned paper to top (see photo). Adhere cranberry ribbon over seam where papers meet. Adhere photo.

❸ Print quote and "Mothers" on ivory cardstock, leaving space between them. Cut quote into tag shape, and shade with brown chalk. Accent with sage and maroon ribbons, knotting maroon ribbon and securing ends behind tag. Attach to page with grommet, using eyelet setting tools.

❹ Cut out "Mothers" and place in label holder. Adhere to calendar.

June

Designer: Wendy Sue Anderson

SUPPLIES

Cardstock: black, blue, tan

Transparency sheet

Photo

Accents:
   Black square brads: Tacks, *Chatterbox*
   Black gingham ribbon: *Making Memories*
   Heart punch: *EK Success*
   Black metal-rimmed tag: *Making Memories*

Font: CK Cute, "Creative Clips & Fonts by Becky Higgins" CD, *Creating Keepsakes*

Watermark ink: VersaMark, *Tsukineko*

Clear embossing powder: *Stampendous!*

Heat tool

INSTRUCTIONS

❶ Cut calendar top from black cardstock.

❷ Create footprints by rubbing child's feet with ink and placing on blue cardstock. Sprinkle embossing powder on footprints and heat set. Mat with calendar top.

❸ Print poem on transparency sheet and adhere to calendar. Place adhesive where border accent will hide it, or use invisible vellum adhesive.

❹ Cut strip of tan cardstock and mat with black cardstock. Tie ribbon around strip and adhere to calendar. Accent with brads and metal-rimmed tag.

❺ Punch heart from red cardstock. Apply watermark ink and embossing powder and heat set. Adhere to tag.

❻ Mat photo with black cardstock and adhere to calendar.

July

Designer: Nancy Church

SUPPLIES

Cardstock: cream, red

Vellum

Photo

Brown snap: *Making Memories*

Alphabet stamps: Printer's Type, Printer's Type Lowercase, *Hero Arts*

Dye ink: Not Quite Navy, *Stampin' Up!*

Heart on tag clip art image: "Creative Clips & Fonts for Everyday Celebrations" CD, *Creating Keepsakes*

Font: CK Stenography, "Fresh Fonts" CD, *Creating Keepsakes*

Brown chalk: Chalklets, *EK Success*

Other: sewing machine, white thread

INSTRUCTIONS

❶ Cut calendar top from red cardstock. Machine-stitch edges with thread, then shade thread with chalk.

❷ Mat photo with cream cardstock. Stamp caption on cream cardstock with alphabet stamps. Machine-stitch caption to photo piece. Machine-stitch edges and shade thread with chalk.

❸ Print tag image on cream cardstock; trim. Print "The heart of America is the home" on vellum; trim to tag shape. Machine-stitch vellum tag over cream tag and shade thread with chalk. Secure brad to tag. Adhere to calendar top.

August

Designer: Heather Erickson

SUPPLIES

Gold cardstock

Patterned paper:
   Striped, sun, *Debbie Mumm*
   Brown plaid, *O'Scrap!*

Accents:
   Cream mini buttons
   Copper brads

Brown chalk: *Craf-T Products*

Black pen: ZIG, *EK Success*

Font: CK Stenography, "Fresh Fonts" CD, *Creating Keepsakes*

Circle punches: ⅜", ½" (from 6-Piece Circles Set); Paper Shapers, *EK Success*

INSTRUCTIONS

Shade edges of paper pieces with chalk.

❶ Cut calendar top from sun patterned paper. Adhere to cardstock backing.

❷ Write names of various activities on striped paper. Cut into pieces.

❸ Cut envelope, sun, and flowers, using patterns. Assemble envelope. Adhere to calendar top. Adhere activity pieces inside envelope.

❹ Print poem on striped paper; trim. Assemble sun, and adhere three mini buttons. Adhere poem and sun to calendar top.

❺ Punch ⅜" circle and ½" circle from cardstock. Attach to flower centers, using brads. Adhere flowers to calendar top.

❻ Print "August Daily Activities" on striped paper. Tear edges. Attach to calendar top with brad.

SUN AND FLOWER PATTERNS

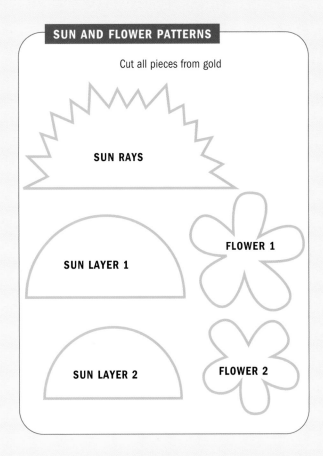

Cut all pieces from gold

SUN RAYS

SUN LAYER 1

FLOWER 1

SUN LAYER 2

FLOWER 2

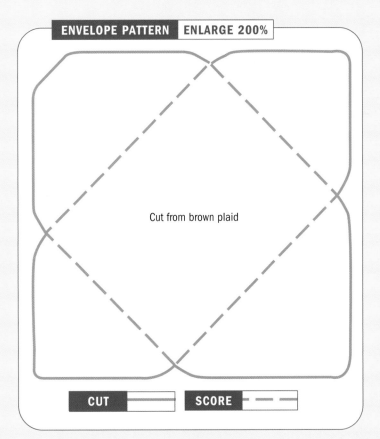

ENVELOPE PATTERN ENLARGE 200%

Cut from brown plaid

CUT ⎯ SCORE ⎯ ⎯

What do you
do in the
Summertime?

Oh, what do you do
in the summertime
when all the world is green?
Do you fish in a stream,
or lazily dream
on the banks as the clouds go by?

Oh, what do you do
in the summertime
When all the world is green?
Do you swim in a pool,
to keep yourself cool,
or swing in a tree up high?

Oh, what do you do
in the summertime
when all the world is green?
Do you march in parades,
or drink lemonades,
or count all the stars in the sky?

Is that what you do?
So Do I!

Dorthy S. Anderson

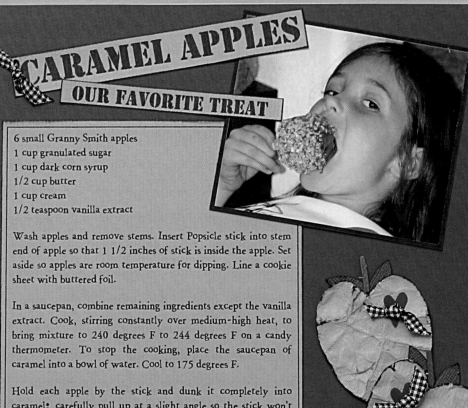

CARAMEL APPLES

OUR FAVORITE TREAT

6 small Granny Smith apples
1 cup granulated sugar
1 cup dark corn syrup
1/2 cup butter
1 cup cream
1/2 teaspoon vanilla extract

Wash apples and remove stems. Insert Popsicle stick into stem end of apple so that 1 1/2 inches of stick is inside the apple. Set aside so apples are room temperature for dipping. Line a cookie sheet with buttered foil.

In a saucepan, combine remaining ingredients except the vanilla extract. Cook, stirring constantly over medium-high heat, to bring mixture to 240 degrees F to 244 degrees F on a candy thermometer. To stop the cooking, place the saucepan of caramel into a bowl of water. Cool to 175 degrees F.

Hold each apple by the stick and dunk it completely into caramel; carefully pull up at a slight angle so the stick won't dislodge. Gently twirl stick so excess caramel will drip off. Place apple on buttered foil. Caramel will harden completely within a few minutes. If caramel cools to below 150 degrees F, it will become too thick to cover apples easily; in this case, reheat it in a double boiler.

September

Designer: Wendy Sue Anderson

SUPPLIES

Cardstock: black, brick red, brown, dark green, light green

Photo

Black gingham ribbon: *Making Memories*

Heart punch: *EK Success*

Black dye ink: Memories, *Stewart Superior*

Fonts:
  CK Stenography, "Fresh Fonts" CD, *Creating Keepsakes*
  Stencil font, www.fontseek.com

Adhesive: *Glue Dots International*

Other: ¹⁄₁₆" circle punch, cosmetic sponge

INSTRUCTIONS

❶ Cut calendar top from brick red cardstock.

❷ Print title and recipe on light green cardstock. Trim and ink edges. Adhere recipe to calendar top.

❸ Mat photo with black cardstock and adhere to calendar top.

❹ To make apple accents, cut out apples, using pattern. Sponge edges with ink. Wet and crinkle apple pieces; let dry. Punch hearts from brick red cardstock. Tie two small pieces of ribbon and attach to hearts with adhesive dots. Assemble accents and adhere to calendar top.

❺ Adhere title to calendar top, punch holes in left side, and tie ribbon.

APPLE PATTERN

APPLE PATTERN
Cut 2 from light green

LEAVES
Cut 4 from dark green

STEM
Cut 2 from brown

Pattern from "The Best of Creative Lettering Super Combo" CD, *Creating Keepsakes.*

October

Designer: Nancy Church

SUPPLIES

Burnt orange cardstock

Black striped paper

Photo

Purple fibers: Dazzle Thread, *Magic Scraps*

Foam squares: *Making Memories*

Star punches: Star Trio, Twinkling Star, *Posh Impressions*

Quote: Tiny Tales Vellum; Halloween, *My Mind's Eye*

INSTRUCTIONS

1. Cut calendar top from striped paper; adhere to cardstock backing.

2. Mat photo and vellum quote with cardstock. Cut moon from cardstock, using pattern. Punch stars from cardstock. Wrap fibers around quote and moon accents.

3. Adhere pieces to calendar top.

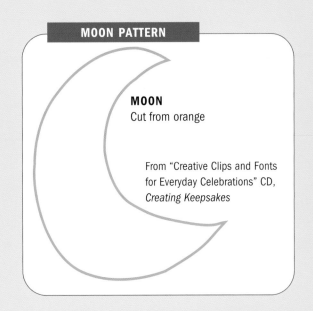

MOON PATTERN

MOON
Cut from orange

From "Creative Clips and Fonts for Everyday Celebrations" CD, *Creating Keepsakes*

November

Designer: Wendy Sue Anderson

SUPPLIES

Cardstock: brown, dark red, orange

Textured cardstock: blue, burnt red, green

Photo

Accents:
Antique eyelets: *Making Memories*

Olive gingham ribbon: *Making Memories*

Pigment ink: Chestnut; ColorBox, *Clearsnap*

Font: CK Daydream, "Creative Clips & Fonts by Becky Higgins" CD, *Creating Keepsakes*

Other: black pen, cosmetic sponge, eyelet-setting tools, sewing machine, thread

INSTRUCTIONS

❶ Print "Thanksgiving is not a time of the year . . . but an attitude of the heart." on burnt red textured cardstock. Cut into calendar top; sponge edges with ink.

❷ Cut 2" squares from dark red, green textured, blue textured, and orange cardstock; rub edges with ink. Machine-stitch to calendar top.

❸ Cut turkey from cardstock, using pattern. Sponge edges with ink. Assemble turkey and add eyes with pen. Adhere to calendar top.

❹ Mat photo with blue textured cardstock; sponge edges with ink. Adhere to calendar top.

❺ Set eyelets in calendar top. Thread ribbon through eyelets and tie.

Thanksgiving is not a time of the year... but an attitude of the heart.

TURKEY PATTERN

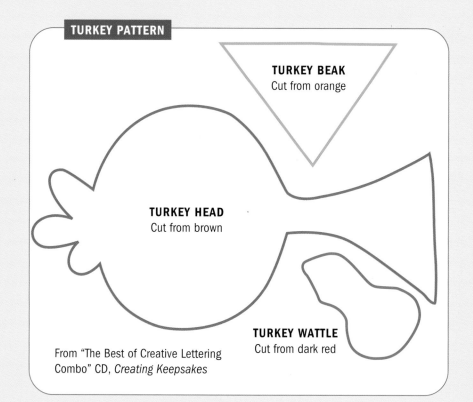

TURKEY BEAK
Cut from orange

TURKEY HEAD
Cut from brown

TURKEY WATTLE
Cut from dark red

From "The Best of Creative Lettering Combo" CD, *Creating Keepsakes*

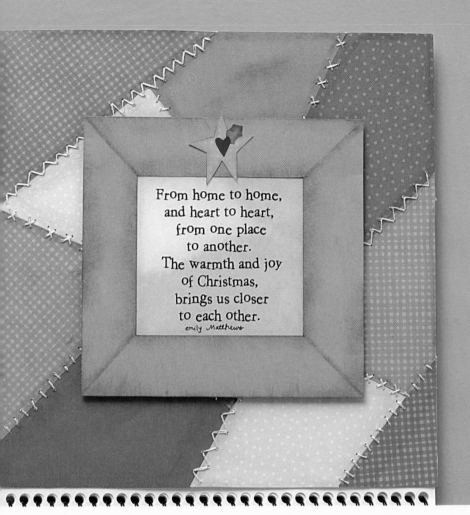

December

Designer: Heather Erickson

SUPPLIES

Cardstock: brown, maroon, white, *O'Scrap!*

Patterned paper: maroon plaid, maroon dot, green plaid, yellow dot, *O'Scrap!*

Vellum

Star sticker: Merry Days; Simple Squares, *O'Scrap!*

White embroidery floss: *DMC*

Font: CK Constitution, "Fresh Fonts" CD, *Creating Keepsakes*

Brown chalk: *Craf-T Products*

Other: foam dots, needle

INSTRUCTIONS

❶ Cut calendar top from white cardstock. Adhere various pieces of cardstock and patterned paper to create quilted look.

❷ Stitch seams with floss to accentuate quilted look.

❸ Cut frame from brown cardstock; shade with chalk.

❹ To make quote accent, print quote on vellum and adhere frame to quote; trim. Cut star from sticker and adhere to frame. Adhere quote accent to calendar top with foam dots.

ASSEMBLE THE CALENDAR

Once you've completed the calendar tops and printed the calendar months from the downloadable master file at *www.PaperCraftsMag.com/projects*, bind the tops and calendars together. Most photocopy and office supply stores provide this service at a minimal cost.

Messages of Affection

Everyone needs to feel appreciated. So this Valentine's Day,
tell people how much they mean to you with handmade cards.

He Loves Me...

Designer: Alice Golden

SUPPLIES

Textured cardstock:
(Aloe Vera) *Bazzill Basics Paper*
(Tsumugi Pastel Green) *Hanko Designs*

Patterned paper: (Pink Dot, Pink Stripe) Scrappy Chic Collage Paper Collection, *Me and My Big Ideas*

Transparency sheet: *3M*

Acrylic paint: (Celery) Springtime Scrapbook Colors, *Making Memories*

Color medium: (Dark Pink chalk) Surprise Chalklets, *EK Success*

Accents: (Pink Daisy Blossoms) *Making Memories*

Fasteners: (Pewter decorative brads) *Making Memories*

Font: (P22 Typewriter) *www.p22.com*

Adhesive:
(Scrapper's Spray) *Creative Imaginations*
(glue stick)

Tools: ruler, scissors, computer and printer, chalk applicator, paintbrush, hole punch

Finished size: 6¼" x 4½"

FRONT OF CARD

❶ Make card from Pastel Green cardstock.

❷ Cut and tear patterned papers to fit card front and adhere (see photo).

❸ Type text in circular pattern (see "Create Circular Text"). Reverse text and print on rough side of transparency sheet. *Note: When transparency sheet is turned smooth side up, text will be in right direction.* Trim transparency sheet to fit card and adhere with spray adhesive.

❹ Lightly chalk flower centers and ends of a few petals. Cut one petal from first daisy, two from second, three from third, and all but one from fourth.

❺ Paint brads and, while paint is still wet, rub some off with your finger to expose metal. Let dry.

❻ Attach first three daisies to card with brads. *Note: To make attaching each brad easier, punch hole through transparency first.* Adhere petals next to corresponding flowers.

INSIDE CARD

❶ Trim Aloe Vera cardstock to fit inside card. Print the following sentiment:

"Hope your Valentine's Day is everything you want it to be!"

❷ Attach fourth daisy with remaining brad.

❸ Fold piece in half and adhere inside card. Adhere petals.

CREATE CIRCULAR TEXT

❶ Open a new document in Microsoft Word. *Note: Be sure drawing toolbar is displayed.*

❷ Select WordArt button (tilted blue "A" on the drawing toolbar).

❸ Select the WordArt style you want, then type your text in the box.

❹ To select the text formation, click on the "ABC" button on the WordArt toolbar. Click and drag the squares around the shape to alter it as desired.

❺ To reverse the text, click the "Draw" button on the drawing toolbar and select "Rotate or Flip" on the drop-down menu. Select "Flip Horizontal."

DESIGNER TIPS

▪ Write or stamp the text on the transparency instead of printing it. Be sure to use a permanent marker (for writing) or solvent ink (for stamping) so the words won't rub off.

▪ For a more realistic look, adhere only part of the petal to the card and curl up the other edge with your finger.

▪ Adding an inside layer to your cards is a good way to cover up the back side of brads, eyelets, staples, or stitching.

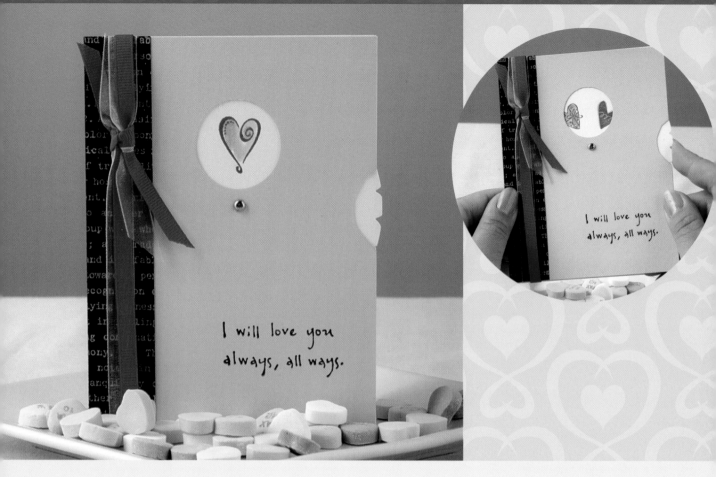

Always, All Ways

Designer: Julie Ebersole

SUPPLIES

Cardstock: (black, pink, white)

Rubber stamps:
(By Definition, hearts from Teeny Tinies, Figures of Speech, Mini Messages, A Greeting for All Reasons, and Good Times sets) Stampin' Up!
(Always, All Ways) Penny Black

Dye ink: (Basic Black, Real Red) Stampin' Up!

Pigment ink: (White) Stampin' Up!

Fastener: (gold brad)

Fibers: (red grosgrain ribbon, pink organdy ribbon)

Adhesive

Tools:
(circle cutter) Coluzzle, Provo Craft Watercolor paintbrush, ruler, needle tool, scissors, decorative edge scissors (see "Notched Scissors"), 1¼" circle punch

Other: pencil

Finished size: 4¼" x 5½"

ASSEMBLE

1 Make card from white cardstock. Punch half circle notch in front edge (see Figure a).

2 To make front panel, cut pink cardstock to fit card front. Punch half circle notch in front edge, aligned with notch on card. Stamp sentiment on bottom of panel with Basic Black.

3 To make heart wheel, cut 4" circle from white cardstock and trim with decorative edge scissors. Pierce center of circle with needle tool (see Figure b).

4 Align wheel on panel so circle edge protrudes from notch. Mark wheel's hole on panel with pencil (see Figure c).

5 Pierce hole through panel as marked, using needle tool. To make window, punch circle above pierced hole (see Figure d).

6 Attach wheel behind panel with brad (see Figure e). Note: Spin wheel by running finger along edge of wheel that protrudes from notch.

DECORATE

1 Stamp heart on wheel through window in panel. Rotate wheel and stamp another heart. Repeat until images fill window upon each rotation.

2 Paint pink accents on hearts, using mix of Real Red and White ink and water.

3 Apply adhesive to edges of panel and adhere to card. Note: Apply adhesive to edges only. Otherwise, wheel won't turn.

4 Stamp By Definition on black cardstock with White. Trim into strip and adhere to left side of card.

5 Tie ribbon around front card flap.

NOTCHED SCISSORS

Scissors that create a notched pattern work best for this project. Here are some options:

- Zipper Paper Shapers from Fiskars
- Scallop edge scissors, available from most manufacturers (trim the top off the scalloped edge with straight scissors)

a Punch notch

b Trim wheel, pierce hole

c Mark wheel hole on panel

d Pierce hole, punch window

e Attach wheel

Put your feelings into words.

Having a hard time expressing yourself? To cure your writers' block, we collected some quotations that are perfect for your Valentine cards.

Grow old along with me, the best is yet to be.
—Robert Browning

I love you not only for what you are, but for what I am when I am with you.
—Elizabeth Barrett Browning

Love does not consist of gazing at each other, but in looking together in the same direction . . .
—Antoine de Saint-Exupery

If I know what love is, it is because of you . . .
—Herman Hesse

Love is when you go out to eat and give somebody most of your French fries without making them give you any of theirs.
—A child

Blessed is the season which engages the whole world in a conspiracy of love . . .
—Hamilton Wright Mabie

If it's wrong to love you, then my heart just won't let me be right.
—Unknown

Set in Adobe Garamond by Adobe Systems Inc.

Love doesn't make the world go 'round; love is what makes the ride worthwhile . . .
—Franklin P. Jones

Designer: Deanna Hutchison

SUPPLIES

Textured cardstock: (Brownie) *Bazzill Basics Paper*

Patterned paper:
(Brianna) Brenda Walton, *K&Company*
(Phonique Blanc) *7gypsies*

Vellum: (Dictionary) Journey Collection, *K&Company*

Dye ink: (Van Dyke Brown) Nick Bantock Collection, *Ranger Industries*

Paper accent: (walnut ink-stained tag) *7gypsies*

Accents:
(elastic cord) *7gypsies*
(mica tiles) *USArtQuest*
(skeletonized leaf) *Black Ink*

Stickers: ("love" definition) Defined, *Making Memories*

Fasteners: (antique brass brads, eyelets) *Making Memories*

Adhesive:
(paper adhesive) *USArtQuest*
(foam squares) *Therm O Web*
(adhesive dots) *Glue Dots International*

Fibers: (brown ribbon)

Tools:
(Aging Sponges) *Foofala*
ruler, scissors, eyelet-setting tools, craft knife

Finished size: 5½" x 4"

FRONT PIECE

❶ Make card from cardstock. Cut Brianna paper to fit card front, positioning gingham pattern on top.

❷ Cut pieces from floral patterned area of Brianna paper to fit left edge and bottom right corner of card; tear inside edges and adhere. *Note: Leave inside edges of paper open for tucking accents underneath.*

❸ Set eyelets in left corners. Ink elastic cord. Adhere one end of cord next to bottom eyelet, using adhesive dot. Thread other end through top eyelet and adhere end in back with adhesive dot.

❹ Gently daub ink on leaf with sponge and adhere to piece. Tie ribbon through tag hole and adhere across top of piece, adhere ribbon end in back (see photo).

❺ Trim and tear Love and Always definitions from vellum; attach to piece with brads. Trim and tear Love definition sticker and adhere to bottom.

❻ Adhere piece to card. Ink edges and random areas of card.

LOVE ACCENT

❶ Tear out letters from Phonique Blanc paper to spell "LOVE"; ink edges.

❷ Adhere letters to card with foam squares.

❸ Separate mica into thin layers with craft knife. Adhere over letters, using paper adhesive.

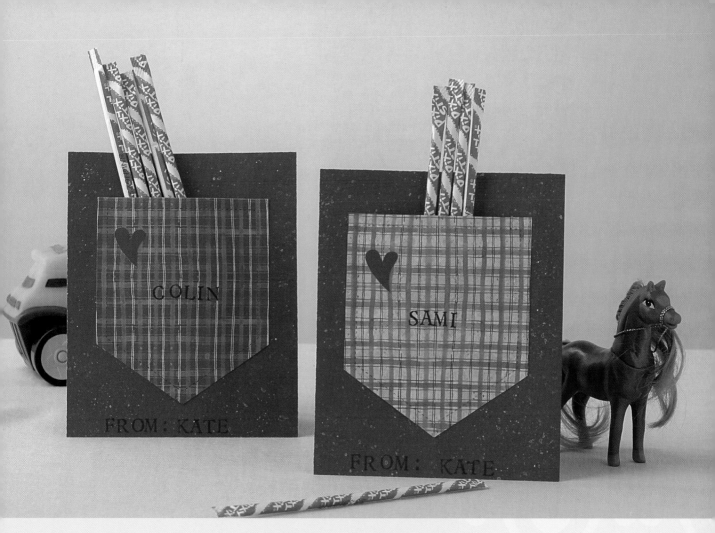

Child's Pocket Valentine

Designer: Nicole Keller

SUPPLIES

Patterned paper: (Wild Berry Plaid, Wild Berry Splatter) *Bo-Bunny Press*

Rubber stamps: (Antique Uppercase) Stamp Craft, *Wal-Mart*

Pigment ink: (Matte Black) Brilliance, *Tsukineko*

Candy: (Pixy Stix) *Nestle*

Adhesive

Tools:
    (Large Pocket Die, die-cutting machine) Sizzix, *Provo Craft*
    (heart punch) Posh Impressions, *Plaid*
    scissors, ruler

Finished size: 5" x 6"
(card does not open)

INSTRUCTIONS

❶ Cut card to finished size from Wild Berry Splatter paper.

❷ Die-cut pocket from Wild Berry Plaid paper. Apply adhesive along side and bottom edges and adhere to card. *Note: Don't apply adhesive to top of pocket or it won't hold candy!*

❸ Punch solid red heart from reverse of Wild Berry Splatter. Adhere to pocket.

❹ Stamp recipient's name on pocket, and name of giver below pocket.

❺ Tuck candy in pocket.

TIME-SAVING TIP

Here's a fast way to make several cards at once: Cut the cards, then the pockets, then punch the hearts. Adhere the pieces together to make cards, then stamp and stuff the pockets.

Bonus Ideas

- Fill the pocket with lollipops, sticks of gum, or flat candy bars.

- Make Christmas pocket cards, using holiday patterned paper. Fill the pockets with candy canes.

- Turn the pocket cards into party invitations. Print the party details on a piece of paper.

Love Ransomed

Designer: Teri Anderson

SUPPLIES

Textured cardstock: (Haley)
Bazzill Basics Paper

Patterned cardstock:
    (Walnut Large Paisley)
    Making Memories
    (Sommes) *7gypsies*

Notebook paper: *MeadWestvaco*

Chalk ink: (Charcoal) ColorBox,
Clearsnap

Accents: (gold paper clips) *Boxer
Scrapbook Productions*

Stickers:
    (Funky Brush alphabet, Italic
    alphabet, "main squeeze")
    Wordsworth
    (Ransom alphabet)
    Karen Foster Design

Fibers: (black polka dot ribbon)
May Arts

Adhesive

Tools: ruler, scissors

Finished size 4¼" x 6"

INSTRUCTIONS

① Make card from Haley cardstock.

② Trim and tear two pieces of each patterned cardstock to fit card front. Adhere pieces together and ink outside edges. Wrap ribbon around opposite corners, adhering ends in back. Adhere to card.

③ Crumple and flatten notebook paper; ink edges. Spell sentiment with stickers (see photo). Add paper clips and adhere to card.

Bonus Idea

Be creative in selecting the letters for your ransom note.
Combine letters cut from magazines and newspapers, alphabet stamps, and leftover stickers.

Love Charm

Designer: Bev Kish

SUPPLIES

Cardstock: (black, pink)

Vellum: (Pastel Pink) *WorldWin Papers*

Rubber stamps:
(Amore Heartprint) *Hero Arts*
(Love and Kisses) *Delta Rubber Stampede*

Dye ink: (Seashell Pink) Sea Shells, *Ranger Industries*

Watermark ink: *Stewart Superior Corp.*

Color medium: (Silver leafing pen) *Krylon*

Accents:
(slide mount) *Gary M. Burlin*
(heart charm) Card Connection, *Charming Thoughts*
(silver jump ring)

Fibers: (pink ribbon) Finishing Accents, *Darice*

Adhesive:
(foam tape) *3M*
(clear craft glue) Crafter's Pick Incredibly Tacky, *API*

Tools:
(scalloped rectangle punch) *Marvy Uchida*
corner rounder punch, ⅛" hole punch, scissors, ruler

Finished size: 4¼" x 5½"

INSTRUCTIONS

❶ Make card from pink cardstock. Stamp Love and Kisses with watermark ink. Tear approx. ½" from front right edge. Open card and outline torn edge with leafing pen; let dry.

❷ Tear strip of vellum (approx. 4" x ½"). Adhere ribbon to center and outline torn edges with leafing pen; let dry. Adhere to card with clear craft glue. Trim and outline right edge of strip with leafing pen so it's even with right edge of card.

❸ Stamp slide mount at an angle with Amore Heartprint, using Seashell Pink.

❹ Punch scalloped rectangle from black cardstock. Center slide mount over punched-out area and adhere with craft glue. Trim cardstock around slide mount, leaving ⅛" border. *Note: Trim corners with corner rounder punch.* Trace cardstock edges with leafing pen.

❺ Punch hole through slide mount. *Note: Punch hole low enough for jump ring to fit through it.* Attach charm to slide mount with jump ring.

❻ Adhere slide mount to card with foam tape.

Bonus Ideas

Adapt the card to different occasions by changing the colors and charm. Who wouldn't love a Halloween card with a jack-o-lantern charm, orange cardstock, black vellum, and purple ribbon? What about a winter card with a snowflake charm and white cardstock stamped with light blue snowflakes? Check out the charm selection at your local craft store and get inspired!

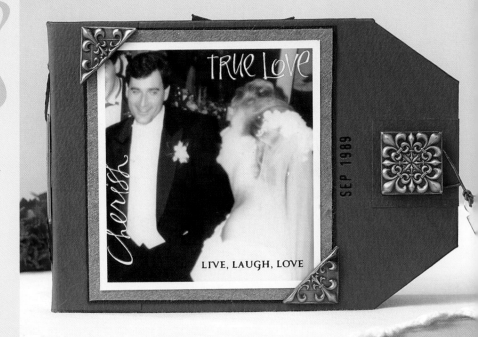

Things I Love About You Tag Book

Designer: Alice Golden

SUPPLIES

Cardstock: (Black Monochromatic) *Bazzill Basics*

Patterned paper:
  (Harlequin Rouge) *7gypsies*
  (antique white crinkle)

Mulberry paper: (Pewter) *Kate's Paperie*

Tag book: (red) Life's Journey, *K&Company*

Color medium: black fine-tip pen

Rubber stamps: (miscellaneous upper/lower case alphabet)

Dye ink: (Black Soot) Tim Holtz Distress, *Ranger Industries*

Permanent ink: (white)

Photos

Paper accents:
  (small white) Paper Tags, *Making Memories*
  (friend Ff printed index card) Synonym Tab, *Autumn Leaves*

Accents:
  (Metal Photo Corners) Architexture Gothic Metal Spandrel, (Metal Decorative Square) Architexture Gothic Metal Pateras, *EK Success*
  (Always metal word strip, love zipper pull, oval label holder, square photo hinge), *All My Memories*

Rub-ons:
  (black, red) Date/Numbers, *Autumn Leaves*
  (Expressions, Remember) Simply Stated Mini Rub-Ons, *Making Memories*

Fibers: (black/white, Red/Black dotted, Cajun ribbon) *Making Memories*

Adhesive: (glue gun, glue sticks)

Tools: heart punch

Finished size: 6½" x 4½"

COVER

❶ Carefully remove button closure from front and fibers from spine.

❷ Thread dotted ribbon through "Always" tag and tie through spine holes to secure pages.

❸ Adhere metal square in place of button with hot glue gun. *Note: Use enough glue so square is raised off book. Cord and tag will wrap around square to keep book closed.*

❹ Trim photo to fit book front, leaving a thin white border around photo edge. Double-mat with gray paper and black cardstock. Embellish with rub-on expressions.

❺ Adhere matted photo and photo corners to cover.

❻ Rub on date along one edge.

❼ Stamp occasion being celebrated on small white tag and ink edges with Black Soot. Tie to end of book closure cording.

INSIDE COVERS

❶ Trim Harlequin Rouge paper to fit inside front and back covers.

❷ Adhere paper to back inside cover. Tie zipper pull with black/white ribbon and adhere.

❸ Write greeting on crinkle paper with pen.

❹ Tear strip from front inside cover paper and tear hole to fit around greeting. Roll torn edges around hole. Adhere over greeting to inside book cover.

❺ Embellish with stamps, ribbon, tag, and label holder.

FIRST PAGE

❶ Double-mat small photo with black cardstock and gray paper; adhere to page.

❷ Attach photo hinge to printed index card and page (see photo).

❸ Punch heart from Harlequin Rouge paper and stamp "1" using white ink. Adhere to page.

Bonus Idea

WEDDING MEMOIRS

This would be a fun gift to give a couple for a special anniversary. Ask friends and family to write about a favorite memory they have of the couple and create a book of these anecdotes.

DESIGNER TIP
The bulkier the tag book becomes, the longer the cording will need to be. The cording should be long enough to wrap around the metal square once or twice.

Simple Sentiments

Select a beautifully worded phrase to include in your book of love.

*Love is a symbol of eternity
that wipes away all sense of time,
removing all memory of a beginning
and all fear of an end.*

—Ikhide Oshoma
set in Typo Upright, Bitstream

Love in its truest form has no language or words,
it just has a thousand and one actions we all wish we could describe.

—Kenneth B. Emery

Love is a sign from the heavens that you are here for a reason.

—J. Ghetto
set in Adobe Garamond

To the world you may be one person, but to one person you may be the world.

—Bill Wilson

Lots of people want to ride with you in the limo, but what you want is someone who will take the bus with you when the limo breaks down.

—Oprah Winfrey
set in Palantino, Adobe

The supreme happiness in life is the conviction that we are loved.

—Victor Hugo

love coupons

Designer: Gretchen Schmidt

SUPPLIES

For card:

Cardstock: white, black, *Making Memories*

Vellum

Tag: *Making Memories*

Pocket template: Deluxe Cuts

Font: Times New Roman, *Microsoft*

Other: crimson dye ink, fibers

For tag:

Alphabet eyelets: *Making Memories*

Other: hole punch, ribbon

For both:

Red cardstock: *Making Memories*

Patterned paper: *Bazzill Basics Paper*

Finished sizes:
   card 4" x 5½"
   tag 2¼" x 4¼"

MAKE CARD

❶ Cut 8" x 5½" cover from red cardstock.

❷ Cut 7½" x 5" lining from patterned paper; adhere to cover. Double-fold to make ¼" spine.

❸ Make pocket from black cardstock using template; adhere inside card.

❹ Print definitions on white cardstock. Trim into cards that fit pocket. Ink edges.

❺ Place cards in pocket.

❻ To make card front, cut 3" x 4½" piece of patterned paper and mat on black cardstock.

❼ Print "coupon book of love" on vellum and adhere to vellum tag. Punch hole in tag and thread fiber through.

❽ Wrap fibers around matted piece and adhere to card front. Secure tag with tape.

Insid

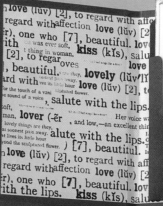

beaded love

Designer: Nichol Magouirk

SUPPLIES

Striped cardstock, pre-printed tag, word borders: Inspire2 by Two Busy Moms, *Deluxe Cuts*

Clear micro beads: *Judi-Kins*

Dimensional adhesive: Diamond Glaze, *Judi-kins*

Extreme eyelet: *Creative Imaginations*

Other: acetate, mini brads, gingham ribbon, hole punch

Finished size 4¼" x 5½"

MAKE CARD

❶ Cut card from striped cardstock. Adhere word borders to front with mini brads.

❷ Cut acetate same size as tag. Punch hole in top.

❸ Cover acetate with adhesive; adhere beads.

❹ Adhere acetate to tag; set eyelet. Tie ribbon; adhere tag to card.

Simple Sentiments

Till I loved I never lived enough.
—Emily Dickinson

When you love someone, all your saved-up wishes start coming out.
—Elizabeth Bowen

Love is a beautiful dream.
—William Sharp

The Eskimos had 52 names for snow because it was important to them; there ought to be as many for love.
—Margaret Atwood

Now I know what love is.
—Virgil

One word frees us of all the weight and pain of life: that word is love.
—Sophocles

be mine

Designer: Alisa Bangerter

SUPPLIES

White cardstock
Striped paper: *Thank You Ink*
Vellum: *Keeping Memories Alive*
Chalk: *Craft-T Products*
Alphabet pebbles: *Making Memories*
Ribbon: *Offray*
Heart Button: *Making Memories*
Pink vellum tag: *Making Memories*
Other: hole punch, string, sewing needle, thread

Finished size 4¼" x 5¾"

❶ Make card from white cardstock and cover with striped paper.

❷ Tear a 1½" x 5¾" vellum strip. Chalk long edges and glue to card.

❸ Punch hole in vellum tag and tie on string. Apply chalk to button and stitch to tag.

❹ Wrap ribbon around card front and tie bow, catching in ends of string.

❺ Spell "be mine" with alphabet pebbles.

i'm falling for you

Designer: Jenny Grothe

SUPPLIES

Cardstock: red, white, *Provo Craft*
Patterned paper: *Pebbles*
Vellum
Brads: *Making Memories*
Font: Cocktail, downloaded from the Web
Foam stickers: *Fibre Craft*
Ribbon: *Stampin' Up!*

Finished size 4¼" x 5½"

❶ Make card base. Adhere red paper.

❷ Adhere ribbon to pink pattern paper, tucking ends under. Adhere to card.

❸ Stamp words on vellum, cut out, and adhere with brads.

❹ Adhere foam hearts stickers.

soul mate

Designer: Jenny Grothe

SUPPLIES

Cardstock: brown, ivory, *Provo Craft*
Rusty tin hearts: *Provo Craft*
Alphabet stamps: *PSX*
Ink: *Tsukineko*
Tan foam square: *Fibre Craft*
Fibers: *On the Surface*

Finished size 5½" x 4¼"

❶ Make brown cardstock base. Tear.

❷ Cut ivory cardstock to fit, tear edge, adhere foam square.

❸ String fibers through rusty tin hearts. Wrap around ivory cardstock piece and adhere on back side.

❹ Adhere ivory cardstock piece to card.

pierced paper valentine

Designer: Darla McFarland

SUPPLIES

Cardstock: blue-gray, cream, navy, sage

Hydrangea die cut: *Anna Griffin*

Navy tulle ribbon: *Offray*

Adhesive foam squares: *Therm O Web*

Paper piercing tool: *Making Memories*

Other: piercing mat or foam-backed mouse pad (turned face down)

Finished size 8¼" x 9"

MAKE CARD

❶ Create pierced heart design on cream cardstock following "How to Pierce Paper."

❷ Cut out and triple mat heart on navy, blue-gray, and sage cardstock (see photo).

❸ Adhere hydrangea die cuts in three-dimensional layers using adhesive squares.

❹ Tie bow and adhere to top.

HOW TO PIERCE PAPER

❶ Transfer pattern lines to back of cream cardstock.

❷ Pierce holes along pattern lines at about ⅛" intervals using piercing tool. Make slightly larger holes at dots by wiggling tool in hole.

❸ Turn piece over to see finished design. Holes will have ridges around edges. For variety, punch some holes from front to eliminate ridges.

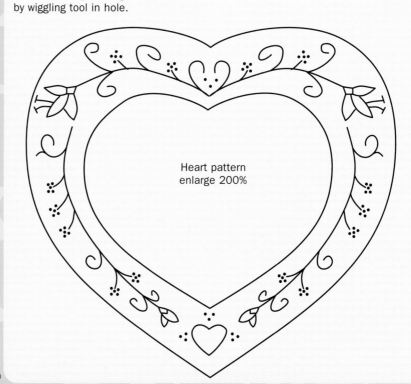

Heart pattern
enlarge 200%

kisses and hugs

Designer: Linda Beeson

SUPPLIES

cardstock: cream, red

Striped paper: *Pixie Press*

Heart patterned paper: *Paper Adventures*

Primitive heart punch: *Emagination Crafts*

Large silver flower eyelet: *Creative Imaginations*

Silver wire: *The Beadery*

Fibers: *DMC*

Fonts: Mom's Typewriter, Scriptina; *www.dafont.com*

Tag template: *Deluxe Cuts*

Other: "love" definition from dictionary, red chalk, red heart eyelet, silver charms

Finished size 4¼" x 5½"

TAG

❶ Photocopy and enlarge "love" definition from dictionary on cream cardstock.

❷ Cut tag from cardstock, using template. *Note: Position definition at an angle.*

❸ Tear edge of heart patterned paper; adhere to tag.

❹ Punch red heart. Strings charms on wire and wrap around heart. Adhere to tag.

❺ Set large flower eyelet in top of tag. Wrap fibers around eyelet.

a heart to adore

Designer: Alison Beachem

SUPPLIES

Cardstock: medium pink, light pink, white

Patterned vellum: *Chatterbox*

Rub-on letters: *Making Memories*

Ribbon: *Offray*

Shaved ice and tiny glass marbles: *Magic Scraps*

Foam tape: *3M*

Other: acetate (transparency)

Finished size 5¾" square

MAKE CARD

❶ Make card from medium pink cardstock.

❷ Mat 5½" square light pink cardstock on white.

MAKE SHAKER BOX

❶ Cut heart frame from white cardstock using pattern.

❷ Cut hearts from vellum and acetate using pattern outline only.

❸ Spell "adore" on acetate heart with rub-on letters.

❹ Adhere a border of foam squares to edge of vellum heart. Place shaved ice and glass marbles inside.

❺ Adhere acetate heart, then cardstock frame on top (see Figure a).

❻ Adhere shaker box to cardstock square. Tie with ribbon and adhere to card.

❼ Make envelope from light pink cardstock (see figure b).

a

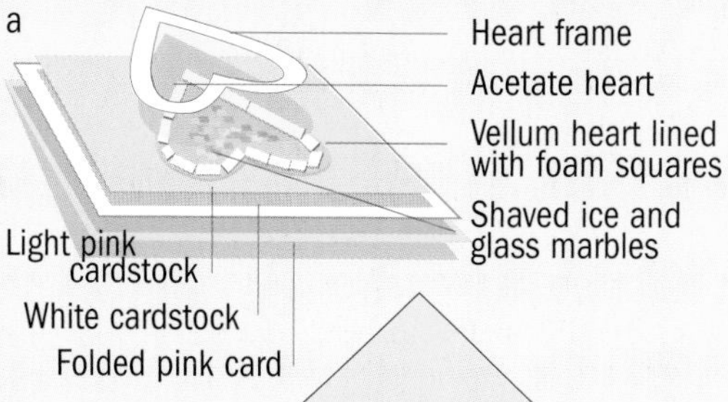

Heart frame
Acetate heart
Vellum heart lined with foam squares
Shaved ice and glass marbles

Light pink cardstock
White cardstock
Folded pink card

b

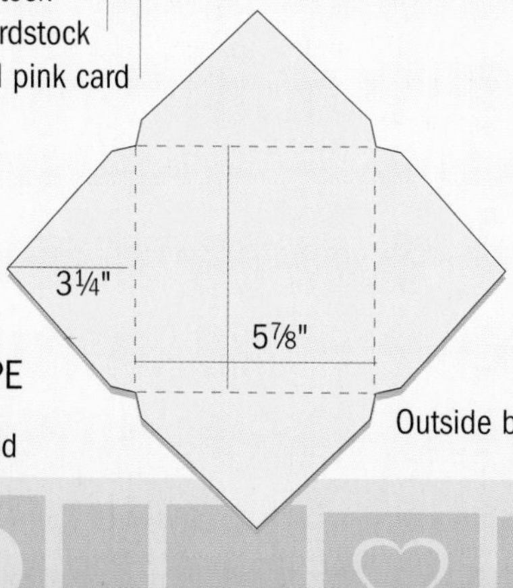

3¼"

5⅞"

MAKE ENVELOPE

cut and fold

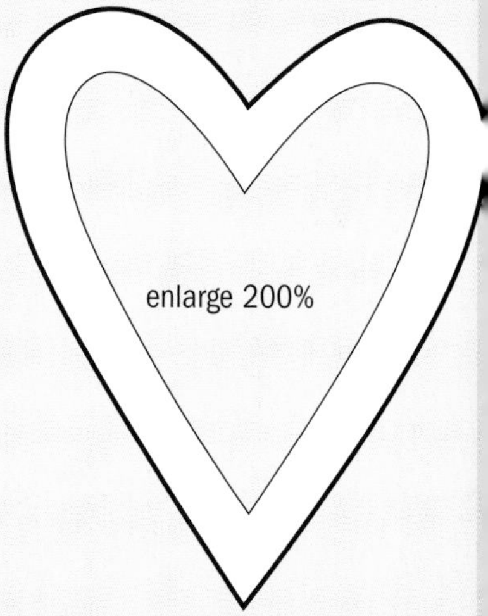

enlarge 200%

Heart frame - cut 1 from white cardstock
Outside border - cut 1 each from vellum and acetate

Baby, I love your...

toes   smile   laugh

hugs   lips   kiss

i love your everything

Designer: Lori Allred

SUPPLIES

White cardstock

Duo-patterned paper: Wild Berry plaid, *Bo-Bunny Press*

Font: Flea Market, *www.twopeasinabucket.com*

Heart charm, beads: *Making Memories*

Ribbon: *Close to My Heart*

4" shaker box: *Idea Tool Box*

Finished size 6" square

MAKE CARD

❶ Cut 6" x 12" piece duo-patterned paper for card base; fold.

❷ Cut and adhere 5" square of white cardstock to card.

❸ Thread charm on ribbon and tie around card front.

❹ Cut and adhere 4¼" square of patterned paper to card, reverse side up.

❺ Print words for inside of shaker on white cardstock; trim.

❻ Fill shaker box with beads and printed words. Adhere to card.

❼ Print "Baby, I Love Your..." on white cardstock and trim into 4" square frame.

❽ Adhere frame to shaker box front.

about us

Designer: Alison Beachem

SUPPLIES

White cardstock

Textured cardstock: pink, white, *Bazzill Basics Paper*

Pink patterned paper: striped, floral

CD tri-fold cover: *Pinecone Press*

Black ink: Clearsnap

Alphabet stickers: *Creative Imaginations*

Alphabet stamps: All Night Media, *Plaid*

Eyelet: *Prym-Dritz*

Snaps: *Making Memories*

Metal-rimmed tags: *Avery*

Font: Glitter Girl, www.twopeasinabucket.com

Other: gingham ribbon, charm, photos

Finished size 5" square
    5" x 15¾" when opened

MAKE COVER

❶ Unfold cover and adhere striped paper to outside. Cover inside with floral paper (see Figure a).

❷ Fold and adhere diagonal flap to inside.

❸ Mat photos on pink textured cardstock and adhere to inside (see photo).

❹ Print song titles on white cardstock. Trim and mat on pink textured cardstock; set snaps. Adhere inside cover (see photo).

Evergreen

Just the way you are

Groovy Kind of Love

as time goes by

calico skies

you remember when we met

Heart Pattern
cut 1 from
pink cardstock

Inside

❺ Make 4⅜" x 2½" tag with textured white cardstock. Set eyelet in tag. Add charm and ribbon; adhere to front.

❻ Cut heart from pink textured cardstock and adhere to tag.

❼ Spell "SONGS" across tag with alphabet stickers.

❽ Stamp "ABOUT" across heart.

❾ Adhere "U" and "S" stickers to metal-rimmed tags and adhere to tag.

❿ Wrap ribbon around cover and tie on inside.

a

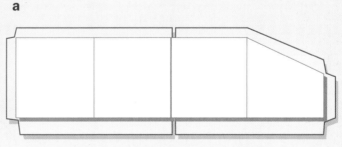

Wrap CD-tri-fold cover with pink patterned paper

scary love

Designer: Alisa Bangerter

SUPPLIES

Red cardstock

Alphabet stickers for "scary": Sonnets, *Creative Imaginations*

Heart tag: *Making Memories*

Foam mounting squares: *Therm O Web* (for spider)

Glue dots: *Glue Dots International*

Fiber: *EK Success*

Font: CK Newsprint, "Fresh Fonts" CD, *Creating Keepsakes*

Other: plastic spider

Finished size 4" x 5½"

1 Print "I love you so much it's" on red cardstock and fold to make card base.

2 Add "scary" alphabet stickers.

3 Attach fiber to heart tag. Adhere tag and fibers to card with glue dots.

4 Adhere spider with foam mounting square.

perfect match

Designer: Stacy Mcfadden

SUPPLIES

Cardstock: brown, terra cotta, cream
Alphabet tiles: *Foofala*
Oval Punch: *Carl Manufacturing*
Font: Facelift, www.scrapvillage.com
Other: brown chalk, alphabet stamps, black ink, stapler

Finished size 4" x 4½"

MAKE MATCHBOOK

① Cut 4" x 10" rectangle from brown cardstock. Chalk edges.

② Make flap by folding up 1" of a short side. Fold 4" and 4⅜" from opposite side to make spine.

③ Cut 3¾" square from cream cardstock. Stamp "We're a perfect match" across square. Cut into fringe at ⅜" intervals for matches (see photo).

④ Punch nine ovals from terra cotta cardstock; adhere to fringe ends for match tips.

⑤ Insert matches under flap and staple.

Inside

my heart beets for you

Designer: Nichole Heady

SUPPLIES

Cardstock: black, red, white, natural
Ink: Old Olive and Ruby Red, *Stampin' Up!*
Stamp sets: Botanicals, Fresh Flowers, Classic Alphabet, *Stampin' Up!*
Mini-fasteners: *Stampin' Up!*
Font: Favero, "Write Me a Memory" CD, *Stampin Up!*
Hole punch: *Fiskars*

Finished size 4¼" x 5½"

① Make card base from natural cardstock.

② Mat red cardstock square with black. Stamp beet on white cardstock, tear out and adhere.

③ Punch holes in corners of square. Attach square to card with mini-fasteners.

④ Stamp sentiment as shown in photo.

bee mine valentine

Designer: Teresa Snyder

SUPPLIES

Cardstock: white, gold, deep red, black, *Pebbles in My Pocket*

Lightweight vellum: *Pebbles in My Pocket*

Fine-tipped black pigment pen: *EK Success*

Gold lollipop: *Startup Candy Company*

Heart punch: *EK Success*

Font: Fairy Princess, *www.twopeasinabucket.com*

Other: ¼" hole punch, scissors, pencil, paper cutter

Finished size 4½" tall

1. Use pattern to cut one body from gold cardstock. Punch holes at each end for stick.

2. Cut strips of black cardstock and glue to body; trim.

3. Use pattern to cut two wings from vellum. Line edges with the pen. Glue to back of body.

4. Print "bee mine" on white cardstock and tear into a small rectangle. Punch heart from red cardstock and glue to the rectangle; glue to body.

5. Thread lollipop stick through holes.

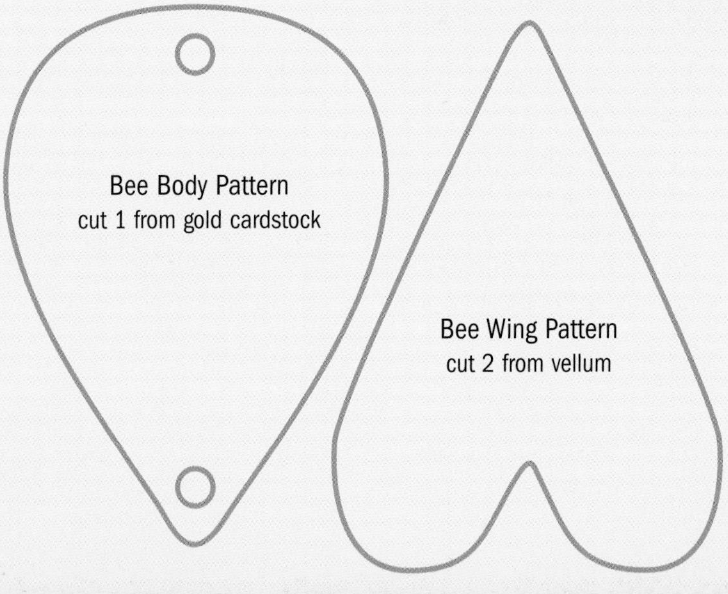

Bee Body Pattern
cut 1 from gold cardstock

Bee Wing Pattern
cut 2 from vellum

wild thing CD case

Designer: Julie Medeiros

SUPPLIES

Cardstock: black, yellow

Book plate: *Making Memories*

Snaps: *Making Memories*

Adhesive-backed fastener: *Velcro*

Font: Typewriter, *www.twopeasinabucket.com*

Other: animal print ribbon, button or decorative closure, chalk, sandpaper, plastic CD case

Finished size approx. 5¼" square

MAKE COVER

① Cut cover from black cardstock, distress with sandpaper, fold around CD case.

② Print sentiments on yellow cardstock. Tear and chalk edges. Adhere to cover with brads.

③ Adhere button and Velcro to ribbon; fasten around CD case.

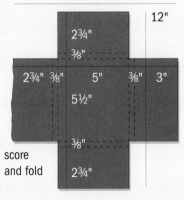

12"

2¾"

⅜"

2¾" ⅜" 5" ⅜" 3"

5½"

⅜"

2¾"

score and fold

Table For Two

Designer: Melanie Brower

SUPPLIES

Cardstock:
(Hot Girl Original Stripes/Orange, Hot Girl Squiggle Worm/Pink) *Scrapworks* (white)

Patterned paper: (Fire Plaid) *KI Memories*

Vellum: (white)

Color medium: (black fine-tip pen)

Fasteners: (Berry, Tangerine brads) *Making Memories*

Fonts: (assorted)

Adhesive: (repositionable double-sided tape)

Tools: computer and printer, scissors, ruler

Other: pencil

Finished sizes:
invitation 4¼" x 5½"
heart pocket 6½" x 6"
napkin ring 7" x 2" open

INVITATION

Invitation does not open.

① Cut Original Stripes cardstock to finished size.

② Print "Favorite" on white cardstock.

③ Type text of invitation (see "Favorite Things Invitation"). Select "Favorite" and make the font white. Select individual words and apply fonts and sizes of your choice. Print on vellum. Cut white cardstock and vellum to 4" x 4¾".

④ Adhere Orange square to white cardstock below "Favorite." Adhere strip of Pink cardstock under invitation information.

⑤ Attach vellum and white cardstock to card with eyelets.

⑥ Cut heart band from Pink cardstock, using pattern. Wrap around invitation. Write "to:" and draw heart and edging.

WOVEN HEART POCKET

① Cut Pink cardstock to 5½" x 8" and fold in half. Mark a stop-cutting line 4" from fold (see Figure a).

② Mark four 1" strips from the bottom to the stop-cutting line. Draw arch of heart (see Figure b). Cut strips and arches following pencil marks.

③ Repeat steps 1–2 with Orange cardstock.

④ Weave strips through each other beginning with strips #1 and A (see Figure c). When complete, push woven strip towards stop cutting line. Continue weaving with strips #2 and B—#4 and D.

⑤ Secure strip ends with adhesive; fill pocket with treats.

NAPKIN RING

① Make napkin ring, using pattern.

② Wrap around napkin and slip one cut heart over the other to secure.

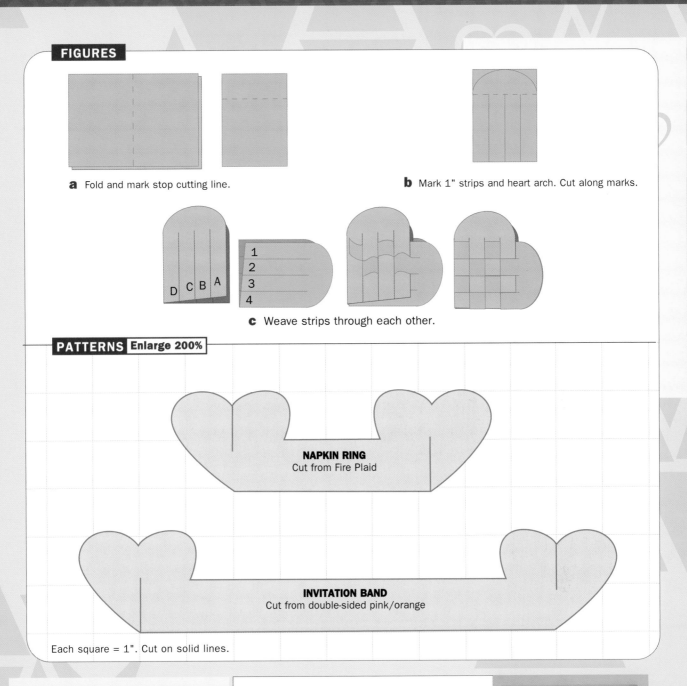

a Fold and mark stop cutting line.

b Mark 1" strips and heart arch. Cut along marks.

D C B A

1
2
3
4

c Weave strips through each other.

PATTERNS Enlarge 200%

NAPKIN RING
Cut from Fire Plaid

INVITATION BAND
Cut from double-sided pink/orange

Each square = 1". Cut on solid lines.

FAVORITE THINGS INVITATION

My Favorite Things...
Clean crisp sheets
Summer river trips
Motorcycle rides up the canyon
Big Surprises
Eating ice cream and watching T.V.
Throwing any kind of party
and
Conversing over a quiet dinner
With you.
Please join me for a romantic
dinner for two
this evening at 6pm

Bonus Ideas

■ Layer coordinating cardstock for placemats. Write questions around the edges
to stimulate dinnertime conversation.
Add pictures or phrases to the reverse
for a double-sided placemat. Laminate
placemats for durability.

■ Make heart decorations for the table.
Cut two matching hearts from cardstock.
To make them stand, trim the point
from each heart. Cut a slit halfway up
one heart and halfway down the other heart. Slide hearts together.

Sweet on you

Hand-packaged treats and sweet remembrances make Valentine's Day special.

Love Candy Bar Wrapper

Designer: Darcy Christensen

SUPPLIES

Red cardstock

Script patterned paper: *7gypsies*

Metal-rimmed vellum tag: *Making Memories*

Red adhesive tile: *EK Success*

Alphabet stickers: *Creative Imaginations*

Double-sided tape: *3M*

Other: brad, king-size candy bar

Finished size 7¼" x 4⅜"

INSTRUCTIONS

❶ Make outer wrapper from red cardstock, using the manufacturer's candy wrapper as a pattern.

❷ Tear script patterned paper and adhere to wrapper.

❸ Adhere alphabet stickers to red tile. Adhere tile to vellum tag.

❹ Attach tag to wrapper with brad. Wrap candy bar.

Be Mine Tent Wrap

Designer: Darcy Christensen

SUPPLIES

White cardstock

12" x 12" patterned paper: *Treehouse Designs*

Pink chalk: *Craft-T Products*

¼" hole punch: *McGill*

Heart eyelets: *Making Memories*

Pen: *EK Success*

Ribbon: *Offray*

Other: paint chip card, crochet thread

Sweets for You Pouch

Designer: Darcy Christensen

SUPPLIES

Cardstock: pink, white with pink stripes, *SEI*

Metal-rimmed tag: *Making Memories*

Rectangle punch: *McGill*

Corner rounder punch: *The Punch Bunch*

Adhesive dots: *Glue Dots International*

Ribbon: *Offray*

Font: CK Constitution, "Fresh Fonts" CD, *Creating Keepsakes*

Other: thread, cellophane bag of candy

Finished size 4½" x 8"

INSTRUCTIONS

❶ Cut, score, fold and stitch pouch as shown in diagrams.

❷ Stamp tag and adhere with glue dots (see photo).

❸ Punch holes, thread ribbon, tie bow.

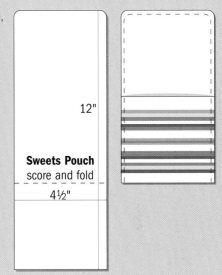

Sweets Pouch
score and fold
4½"
12"

Tent Wrap
score and fold

4½"   3"   4½"

6⅜"   5¾"

Finished size 6⅜" x 4½"

❶ Adhere patterned paper to white cardstock. Cut and fold as shown in diagram.

❷ Tear and fold paint chip card for flap. Punch hole through flap and tent. Attach eyelet and bow.

❸ Cut out tag. Adhere paper strips, chalk edges, set eyelet, and write message. Attach to bow with crochet thread.

PAINT CHIP CARDS

Whoever thought of incorporating paint chip cards in paper crafts is a genius! Paint chip cards from the hardware store make unusual accents that are guaranteed to start a conversation. They come in every color under the sun and have infinite crafting possibilities. You can cut the cards apart, tear the edges, punch out shapes, or embellish them with stamps, stickers, brads, or fibers.

GIFT IDEAS

Fill your tent wrap with a bag of candy, potpourri, or bath salts. Secure the gift to the tent bottom with double-sided tape.

Vellum Candy Packets

Heart Strings

Designer: Nichol Magouirk

SUPPLIES

White cardstock

Patterned vellum: *Printworks*

Metal-rimmed tag: *Making Memories*

Brads: *Magic Scraps*

Alphabet brad stickers: Bradwear Impress-ons, *Creative Imaginations*

Thread: Coats & Clark

"Love" bead: *Magnetic Poetry*

Heart buttons: *Dress It Up*

Other: small circle punch, string, candy

Finished size 4¼" x 4¾"

MAKE ENVELOPE

trim vellum   11"

| 4¾" | 4¾" | 1½" |

4¼"

MAKE CLOSURE

❶ Insert brad through punched cardstock circle and flap of bag. Repeat below flap.

❷ Attach tag to string; wind string around brads to close bag.

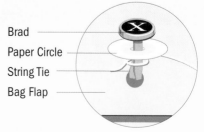

Brad
Paper Circle
String Tie
Bag Flap

Pinked Heart

Designer: Nichol Magouirk

SUPPLIES

Patterned vellum: Over the Moon Press, *EK Success*

Metal label holder: *Making Memories*

Alphabet stamps: *Hero Arts*

Ink: Memories, *Stewart Superior*

Love tag: *Kangaroo and Joey*

Thread: *Coats & Clark*

Pinking scissors: *Fiskars*

Other: small candies

Finished size 5½" x 4½"

❶ Stitch two vellum hearts together, leaving 1½" opening.

❷ Stamp label and adhere label holder. Add tag.

❸ Fill packet with candy; stitch opening closed.

Pinked Heart Pattern
Cut 2 from patterned vellum

Be Mine

Designer: Nichol Magouirk

SUPPLIES

Patterned vellum: Shotz, *Creative Imaginations*

Alphabet stickers: Shotz, *Creative Imaginations*

Mesh heart eyelet: *Making Memories*

Thread: *Coats & Clark*

Adhesive-backed fastener: *Velcro*

Other: lace trim, candy

Finished size 3" x 5¼"

❶ Make envelope as shown in diagram.

❷ Adhere lace trim and heart eyelet to flap.

❸ Add alphabet stickers.

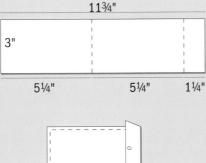

11¾"

3"

5¼"   5¼"   1¼"

Valentine Treat Bags

Designer: Linda Beeson

SUPPLIES

Plaid cardstock: *The Robin's Nest*

Cardstock: red, white

Heart stickers: *Stickopotamus*

Hole punch: *McGill*

Heart template: *Accu-Cut*

Other: ribbon, cellophane bags, candy

Finished size 2¾" x 3½"

❶ Cut and fold cardstock as shown in diagram.

❷ Fill cellophane bag with candy; fold top over twice.

❸ Place candy bag in treat bag, positioning folded top of candy bag inside top of treat bag.

❹ Punch two holes through all layers. Tie with ribbon.

fold up

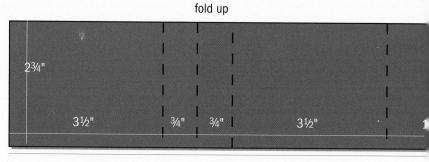

2¾"

3½"   ¾"   ¾"   3½"

9½"

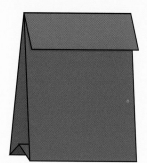

The recipe card image shows:

Red Hot Valentine Popcorn

1 c. butter or margarine
1/2 c. light corn syrup
1 pkg. (9 oz.) red hot
    cinnamon candies
8 qts. popped popcorn

Combine butter, corn syrup, and cinnamon candies in a heavy saucepan. Bring to a boil and stir constantly over medium heat. Boil for 5 minutes. Pour over popcorn and mix well. Pour onto a greased cookie sheet and spread out. Bake at 275 degrees for 1 hour. Stir several times while baking. Remove from oven and allow to cool. Break apart. Store in an airtight container.

Red Hot Valentine Popcorn

Designer: Alisa Bangerter

SUPPLIES

Cardstock: red, white
Vellum: *Keeping Memories Alive*
Font: CK Constitution, "Fresh Fonts" CD, *Creating Keepsakes*
Red chalk: *Craf-T Products*
Heart punch: *Marvy Uchida*
Heart eyelet: *Making Memories*
Fibers: *On The Surface*
Other: black ink, sponge

Finished size 8" x 2⅜"

① Cut red tag.

② Tear strip of white cardstock. Sponge black ink around edges. Adhere heart punch-outs. Adhere strip to tag.

③ Print recipe on vellum. Tear and chalk edges. Adhere to tag.

④ Add eyelet and fibers.

Popcorn Recipe

INGREDIENTS

1 c. butter or margarine

½ c. light corn syrup

1 pkg. (9 oz.) red hot cinnamon candies

8 qt. popped popcorn

Combine butter, corn syrup, and cinnamon candies in a heavy saucepan. Bring to a boil and stir constantly over medium heat. Boil for 5 minutes. Pour over popcorn and mix well. Pour onto a greased cookie sheet and spread out. Bake at 275°F for 1 hour. Stir several times while baking. Remove from oven and allow to cool. Break apart. Store in an airtight container

From *Sweet Surprises for the Holidays* by Alisa Bangerter (Gingerbread Garden, 801/633-3978, *www.gingerbreadgarden.com*)

Love Door Hanger

Designer: Dee Gallimore-Perry

SUPPLIES

All supplies from Creative Imaginations unless otherwise noted.

Patterned paper: (red love) Script Paper Collection, Sandra Magsamen

Transparency sheet: (love) Narratives, English Composition

Door hanger pouch: *Close To My Heart*

Paper accent: (square metal-rimmed tag) Double-Sided, Sonnets

Sticker: (heart) Love & Family Collection, Sandra Magsamen

Fasteners: (red eyelets) Making Memories

Fiber: (Red Swiss Dot Ribbon) *Offray*

Adhesives: (double-sided tape, spray adhesive) no source

Tools: (eyelet-setting tools, scissors, ruler) no source

Finished size 3½" x 7¼"

INSTRUCTIONS

❶ Cover both sides of unassembled door hanger with red love paper and adhere.

❷ Assemble door hanger pouch and cut out doorknob hole. *Note: Place something solid inside pouch to help maintain its shape during assembly.*

❸ Cut transparency sheet to 2½" square; attach to tag with eyelets.

❹ Adhere tag to hanger and heart sticker to tag.

❺ Tie with ribbon. Slip a treat inside.

Hot Chocolate Love

Designer: Kathleen Paneitz

SUPPLIES

Textured cardstock: (red)

Patterned Paper: (Studio K Mustard Collage) K&Company

Dye ink: (Sepia) Archival, Ranger Industries

Sticker: (YOU AND ME) Life's Journey, K&Company

Fastener: (pewter heart brad) Creative Impressions

Font: (CK Stenography) "Fresh Fonts" CD, Creating Keepsakes

Fibers:
   (Always) Printed Twill Ribbon, Creative Impressions
   (black twill ribbon) Wrights

Hot cocoa mix: (Supreme Chocolate) Land O'Lakes

Adhesive

Tools:
   (2¼" square punch) McGill
   ¼" hole punch, computer and printer, scoring tool, ruler, scissors

Finished size 3½" x 6¼"

INSTRUCTIONS

1 Cut patterned paper to 3½" x 12", fold in half, and ink edges.

2 Punch square opening near fold (see photo).

3 Print sentiment on cardstock and trim to 3¾" x 5". Tear and ink bottom edges. Score above sentiment and fold.

4 Place chocolate mix bag in folded patterned paper and position folded cardstock over top. Punch two holes through all layers and tie with black twill ribbon.

5 Cut 12" length of printed twill ribbon. Lift cardstock and loop over black twill ribbon. Secure to paper with brad.

6 Adhere sticker at bottom.

Hug Tag

Designer: Sahily Gonzalez

SUPPLIES

Patterned paper:
   (Dream Wash) Teri Martin, (Blush Wash) Sonnets, Creative Imaginations
   (Tan Wash) Sweetwater
   (Seed Pods, Vintage Dictionary) Rusty Pickle
   (Romance Collage) Two Busy Moms

Paper accent: (square tag)

Rubber stamps: (Antique lowercase alphabet) PSX

Dye ink: (Artprint Brown) Memories, Stewart Superior

Accents: (Hug cork word) Lazer Letterz; (red staples)

Stickers:
   (love, moments) Life's Journey, K&Company
   (Loving) Sticko, EK Success

Fibers: (brown, gold, orange) Fibers by the Yard

Adhesive

Tools: stapler, ruler, scissors, brown pen

Finished size: 5½" square

INSTRUCTIONS

1 Adhere Dream Wash paper to top of tag. Trim Tan Wash and Blush Wash paper and adhere to bottom.

2 Adhere strip of Seed Pod paper below Dream Wash.

3 Cut 3½" square of Vintage Dictionary paper. Add staples along top and right edges; apply adhesive to center of square and adhere to tag.

4 Cut couple from Romance Collage paper; apply adhesive to top and bottom edges and adhere to tag.

5 Stamp and write sayings on tag as desired (see photo).

6 Add sticker, accents, and fibers to tag.

Text on hearts (part of image): "You have encouraged me when I've started to waver. That's why you're one of my favorite", "I'll show my love for you with pleasure, by giving you a Nestle", "You're worth more than", "I think you're the best in the land!", "14 days valentines", "100 GRAND"

14 Days of Valentines

Designer: Cindy Knowles

SUPPLIES

Cardstock:
(Cantaloupe) Double Dipped, *Making Memories*
(kraft)

Patterned paper: (Artsy Plaid), *Wordsworth*

Transparency sheets: (Inkjet Transparency Film) *3M*

Rubber stamps: (alphabet upper case, lower case) Printer's Type, *Hero Arts*

Solvent ink: (Jet Black) StazOn, *Tsukineko*

Pigment ink: (Pink) Cat's Eye, ColorBox, *Clearsnap*

Envelope die cut: (#Z02576 square with rounded flaps) *Accu-Cut*

Accents: (self-adhesive pastel buttons) Button Ups, *EK Success*

Fasteners:
(elastic with metal stays) *7gypsies*
(jean rivets, small eyelets)

Fibers:
(pink twill ribbon) *Boxer Scrapbooks*
(pink gingham ribbon) Craft Narrows, *Michaels*
(pink rickrack) *Wrights*
(orange grosgrain ribbon, white thread)

Font: (P22 Typewriter) *www.P22.com*

Adhesive:
(adhesive dots) 3-D Dots, *EK Success*
(repositionable tape)

Tools:
(1½" square punch) Whale of a Punch, *EK Success*
computer and printer, fine sandpaper or emery board, large hole punch, needle tool, sewing machine, scissors

Other: black pen, wrapped candy and mini candy bars

Finished sizes:
hearts 4½" x 5"
envelope 5" square

HEARTS

Create 14 heart notes; one heart for each day leading up to Valentine's Day.

❶ Draw heart on transparency sheet. Print sentiment on heart, leaving room for candy. Cut out heart.

❷ Secure fibers to transparency heart, using adhesive dots. *Note: Do not put adhesive where you will sew. Sewing through adhesive may make the needle sticky and break the thread.*

❸ Adhere transparency hearts to Artsy Plaid paper with repositionable tape. Tear paper into matching heart shape.

❹ Remove repositionable tape as you zig-zag stitch transparency to paper, catching fibers.

❺ Adhere candy, and button if desired.

ENVELOPES

Make one envelope for each heart.

❶ Cut envelope from kraft cardstock using die.

❷ Stitch around outside edges.

❸ Ink edges with pink.

❹ Punch square from Cantaloupe cardstock. Lightly sand edges. Tear patterned paper into 2" heart shape. Adhere punched square to flap. Adhere torn heart to square, using adhesive dot. Adhere button to heart.

❺ Cut 5" length orange grosgrain ribbon, fold in "V" shape and stamp "14 days" and "Valentines". Adhere ribbon under heart so that message shows.

❻ Attach rivet to bottom flap following manufacturer's instructions.

❼ Punch hole through envelope back and set eyelet.

❽ Adhere side flaps, then bottom flap.

❾ To create closure, thread elastic fastener through eyelet from inside. *Note: To close envelope, pull elastic up and over top, around sides of heart, and secure around rivet.*

DESIGNER TIPS

■ Tearing a heart shape is easier if you start at the point and tear slowly, working upward.

■ To avoid the sewing machine slipping on the transparency sheets, maintain an even pressure with one hand and direct the stitching with the other hand.

CANDY

Use one piece of each candy unless otherwise noted.

Hugs, Kisses (2 of both); Almond Joy, Whoppers; *Hershey Foods,* www.hersheys.com

100 Grand, Chocolate Coins, Crunch Bar, Treasures, Smarties, Sweetarts; *Nestlé,* www.nestleusa.com

Snickers, Twix; *Mars Incorporated,* www.mars.com

Lifesavers, Now & Later; *Kraft Foods,* www.kraftfoods.com

Airheads, www.airheads.com

CANDY SENTIMENTS

Replace words in parentheses with candy.

Day 1
I love your (Kisses)
I love your (Hugs)
They pull on my heart with great big tugs!

Day 2
You're worth more than (100 Grand)
I think you're the best in the land!

Day 3
I hope that we will never part,
and that we will stay real (Sweetarts)!

Day 4
Don't you fret and don't you (Snicker)
Don't let my love upset your ticker!

Day 5
You're so sweet, as sweet as honey.
I love you more than chocolate (Chocolate Coins)

Day 6
You are a (Smartie)
You're full of brains.
I know you'll go far,
You'll make BIG gains.

Day 7
To show my love, oh boy! Oh boy!
I'm giving you this (Almond Joy)

Day 8
No one can come (Twix) you and me
Because you're as special as can be!

Day 9
I don't tell (Whoppers)
I don't tell lies.
You're an important part of our family ties.

Day 10
I'll love you always, (Now & Later)
I'd even love you at the Equator.

Day 11
I've met (Airheads)
I've met geeks. You're one of a kind;
You're someone UNIQUE!

Day 12
You always help out when I'm in a (Crunch)
That's one of the reasons I love you a bunch!

Day 13
You have encouraged me, when I've started to waiver.
That's why you're one of my favorite (Lifesavers)!

Day 14
I'll show my love for you with pleasure,
By giving you a chocolate (Treasure).

Friendship Tin

Designer: Kelly Anderson

SUPPLIES

Tin box and miniature glass-topped canisters: Watchmaker's case, *Lee Valley*

I love you eyelet: *Making Memories*

Metal-rimmed vellum tags: *Making Memories*

Black script paper: *7gypsies*

Love enamel plaque: *7gypsies*

Black polka-dot ribbon: *Midori*

Other: cardboard sheet, assorted paper, cardstock, tissue paper, ribbon, decorative paper clips, fabric, jewelery adhesive; memorabilia such as photos, buttons, charms, miniature frames, and vintage accents

Finished size approx.
  5½" x 6½" x 1"

DECORATE LID

❶ Cut two pieces of cardboard to fit box lid.

❷ Cover with patterned paper; decorate as desired.

❸ Adhere one piece of cardboard to top of box lid and one inside box lid.

FILL BOX

❶ Line box bottom with paper.

❷ Cut photos to fit some canister lids.

❸ Fill remaining canisters with paper, fabric, or tissue paper, plus memorabilia. Glue in place.

❹ Adhere canisters to box bottom with jewelry adhesive.

BEST FRIENDS MEMORABILIA

Fill your best friends box with small reminders of your friendship. Here are some ideas:

■ Charms, magnets, postage stamps, or stickers that represent a shared hobby or interest

■ Fabric swatches or buttons from clothing you shared

■ Significant newspaper clippings

■ Miniature photocopies of letters, yearbook signatures, birthday invitations, graduation and wedding announcements

■ Paper and ribbon in your favorite colors

■ The quarter you still owe your friend for that ice cream cone

■ Small keepsakes like concert tickets, dried flowers, receipts, or keys

Open

Book Necklace

Designer: Laurie D'Ambrosio

SUPPLIES

Black cardstock scrap

Silver vellum

Mini frame necklace: *PSX*

Heart stamp: Spiral heart 653989, *PSX*

Silver embossing ink: *Ranger Industries*

Silver embossing pen: *Ranger Industries*

Embossing powder: Silver Detail, *Ranger Industries*

Embossing heat tool: *Darice*

⅛" hole punch: *Fiskars*

Deckle-edge scissors: *Fiskars*

Glue stick: *Tombow*

Other: eyelet, 2 small photos

Finished size 2" x 2¼"

❶ Stamp and emboss heart on vellum; trim. Set eyelet.

❷ Pat inside frames on embossing pad; emboss.

❸ Write message inside book spine with embossing pen; emboss.

❹ Adhere heart and black cardstock strips to cover.

BONUS IDEA

Insert small personal messages or quotations in the frames instead of photos.

St. Patrick's Day

Bonus Idea

Use the same papers and techniques to create a whole table ensemble of place cards, gift bags, and gift boxes.

For the luck of the Irish We hope you can attend our annual

St. Patrick's Day Party!

Ryan

Thank you

Shamrock Party Invitation

Designer: Michelle Tardie

SUPPLIES

Cardstock: cream

Paper: (Summer Green, Wineberry) *The Robin's Nest*

Pigment ink: (gold) Colorbox, *Clearsnap*

Embossing powder: (clear) Ultra Detail, *Mark Enterprises*

Color medium: (Gold Metallic Rub-on) Kit #1, *Craf-T Products*

Paper accent: shipping tag

Stickers: (Apple rectangle) Pure Juice Frames & Tags, *Memories Complete*

Fasteners:
   (gold safety pin) *Singer*
   (cream rivet) *Chatterbox*

Fibers: (green gingham ribbon) *Offray*

Font: (CK fable) "Creative Clips and Fonts for Special Occasions" CD, *Creating Keepsakes*

Adhesive: (narrow double-sided mounting tape) Scotch, *3M*

Tools: computer and printer, small circle punch, heat tool, scissors, ruler

Other: baby powder

Finished size: 3¼" x 8"

INSTRUCTIONS

❶ Make card from cardstock and lightly ink all edges.

❷ To create pocket, sprinkle baby powder on back of green rectangle sticker to neutralize stickiness. Punch half circle at top. Adhere sides and bottom of sticker to slightly larger piece of Summer Green, using double-sided tape. Adhere piece to card front.

❸ Print invitation on shipping tag; lightly ink edges and emboss. Add metallic rub-on. Set rivet in tag hole, tie ribbon, and attach pin.

❹ Cut large shamrock, using pattern. Crumple shamrock, then smooth. Lightly ink edges, heat emboss, and accent with metallic rub-on. Tie ribbon around stem. Adhere shamrock to pocket with mounting tape.

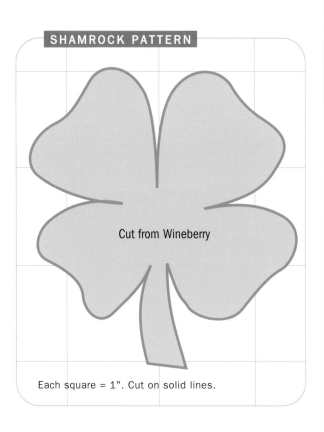

SHAMROCK PATTERN

Cut from Wineberry

Each square = 1". Cut on solid lines.

Lucky To Have You Card

Designer: Kim Hughes

SUPPLIES

Cardstock:
  (Garden Green) *Stampin' Up!*
  (Hunter Green, Sunflower Yellow) *Bazzill Basics Paper*

Patterned paper: (green/yellow)

Transparency sheet

Foam stamps: (Philadelphia alphabet) *Making Memories*

Acrylic paint: (Hunter Green)

Stickers: (Scrapbook alphabet) Alphabitties, *Provo Craft*

Fibers: (green gingham ribbon) *Michaels*

Adhesive: (Memory Book Glue Dots) *Glue Dots International*

Tools:
  (Shamrock Punch) *Marvy Uchida*
  paintbrush, scissors, ruler

Finished size: 4¼" x 5½"

INSTRUCTIONS

1. Make card from Garden Green cardstock.

2. Cut Sunflower Yellow cardstock to 4" x 3¼" and stamp "Lucky" using paint. Adhere to top of card.

3. Cut patterned paper to 4" x 2" and adhere to bottom of card.

4. Adhere ribbon where papers meet; adhere ribbon ends to card back and inside.

5. Punch shamrocks and adhere.

6. Apply letter stickers to transparency sheet; paint and let dry. To mount letters correctly on card, begin with "u" and spell backwards.

7. Cut two pieces of Sunflower Yellow to 4¼" x 5½" and adhere to card inside and back to cover ribbon ends.

Bonus Ideas

This card can be adapted for any occasion with just a few changes in paper, ribbons, punches, and wording.

- Stamp "Easter" and adhere bunny or egg accents.

- Use beautiful floral ribbons and papers, and stamp "Mom" for Mother's Day or birthday.

- Create pink or blue cards, stamp "Baby," and use for a baby shower.

Spring Greetings

Send cheerful messages to celebrate Mother's Day, Easter, and the arrival of spring.

Spring Flowerpot

Designer: Wendy Johnson

SUPPLIES

Rubber stamp: (Small Solid Daisy) *Impress Rubber Stamps*

Dye ink: (Pretty in Pink, Lavender Lace) *Stampin' Up!*

Cardstock: (pink, white)

Patterned paper: (solid yellow)

Fibers: (green floss) *DMC*; (lavender ribbon) *Making Memories*

Font: (GeeokHmk) *Hallmark*

Dimensional glaze: Crystal Effects, *Stampin' Up!*

Adhesive

Tools: (Plant Pots die #38-0212, die-cutting machine) Sizzix, *Ellison/Provo Craft*; scissors, paintbrush, needle, computer and printer

Other: sandpaper

Finished size: 4¼" x 5½"

DIMENSIONAL GLAZE TECHNIQUE

1. Stamp Small Solid Daisy two times with Pretty in Pink and three times with Lavender Lace on white cardstock.

2. Apply dimensional glaze to each flower; let dry.

3. Cut out flowers, bending petals slightly for dimension.

MAKE CARD

1. Make card from pink cardstock.

2. Cut white cardstock slightly smaller than card front.

3. Straight-stitch five stems on white cardstock rectangle with floss and adhere to card.

4. Die-cut pot from yellow paper; sand edges and adhere over stem bottoms.

5. Adhere flowers to stem tops.

6. Tie ribbon bow and adhere to pot.

7. Print "Mother" on white cardstock and trim into tag shape; mat with pink cardstock. Adhere tag just under bow.

Simple Sentiments

Spring is a heart full of hope
and a shoe full of rain.

Spring in the world!
And all things are made new!

—Richard Hovey

Easter tells us that life is to be interpreted not simply in terms of things but in terms of ideals.

—Spanish Proverb

Mother's love is the fuel that enables a normal human being to do the impossible.

—Marion C. Garretty

An ounce of mother
is worth a
pound of clergy.

—Spanish Proverb
FilosofiaUnicase

Mothers are flowers in the garden of life.

Lilac Garden Journal

Designer: Kathleen Paneitz

SUPPLIES

Rubber stamp: French Script, *Stampin' Up!*

Black ink: *PrintWorks*

Purple ink: VersaColor, *Tsukineko*

Composition notebook: *Wal-Mart*

Computer font: CK Elegant, "Fresh Fonts" CD, *Creating Keepsakes*

Purple mini brads: *Magic Scraps*

Gold bookplate: *Two Peas in a Bucket*

Laminate: *Therm O Web*

Black gingham ribbon: *Offray*

Other: lilac photo, 5¾" x 4" canvas, 6½" x 9¾" and ½" x 2½" cream cardstock, scissors, adhesive

Finished size 9¾" x 7½"

INSTRUCTIONS

❶ Stamp script on large cream cardstock with black. Adhere to notebook; trim excess.

❷ Transfer photo to laminate (see "How to Transfer a Photo to Laminate").

❸ Adhere image to canvas. Fray canvas edges; adhere to notebook.

❹ Print "my garden journal" on small cream cardstock. Center in bookplate, attach with brads.

❺ Press ribbon into purple ink. Let dry; tie around notebook.

HOW TO TRANSFER A PHOTO TO LAMINATE

❶ Make color copy of photo. Cut laminate to photo size. Peel backing off laminate.

❷ Press photo onto laminate. Burnish. Trim excess laminate. *Note: Leave ⅛" border around photo.*

❸ Soak laminated photo in warm water for several minutes.

❹ Remove and peel photocopy away from laminate. *Note: The image should be transparent.*

Bloom Canister

Designer: Summer Ford

SUPPLIES

Rubber stamps: (French Writing) *Inkadinkado;* (Berryvine Border) *Stampabilities;* (Classic alphabet) *Stampin' Up!*

Foam stamps: (Philadelphia Lowercase alphabet) *Making Memories*

Watermark ink: VersaMark, *Tsukineko*

Pigment ink: (white)

Chalk ink: (Dark Moss) ColorBox, *Clearsnap*

Paint: (Spotlight) Cityscape, Scrapbook Colors, *Making Memories*

Paper: (Green) *Anna Griffin*

Fiber: (green) *Great Balls of Fiber*

Accent: (pewter flower) The Jewelry Shoppe, *Crafts Etc.*

Tin can

Adhesive

Tools: scissors

Finished size: 4¾" x 4" diameter

INSTRUCTIONS

❶ Cut Green paper to fit around can.

❷ Stamp French Writing randomly on paper with watermark ink. Stamp Berryvine Border with Dark Moss and white at top and bottom of Green paper.

❸ Stamp "bloom" with Spotlight and foam stamps on center of stamped paper; let dry.

❹ Stamp "where you're planted" over "bloom" with Dark Moss and Classic alphabet.

❺ Adhere stamped strip to can.

❻ Wrap fiber around can top; string pewter flower on fiber and tie bow.

BONUS IDEA

Create a garden poke with the guest's name stamped on it to place in each can. Then place them around the table for cute place cards and party favors all in one.

Pressed Flower Pot

Designer: Livia Mcree

SUPPLIES

Rubber stamp sets and acrylic block: *Stampendous!* (Perfectly Clear Pop Flowers, Whimsy Alphabet)

Ink: Pearlescent Ivy, Brilliance, *Tsukineko*

Deckle-edge scissors: *Fiskars*

Other: green cardstock, light-colored handmade paper, natural greeting card, small pressed yellow daisy, terra cotta raffia, scissors, adhesive

Finished size: 5" x 7¼"

MAKE THE POT

❶ Layer strips of raffia on pre-glued cardstock. *Note: Push sides of strips together as you lay them down to eliminate gaps.*

❷ Cut 1⅜" tall pot shape from cardstock, 1⅝" wide at rim.

STAMP

❶ Stamp flower stem and leaves on light-colored paper.

❷ Arrange the letter stamps to stamp "spring" on green cardstock.

ASSEMBLE

❶ Adhere pot, flower to card.

❷ Trim flower; trim green cardstock with deckle-edge scissors.

❸ Layer and adhere to card.

Butterfly Pressed Flowers

Designer: Livia Mcree

SUPPLIES

Rubber stamps and acrylic block: Perfectly Clear Doodle Bugs, *Stampendous!*

Ink: Pearlescent Ivy, Brilliance, *Tsukineko*

Deckle-edge scissors: *Fiskars*

Other: green cardstock, handmade paper, cream card, pressed viola or larkspur petals, craft knife, tweezers, adhesive, small paintbrush, scissors

Finished size: 4½" x 7"

INSTRUCTIONS

❶ Trim ½" from width of card.

❷ Stamp butterfly bodies, antennae, dotted trails on green cardstock.

❸ To make butterflies, cut apart one larger and one smaller petal for each wing, layering smaller petal over larger petal. *Note: Use tweezers to handle petals.*

Everything Easter

Hop on down the bunny trail to make our spring-fresh baskets, bunnies, and egg-inspired greetings.

A tisket, a tasket
Make a nifty gift box or basket.

Bunny Basket

Designer: Mary Ayres

SUPPLIES

Cardstock: pink, light pink, orange
140 lb. watercolor paper
Pink craft thread: *DMC*
Fabric adhesive: *Beacon Adhesives*
Adhesive pen: Zig, *EK Success*
Cloud decorative-edge scissors: *Fiskars*
Circle punches: ⅛", ¼", ⁵⁄₁₆", *Fiskars*
Other: green paper raffia, silver wire, pink gingham ribbon, 18 pink eyelets

Finished size 6½" x 4½" x 3"

CARROT

See Figure a.

❶ Transfer carrot pattern to orange cardstock; cut out, using decorative-edge scissors. Insert eyelets next to indentations on edges.

❷ Insert long thread length through bottom two eyelets; weave thread through side eyelets. Knot and adhere thread ends in back.

❸ Insert 10" thread length through top eyelet. Wrap around center of raffia pieces; tie thread ends into bow. Bend raffia ends upward and glue in place.

BUNNY

❶ Transfer bunny pattern to watercolor paper. Cut out and score as indicated. Fold paws inward.

❷ Set eyelets as indicated. *Note: Make*

sure eyelets on paws face outward when paws are folded.

❸ Punch two ¼" circles from pink, and two ⁵⁄₁₆" circles from light pink cardstock. Adhere small circles to large ones; adhere to bunny for cheeks.

❹ Adhere carrot to bunny; tie paws together with thread as shown in photo.

❺ Adhere gingham bow to neck.

BASKET

See Figure b.

❶ Transfer basket pattern to watercolor paper. Cut out and score as indicated.

2 Insert eyelets as indicated. *Note: Make sure eyelets face outside of basket.*

3 Adhere flaps to adjacent sides to create basket. Adhere bunny to basket. *Note: Bottom edge of bunny should be even with bottom edge of basket.*

4 Insert wire through eyelets in basket sides; bend ends back around wire. Shape into handle.

DESIGNER TIP

Fabric adhesive has a stronger bond than many paper adhesives, so it's ideal for assembling your bunny basket.

BONUS IDEA

Make the bunny into a card. Write a message on the inside of the paws.

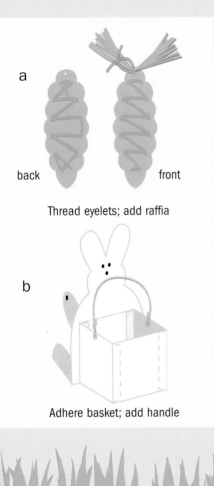

a

back   front

Thread eyelets; add raffia

b

Adhere basket; add handle

Enlarge all patterns 200%

BUNNY PATTERN

CARROT PATTERN

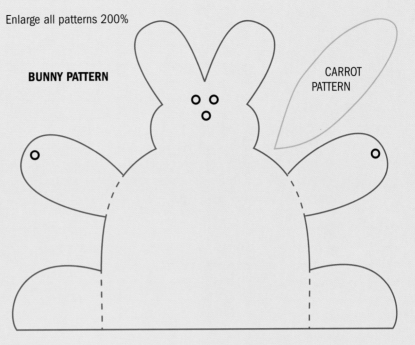

9"

BASKET PATTERN

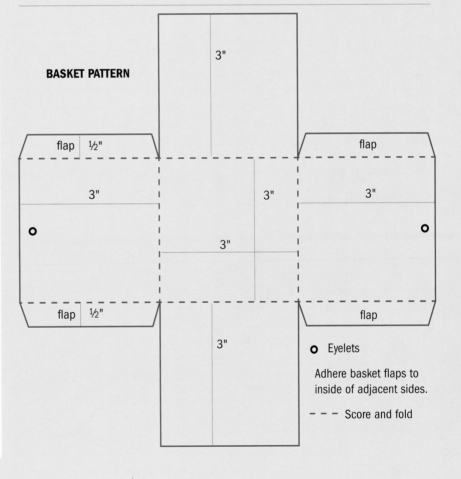

3"

flap ½"   flap

3"   3"   3"

3"

flap ½"   flap

3"

○ Eyelets

Adhere basket flaps to inside of adjacent sides.

- - - Score and fold

Stitched Bunny

Designer: Jana Millen

SUPPLIES

White cardstock

Textured cardstock: lavender, light green, *Bazzill Basics Paper*

Light green patterned paper: Chloe Collection, *K&Company*

White eyelets: *doodlebug design*

Embroidery floss: black, pink, white, *DMC*

Font: 2Peas Tiny Tadpole, *Two Peas in a Bucket*

Other: green gingham ribbon, tapestry needle

Finished size 5½" x 4"

BACKGROUND

① Make white card base.

② Cut 3" x 4" piece of patterned paper.

③ Print "Happy Easter" on light green cardstock. Trim to 3" x 4". Adhere to patterned paper piece, overlapping bottom by ½".

④ Wrap ribbon around center of piece. Adhere ends in back.

⑤ Add eyelets to corners.

⑥ Adhere to card base.

STITCHED PIECE

① Attach bunny pattern to lavender cardstock. Punch holes ¼" apart along pattern lines.

② French knot eyes with black. Backstitch design as shown in photo.

③ Trim stitched piece; mat with white cardstock. Adhere to card.

BACKSTITCH

Up at 1, down at 2, up at 3, down at 1, stitching back to meet previous stitch.

FRENCH KNOT

Up at 1, wrap thread once around needle, down at 1.

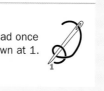

BUNNY PATTERN

● Stitching entry and exit holes

Faux Weave Paper Basket

Designer: Kathleen Paneitz

SUPPLIES

Cork weave patterned paper: Layer it On, *Creative Imaginations*

Gold eyelets: *Creative Imaginations*

Double-sided tape: Terrifically Tacky Tape; Art Accentz, *Provo Craft*

Other: chipboard, purple grosgrain ribbon, multi-colored plaid ribbon

Finished size 5" x 5" x 5"

INSTRUCTIONS

This basket looks woven, but don't be fooled. You can make it in minutes with weave-patterned paper!

1. Cut 21" x 5" strip of chipboard. Score strip every 5" to create four sides, plus 1" tab on one end.

2. Wrap the strip with patterned paper; fold along scored lines. Adhere 1" tab in back.

3. Cover bottom piece with patterned paper and adhere inside basket (see figures a and b).

4. Cut chipboard handle (see Figure c).

5. Sandwich handle between two lengths grosgrain ribbon, allowing at least 2" of ribbon on each end; adhere.

6. Set eyelets in basket. Slip ribbon ends through eyelets; knot each pair of ends outside basket (see Figure d).

7. Tie multi-colored plaid ribbon around box.

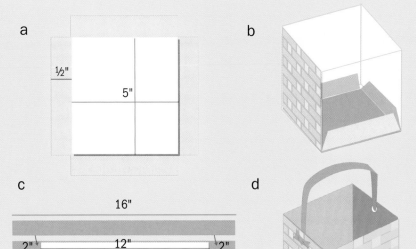

a

½"

5"

b

c

16"

2"   12"   2"

d

Egg expressions

Our Easter egg hunt
yielded spring-fresh
cards and tags.

Easter Greetings Card

Designer: Darcy Christensen

SUPPLIES

Hot pink cardstock

Pink cardstock squares: Double Mats, *Scrapbook Wizard*

Pink plaid paper: *Scrapbook Wizard*

Vellum

Embossed egg die cuts: Embossible Designs, *We R Memory Keepers*

Font: Funky Fresh, *www.itcfonts.com*

Pink brads: *Making Memories*

Other: white thread, sewing machine, adhesive foam squares

Finished size 5½" x 6¾"

INSTRUCTIONS

1 Make hot pink card base. Tear bottom front edge.

2 Cut patterned paper to fit card.

3 Zigzag-stitch cardstock squares to paper. Adhere egg die cuts with adhesive foam squares.

4 Print "Easter Greetings" on vellum; cut into strip. Layer over patterned paper.

5 Adhere to card front and set brads.

Spring Green Egg Card

Designer: Maria Larson

SUPPLIES

Cardstock: light sage green, sage green, *WorldWin*

Dark sage green textured cardstock: *Bazzill Basics Paper*

Pink eyelets: *doodlebug design*

Yellow button: *SEI*

Egg die cut: Eggs/Frame Sampler, *O'Scrap!*

Font: CK Cute, Becky Higgins' "Creative Clips & Fonts" CD, *Creating Keepsakes*

Other: adhesive dot, adhesive foam squares

Finished size 5½" x 4¼"

INSTRUCTIONS

1 Make sage green card base.

2 Print "Happy Easter" on textured cardstock. Trim to 1" x 2½".

3 Cut 2½" square of textured cardstock. Adhere egg die cut to square with adhesive foam squares. Adhere button with adhesive dot.

4 Cut ½" x 5½" strip of textured cardstock. Add eyelets.

5 Cut light sage green cardstock to same sizes as textured cardstock pieces.

6 Assemble card as shown in photo.

Easter Egg Tag

Designer: Maria Larson

SUPPLIES

Cardstock: Honeydew, Lavender, Soft Rose, Willow, *Pebbles in My Pocket*

Vellum

Egg punch: *EK Success*

Alphabet rub-on transfers: *Making Memories*

Ribbon: light green, pink, *Making Memories*

Other: hole punch, white gable box (optional)

Finished sizes:
   tag 3" x 6",
   box 8" x 8" x 4¾"

INSTRUCTIONS

1 Cut 2½" x 5¾" tag from Lavender cardstock. Mat with Soft Rose cardstock.

2 Spell "easter" with rub-on letters.

3 Cut ¼" wide vellum strip; adhere to left side of tag. Adhere egg punch-outs over strip.

4 Punch hole in right side; add ribbon.

5 Optional: Adhere tag to box. Adhere ribbon along box top and bottom.

Delightful Daisies Basket

Designer: Judi Andersen

SUPPLIES

Cardstock: (Barely Banana) *Stampin' Up!*

Textured cardstock: (Dahlia) *Bazzill Basics Paper*

Patterned paper: (Sherbet Stripe) *Doodlebug Design*

Accents:
(purse charm) Art Accentz Changlez, *Provo Craft*
(purple bead chain) *Making Memories*
(jump ring)

Fasteners: (pastel eyelets) Soft Subtles, *Stampin' Up!*

Fibers:
(Lavender wired fuzzy ribbon, Maize grosgrain ribbon) *Midori*
(white thread)

Punch: (Daisy) *EK Success*

Adhesive: (double-sided tape) Sticky Strip, *Stampin' Up!*

Tools: eyelet-setting tools, scissors, sewing machine, ruler

Finished size: 5" x 3½" x 2¼"

INSTRUCTIONS

1 Cut basket and liner pieces, using pattern. Sew basket on stitching lines. Score, fold, and assemble.

2 Adhere liner pieces inside basket sides; trim excess.

3 Adhere fuzzy ribbon to basket with narrow tape. *Note: Cut tape to ⅛" if necessary.*

4 Cut two 10" lengths of fuzzy ribbon for handles. Punch holes as indicated on pattern, insert ribbon ends, and twist ends around handle to secure.

5 Punch daisies from Barely Banana cardstock. Attach to basket with eyelets.

6 Tie Maize ribbon to handle.

7 Attach jump ring to purse charm. Loop charm on metal chain and secure around handle.

DESIGNER TIP

You can make your own wired fuzzy ribbon by wrapping fuzzy yarn around 22–26 gauge wire, doubling the yarn if necessary.

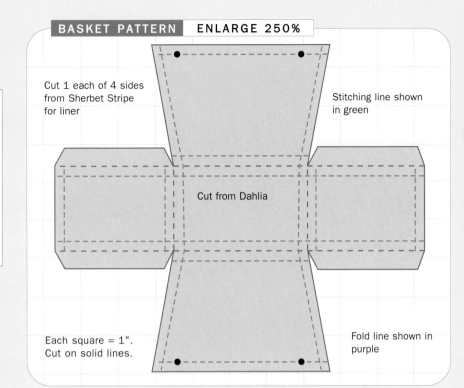

Cut 1 each of 4 sides from Sherbet Stripe for liner

Stitching line shown in green

Cut from Dahlia

Each square = 1". Cut on solid lines.

Fold line shown in purple

Bonus Idea

BEACH BAG

This pattern would make a cute beach bag for a summer themed gift or favor. In place of the purse charm, attach a flip-flop or shell charm to the bag.

Egg Wrappers

Designer: Nancy Church

SUPPLIES

Cardstock: (white)

Patterned paper: (Baby Blue Gingham, Baby Pink Gingham, Spring Green Dot/Stripe double-sided) *Pebbles Inc.*

Stickers: (Easter borders) Snip Its, *Pebbles Inc.*

Adhesive: double-sided tape

Tools: scissors, ruler

Other: candy, plastic eggs

Finished size: 1¾" diameter x 1½"

INSTRUCTIONS

❶ Fill egg with candy.

❷ Cut patterned paper to 7" x ¾" strip. Wrap around egg and secure with tape.

❸ Cut square piece from border sticker. Adhere to white cardstock and trim to fit. Adhere piece to paper strip.

Bonus Idea

Egg stands are a great way to display dyed Easter eggs. Just cut a shorter paper strip for the band. Tape the sticker square flush with the bottom of the egg stand.

Eggstra Special Brunch Invitation

Designer: Alice Golden

SUPPLIES

Cardstock: (Black) *Bazzill Basics Paper*

Patterned paper: (Summer Green Watercolor Ribbed, Lavender Watercolor Ribbed) *The Robin's Nest*

Sticker: (basket from Easter Hats) *Bisous Stickers*

Fibers: (pink satin ribbon)

Font: (Mister Giggles) www.twopeasinabucket.com

Adhesive: double-sided tape, foam tape

Tools: scissors, ruler

Finished size: 4⅛" x 7⅞", card does not open

INSTRUCTIONS

❶ Print invitation on Summer Green paper, leaving space in center for sticker. Trim to 2¾" x 6¼" and mat with black.

❷ Make ribbon photo corner by placing 1½" length of ribbon diagonally on corner and taping ends in back. Repeat for all corners. Adhere to 4" x 7¾" piece of lavender paper and mat with black.

❸ Cut out basket sticker and adhere to invitation with foam tape.

Simple Sentiments

Pick a clever quip to wish someone a happy Easter.

There's nobunny like you.

Hope you have an egg-stra special Easter!

You're a good egg.

set in Serifa, Adobe

Have a 24-carrot day!

Monogrammed Easter Basket Tags

Designer: Wendy Sue Anderson

SUPPLIES

Cardstock:
(Baby Pink Check/Solid, Hawaiian Blue Check/Solid, Soft Yellow Check/Solid, Mossy Green Dot) *O'Scrap!*

(ivory)

Pigment ink: (Sand) *Stewart Superior Corp.*

Paper accents: (Eggs) Easter, Samplers, *O'Scrap*

Accents: (Belfast Moulding Strips, Eyelet Letters, Wave Moulding Corners) *Making Memories*

Fasteners: (silver safety pins) *Making Memories*

Fibers: (green gingham, ivory picot, pink gingham, yellow gingham ribbons), *May Arts*

Adhesive: double-sided tape

Tools: scissors, ruler, ⅛" hole punch

Finished size: 2¼" x 3½"

INSTRUCTIONS

1 Cut tags from patterned paper, using pattern; ink edges.

2 Cut patterned papers to create background designs for tags, ink edges and adhere. Mat tags with ivory cardstock.

3 Cut out eggs, ink edges, and adhere to tags.

4 Punch holes in tag tops; thread ribbons through. Pin metal letters to ribbons.

DESIGNER TIPS

- Speed up productivity by making tags assembly-line style.

- These tags are a great way to use those scraps you've been saving!

- Let the kids choose which egg they want on their tag.

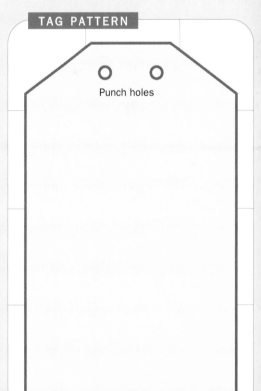

TAG PATTERN

Punch holes

Each square = 1". Cut on solid lines.

Easter Bunny Picnic

Designer: Wendy Sue Anderson

SUPPLIES

FOR EGG HOLDERS, PLACE CARDS, AND FOOD PICKS:

Blue cardstock

Striped paper: pink, green, blue, purple, *doodlebug design*

FOR CENTERPIECE:

Striped paper: pink, green, blue, purple, *doodlebug design*

Embroidery floss to match papers: *Making Memories*

Gift shred: Creative Crinkle, *DMD Industries*

Decoupage adhesive: *Plaid*

Other: 3" flower pot, wood skewers, paper piercing tool, embroidery needle, paintbrush, floral foam

FOR CARD:

Cardstock: blue, purple

Striped paper: pink, green, *doodlebug design*

Pink thread: *Making Memories*

Other: paper piercing tool, embroidery needle

FOR ALL:

White cardstock

Bunny accents: Paper Bliss, *Westrim Crafts*

Buttons: *doodlebug design*

Font: Fairy Princess, *www.twopeasinabucket.com*

Adhesive foam dots: *All Night Media*

Finished sizes:
   card 5¼" x 4¼"
   centerpiece approx. 11" high
   place card 2¾" square
   egg holder 2½" square
   food picks approx. 6" high

EGG HOLDER

❶ Cut 2" square from blue cardstock. Mat with white cardstock, striped paper, and white cardstock again.

❷ Adhere bunny to square with adhesive foam dots.

❸ Cut 1" x 7½" strip from striped paper; adhere to back of square (see photo).

❹ Add button to one end of strip. Join strip ends to fit around egg.

CENTERPIECE

❶ Cut nine 1" x 6" strips of striped paper, using all the colors.

❷ Adhere strips to flower pot with decoupage adhesive (see photo). Trim excess paper.

❸ Print "hoppy easter" on white cardstock Pierce and stitch letters as for card. Trim and adhere to flowerpot rim. Add buttons.

❹ Cut six skewers in varying lengths. Adhere two bunnies back-to-back on skewers, using adhesive foam dots.

⑤ Place floral foam in bottom of flowerpot.

⑥ Push skewers into foam. Cover foam with gift shred.

CARD

① Print "hop on over" on white cardstock. Cut into 4¾" x 3⅜" rectangle.

② Punch holes ⅟₁₆" apart along letters, using paper piercing tool.

③ Backstitch phrase with pink floss.

④ Make blue card base.

BACKSTITCH

Up at 1, down at 2, up at 3, down at 1, stitching back to meet previous stitch.

⑤ Mat stitched piece with purple, then white cardstock; adhere to card.

⑥ Cut 3" x 3⅜" piece pink striped paper. Adhere to card below stitched phrase.

⑦ Adhere bunny with adhesive foam dots. Add buttons to corners.

⑧ Print invitation on white cardstock. Trim, mat with green striped paper, and adhere inside card.

PLACE CARD

① Make white card base.

② Cut 2½" square from blue cardstock; adhere to card.

③ Print guest's name on white cardstock. Cut into ⅝" x 2⅜" strip and mat with striped paper.

④ Adhere name to card. Add buttons.

⑤ Adhere bunny to place card with adhesive foam dots.

FOOD PICKS

① Print food name twice on white cardstock. Cut into ⅝" x 2½" strip.

② Adhere strips and bunnies back-to-back on skewers, using adhesive foam dots.

③ Add buttons to one side.

INSTRUCTIONS

❶ Fold light orange cardstock; cut out flip-flop, using pattern.

❷ Stamp card with polka dot stamps and watermark ink.

❸ Outline card with black pen.

❹ Cut yellow cardstock straps, outline with black pen, and adhere to card with pop-up dots.

❺ Stamp flower with black ink, color with pencils, and trim.

❻ Adhere leaves and flower to card; outline with glitter glue.

DRESS UP THOSE SANDALS

This invitation is jazzed up with a little glitter, but you can also add beads, sequins, stitching, or other decorations.

Flip-Flop Fun

Designer: Lisa Spangler

SUPPLIES

Cardstock: light orange, white, yellow

Stamps: flower, small and large polka dot, *Magenta*

Watermark ink: VersaMark, *Tsukineko*

Coal Black ink: Ancient Page, *Clearsnap*

Clear glitter glue

Colored pencils: *Prismacolor*

Adhesive pop-up dots

Other: black fine-tip pen, fine-line black pencil

Finished size approx. 5½" x 2½"

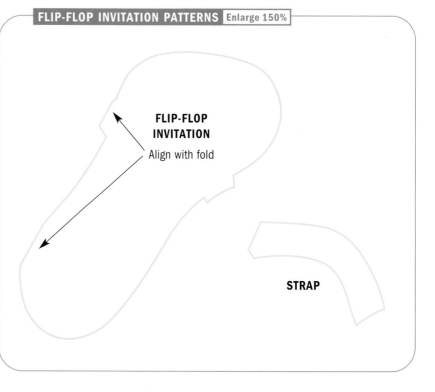

FLIP-FLOP INVITATION PATTERNS Enlarge 150%

FLIP-FLOP INVITATION

Align with fold

STRAP

1 Place mesh on top of two-tone blue cardstock.

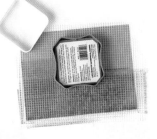

2 Press ink pad directly onto mesh to create fun pattern.

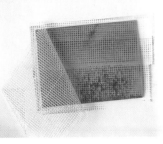

3 Remove mesh and let ink dry. Sand cardstock lightly for distressed look.

4 Tear bottom and punch circle for sun; cut rays with craft knife.

5 Cut strips of yellow handmade paper, and fan out behind opening. Secure with double-sided tape, trimming excess.

6 Stamp "pool party" on piece of handmade paper and adhere to bottom of sun piece.

7 Mount on aqua card base.

Sunny Pool Party

Designer: Denise Pauley

SUPPLIES

Cardstock:
  Aqua
  Two-tone blue, *Paper Adventures*
Yellow handmade paper: Thatch; Little Textures, *Provo Craft*
Alphabet stamps: *PSX*
Blue ink: Sistine Sky; Fresco, *Gary M. Burlin*
Black ink: StazOn, *Tsukineko*
Mesh: *Magic Mesh*
2" circle punch: *Marvy Uchida*
Other: craft knife, double-sided tape

Finished size 5½" x 4"

Burger Bash

Designer: Linda Beeson

SUPPLIES

Cardstock: black, red, white

Hamburger accent: Paper Bliss, *Westrim Crafts*

Barn woods paper frame: This & That Frames & Embellishments, *My Mind's Eye*

Red star eyelets: *Making Memories*

Font: 2Ps Flea Market, *www.twopeasinabucket.com*

Finished size 5" x 6½"

INSTRUCTIONS

❶ Make black card base. Print background text on white cardstock; mat with card base.

❷ Adhere frame and attach eyelets.

❸ Fold red cardstock in half; apply hamburger accent to cardstock. Cut out hamburger shape. *Note: Make sure top fold remains intact so invitation can be opened (see photo).* Adhere back of hamburger card to invitation.

❹ Print information on white cardstock. Cut out and adhere to inside of hamburger card.

AN ABUNDANCE OF ACCENTS

You'll find hundreds of ready-made accents that work for this type of invitation. Use wedding cake accents for a bridal shower, balloons for a birthday party, or snowflakes for a seasonal gathering.

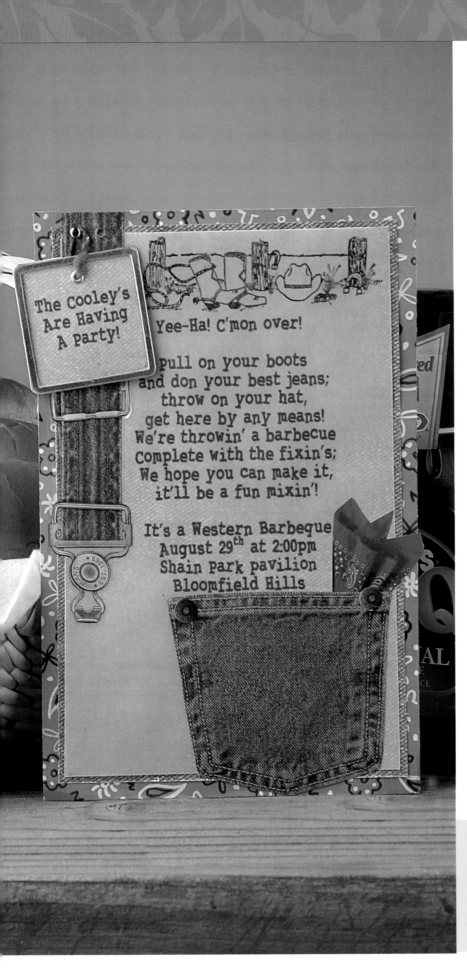

The Cooley's Are Having A Party!

Yee-Ha! C'mon over!

pull on your boots
and don your best jeans;
throw on your hat,
get here by any means!
We're throwin' a barbecue
Complete with the fixin's;
We hope you can make it,
it'll be a fun mixin'!

It's a Western Barbeque
August 29th at 2:00pm
Shain Park pavilion
Bloomfield Hills

Cowboy Cookout

Designer: Ruth Cooley

SUPPLIES

Patterned paper:
  Bandana, *Colors By Design*
  Denim, *The Robin's Nest*
Vellum
Stickers:
  Suspender; Memories in the Making, *Leisure Arts*
  Pocket, *Mrs. Grossman's*
  Bandana, *Mrs. Grossman's*
Western border rubber stamp: *The Happy Stamper*
Metal-edged tag: *Making Memories*
Red fibers: *On the Surface*
Ink: ZiG brush markers, *EK Success*
Font: CK Corral, "Fresh Fonts" CD, *Creating Keepsakes*
Verse: *www.verseit.com*
Other: silver brad, clear embossing powder, eyelet, heat tool, metal-rimmed tag

Finished size 9" x 6"

INSTRUCTIONS

❶ Print invitation in red on vellum. Immediately stamp top border and emboss entire page with clear powder. Color border with markers.

❷ Mat invitation with denim and bandana patterned papers. Add stickers.

❸ Print wording for tag on vellum and emboss. Back with denim, and cut to fit metal-edged tag. Cut paper from tag, and replace with vellum piece. Attach eyelet to tag.

❹ Tie tag with fiber and attach to invitation with brad.

SAYING IT BEST

Visit **www.verseit.com** for pages and pages of great sayings and verses. Use the ideas to spark your creativity and find the perfect way to say it best.

Patriotism

Keep morale high for a member of our armed forces.
Send a handmade card to say "Thanks for your service—you make me proud."

Come Home Soon

Designer: Nancy Church

SUPPLIES

Cardstock: dark blue, light blue, red textured, white, yellow

White embossed star cardstock: *Frances Meyer*

Yellow grosgrain ribbon: *Offray*

Mini adhesive dots: *Glue Dots International*

Font: CK Letter Home, "Fresh Fonts" CD, *Creating Keepsakes*

1¼" square punch

Finished size 5½" x 4¼"

INSTRUCTIONS

❶ Print "Come Home Soon" on white cardstock. Make card base.

❷ Punch one square each from dark blue, light blue, red textured, and white embossed cardstock. Mat with yellow cardstock. Adhere to card.

❸ Loop ribbon and adhere to card with adhesive dots.

HOW TO SEND YOUR CARD

Send a card to a member of the armed forces stationed anywhere in the world. According to government policy, a card must be addressed to a particular person rather than to "any service member," so pick one of these options:

- Choose a service member you already know.

- Sign up through Operation Military Support to receive the name and address of someone who is deployed. Visit *www. operationmilitarysupport .com/request_a_name.htm.*

- Send your card to Military Moms, an organization that mails cards to service members through channels it has established with the military. This is a great way to send large quantities of cards made by school, church, or other groups. Visit *www.militarymoms.net.*

SEND A CARE PACKAGE

Send a care package along with your card through Operation Military Pride. *Visit www.operationmilitarypride.org/ involved.html* for a list of the most requested care package items and guidelines for package shipment. If you would rather make a donation to sponsor care packages, you can do so at this Web site.

Missing You

Designer: Nancy Church

SUPPLIES

Sage green cardstock

Camouflage patterned paper: *Making Memories*

Silver bead chain: *Making Memories*

Silver metal sheet: *Making Memories*

Other: corner rounder, alphabet stamps for metal (available at hardware stores), dimensional adhesive dots, hole punch

Finished size 5½" x 4¼"

INSTRUCTIONS

❶ Make card base with sage green cardstock.

❷ Trim patterned paper slightly smaller than card front. Adhere to card.

❸ Cut two rectangular tags from metal sheet; round corners. Stamp "Missing" and "You" with metal stamps.

❹ Punch hole through each tag; attach to bead chain. Adhere to card with dimensional adhesive dots.

JUST STAMP IT
For a bolder look, stamp the tags using rubber alphabet stamps and black solvent ink. Try StazOn ink from Tsukineko (800/769-6633, *www.tsukineko.com* or the new Palette Hybrid ink from Stewart Superior (800/401-8644, *www.sundayint.com/mall/IPIndex.asp).*

Proud to Be An American

Designer: Nancy Church

SUPPLIES

White cardstock: *Making Memories*

Vellum

Walnut ink: *7gypsies*

Embossed flag: Old Glory Embossibles, *We R Memory Keepers*

Antique copper brads: *Karen Foster Design*

Fonts:
Scrap Twiggy,
www.letteringdelights.com
CK Letter Home, "Fresh Fonts" CD,
Creating Keepsakes

Other: spray bottle, water

Finished size 4¼" x 5½"

INSTRUCTIONS

❶ Dilute walnut ink with water in spray bottle.

❷ Spray cardstock with ink. Let dry. Make card base with dyed cardstock.

❸ Cut out embossed flag; adhere to card center.

❹ Print "Proud to be an American" on vellum. Attach to card with brads.

Pledge of Allegiance

Design: Kathleen Paneitz

SUPPLIES

Rubber stamps: fireworks*, flag*

Ink pads: Black*, watermark*, White*

81/2" x 11" paper:
- Blue cardstock
- Red cardstock
- Vellum*
- White cardstock

Embossing powder: Gold*, White*

Embossing tinsel*: Red, Silver

Silver star brads*

Flag charm

Pens: Red*, Silver*

Embossing heat tool

Miscellaneous items: computer font*, computer with printer, adhesive, paper trimmer or scissors, ruler

*Double D Rubber Stamps fireworks stamp; Stampabilities flag stamp; Tsukineko VersaColor Black and VersaMark watermark ink pads; Printworks White ink pad; Paper Adventures vellum; Mark Enterprises Jeweled Gold embossing powder; Ranger Industries Seafoam White embossing powder and tinsel; Creative Impressions brads; EK Success ZIG Writer Red pen; Sakura Gelly Roll Silver metallic pen; and Two Peas in a Bucket Bad Hair Day font were used in the sample project.

Finished size: 4" x 5¼"

Thank You Gift Holder

Designer: Nancy Church

SUPPLIES

Cardstock: blue, red

Patriotic Plaid patterned paper: *Karen Foster Design*

Red polka dot patterned paper: *Printworks*

White organdy ribbon: *Offray*

Star charms: *Making Memories*

Other: alphabet stickers, magnet tape, small gift to tuck in pocket

Finished size 4¼" x 8¼"

INSTRUCTIONS

❶ Adhere patterned papers back to back. Cut, fold, and adhere sides of pocket (see diagram).

❷ Adhere magnet tape squares to pocket and inside flap (see photo). Note: Substitute a hook and loop closure if you plan to enclose a phone card with a magnetic strip.

❸ Spell "Thank You" with alphabet stickers on red cardstock; cut into strip. Mat with blue cardstock. Adhere to card front.

❹ String star charms on ribbon; tie around top of the card.

GIFT HOLDER DIAGRAM

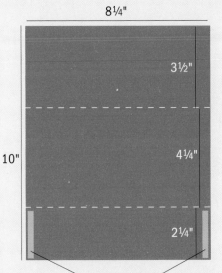

8¼"

3½"

10"

4¼"

2¼"

Adhere edges
Score and fold on dashed lines

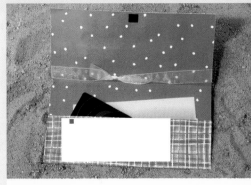

POCKET A GIFT

Tuck a welcome remembrance into your card pocket. *Note: Do not send cash through the mail. Try these ideas:*

- Calling cards

- Coffee or other drink packets

- Sticks of gum

- Small sewing kit

- Crossword puzzles

- Jokes

- Hand-drawn pictures from children

- Small notes of encouragement

- Photos of your family

Accent your priceless memories with stylish album.

Patriotic Journal Cover

Design: Sharon Lewis

SUPPLIES

Rubber stamps: label*, no coward*, postage stamps*, vintage compass*

Taupe dye ink pad*

Crafter's ink pads*: blue, red

Soft Gray shadow ink pad*

8" x 8" spiral bound journal*

12" x 12" paper*:

   2 sheets American flag print (front, back cover)

   2 sheets gold star print (inside covers)

   Cream cardstock

Decoupage adhesive*

Clear embossing pad*

Clear thick embossing powder*

Gold fine glitter*

Embossing heat tool

Tag*

Mini eyelet*

Eyelet setter and hole punch

Brown metallic rub-on*

Hemp

Silver key

Mini pinking scissors*

Computer font*

Miscellaneous items: pencil, paintbrush, computer with printer, hammer

*Inkadinkado label stamp; Wordsworth No Coward Soul Mine stamp; Rubberstamp Ave postage stamp images; Stampabilities vintage compass stamp; Clearsnap Vivid! Taupe dye ink pad and ColorBox crafter's Cerulean and Merlot ink pads; Hero Arts shadow ink pad; 7 Gypsies journal; K&Company printed papers; Plaid Enterprises Mod Podge matte finish; Clearsnap Top Boss embossing pad; Ranger Industries Suze Weinberg's Clear Ultra Thick Embossing Enamel; Creative Beginnings Gold Ultra Fine glitter; American Tag Co. shipping tag; doodlebug design i-let; Craf-T Products metallic rub-on; Fiskars Mini-Pinking Paper Edger scissors; and Microsoft Word Modern no. 20 font were used in the sample project.

Text on the tag in the image:

NO COWARD SOUL MINE
NO TREMBLER IN THE
WORLD'S STORM-TROUBLED
SPHERE : I SEE
HEAVEN'S GLORY SHINE
AND FAITH SHINES EQUAL
ARMING ME FROM FEAR
emily bronte

INSTRUCTIONS

Note: Let the decoupage adhesive dry after each application.

COVER THE ALBUM

❶ Trace the outline of the album cover on the back side of the flag print paper so the section with stars will be at the top left hand corner of the album. *Note: Reverse the pattern for the back cover so the flag will be right side up.* Cut out the squares.

❷ Apply decoupage adhesive with a paintbrush to the journal front and back covers. Adhere the flag print paper to the covers and smooth it out to avoid wrinkles.

❸ Decoupage the gold star print paper on the inside covers.

STAMP THE ALBUM

❶ Print the Longfellow quote on cream cardstock. Stamp the label image around the quote with taupe ink. Cut around the quote to make a tag, and attach an eyelet in the top.

❷ Stamp the postage images on cream cardstock with blue and red inks. Cut around the stamped images with mini pinking scissors. Apply brown metallic rub-on to the edges of the stamped images with your fingers.

❸ Adhere the stamped postage images to the journal cover.

❹ Stamp the No Coward Soul Mine quote on the large tag with taupe ink. Apply metallic rub-on to the tag edges. Tear off the end of the tag.

❺ Stamp the vintage compass on the edge of the tag with gray shadow ink. Place the tag on the front cover and lightly pencil inside of the outline so the line won't show. Remove the tag.

FINISH THE ALBUM

❶ Press the embossing ink pad over the entire front cover, except for the penciled outline where the tag will be.

❷ Sprinkle thick embossing powder over the ink and shake off any excess.

❸ Sprinkle glitter over the embossing powder, and then heat set.

❹ Apply adhesive to both sides of the small tag. Repeat approx. 3–4 times.

❺ Wrap the hemp horizontally around the front cover twice. Thread the hemp through the large embellished tag.

❻ Decoupage the large tag and adhere it to the album cover. *Note: Hold the hemp ends away from the adhesive with one hand.*

❼ Apply 3–4 coats of adhesive to the top of the tag.

❽ Wrap the hemp vertically around the front cover and tie it in a bow. Attach the key and small tag to the hemp ends.

Autumn in the Air

Celebrate fall with a colorful festival of cards and gifts.

Love Those Leaves Card

Designer: Barbara Greve

SUPPLIES

White cardstock

White rice paper: Double Shuen Rice Paper, *Oriental Art Supply*

Gold card

Leaf foam stamp: Maple Leaf; Chunky Stamps, *Duncan*

Acrylic paint: Berry Red, Burnt Orange, Cadmium Red, Cadmium Yellow, Dioxazine Purple, Napa Red, Russet, Shading Flesh, Tangelo Orange; Americana, *DecoArt*

Brown fibers: Adornments, *EK Success*

Glue stick: *Westrim Crafts*

Fabric adhesive: Fabri-Tac, *Beacon Adhesives*

Other: felt or other absorbent fabric (larger than 18" x 14"), foam paint-brushes, palette, paper towels, spray bottle filled with water

Finished size 7" x 5"

STAMP PAPER

Read "Tips from Barbara" before you begin.

❶ Cut an 18" x 14" piece of rice paper; place on absorbent fabric.

❷ Apply different paint color combinations (omit Dioxazine Purple) to stamp with foam brush. Stamp leaves. *Note: Clean stamp between applications.*

❸ Mist paper with water so leaf images fade and colors bleed. Leave corners of paper dry so you can hold them to rotate paper. Let dry.

❹ Loosely crumple paper and paint ridges with Dioxazine Purple. Spray ridges randomly so paint will bleed. Let dry, then smooth paper.

❺ Spray paper again to dampen, and repeat step 2. *Note: Do not spray paper after stamping. Let dry.*

MAKE CARD

❶ Cut large and small rectangles from stamped paper. Adhere to cardstock to make paper sturdier, using glue stick; trim cardstock edges.

❷ Adhere rectangles to card with fabric adhesive.

❸ Tie fibers around left side of card.

TIPS FROM BARBARA

- Keep the rice paper on absorbent paper or fabric during the entire process.

- Handle the rice paper carefully when wet—it tears easily!

- To speed up the drying process, hang the paper in front of a fan.

Bonus Ideas

The leaf-patterned paper has lots of beautiful possibilities. Use it to:

- Wrap a gift.

- Cover albums or notebooks.

- Decoupage a candle or candle chimney.

- Display on a shoji (free-standing) screen.

Simple Sentiments

Add your favorite fall phrase to a card.

Happy Fallidaze!

Everyone must **take time** to sit and watch the **leaves** turn.
—*Elizabeth Lawrence*
Set in Adobe Garamond

No spring nor summer beauty hath such grace As I have seen in one autumnal face.

—*John Donne*

October's poplars are flaming torches lighting the way to winter.

—*Nova Bair*

Bittersweet October.
The mellow, messy, leaf-kicking, perfect pause between the opposing miseries of summer and winter.

—*Carol Bishop Hipps*

Autumn is a second spring when every leaf is a flower.

—*Albert Camus*
Set in Snell Roundhand Blackscript, Adobe

Boo to You!

Designer: Jenny Grothe

SUPPLIES

Rubber stamps:
  (Ghosts) *Penny Black*
  (Boo to You!) *Close To My Heart*

Dye ink:
  (black) Exclusive Inks, *Close To My Heart*
  (orange) *Delta Rubber Stampede*

White cardstock: *Provo Craft*

Patterned paper: (orange polka dot, orange check, black polka dot) *Pebbles Inc.*

Eyelet: copper, *Making Memories*

Mesh: orange, *Magic Mesh*

Pen: black, *Close To My Heart.*

Star buttons: *Dress It Up*

Ribbon: orange, *Making Memories*

Chalk: (Yoyo Yellow, Only Orange) Stampin' Pastels, *Stampin' Up!*

Other: adhesive, scissors, cotton swab or make-up applicator, eyelet-setting tools

Finished sizes:
  Card: 4¼" x 5½"
  Tag: 2" x 4¼"

TAG

1 Make orange check tag. Cut black polka dot rectangle; adhere to tag.

2 Stamp Boo to You! with orange on white cardstock; cut words apart and tear top and bottom edges.

3 Adhere words to tag.

4 Attach eyelet to top of tag; add ribbon.

CARD

1 Make card from white cardstock.

2 Cut orange polka dot paper to fit card front; adhere.

3 Cut strip of black polka dot paper and orange mesh; adhere to center of card.

4 Stamp Ghosts with black on white cardstock; cut out and mat with black polka dot paper and white cardstock. Draw border around Ghosts with pen.

5 Tear edges of white cardstock.

6 Adhere three edges of stamped image to card to create pocket.

7 Adhere star buttons; chalk stamped image. Place tag in pocket.

Pumpkin Patch

Designer: Heidi Passey

SUPPLIES

Rubber stamps:
  (Small Pumpkin) *Penny Black*
  (Pumpkin) *Paper Inspirations*
  (Happy Harvest sentiment) *Close To My Heart*

Dye ink: black, *Delta Rubber Stampede*

Cardstock: (orange, tan) *Gartner Studios*

Patterned paper: (Green Stripe, Black Stripe) *Pebbles Inc.*

Ribbon: orange, *Making Memories*

Eyelets: silver, *Making Memories*

Chalk: (orange, green) Chalklets, *EK Success*

Other: scissors, adhesive, eyelet-setting tools, cotton swab or make-up applicator

Finished size: 4¼" x 5½"

INSTRUCTIONS

1 Make card from tan cardstock.

2 Stamp Pumpkin with black repeatedly on card; let dry. Apply chalk to each image.

3 Stamp Small Pumpkin with black two times on orange cardstock. Cut out and chalk edges with green.

4 Mat both pumpkins with tan and Green Stripe. Attach eyelets.

5 Stamp Happy Harvest sentiment with black on orange cardstock; cut to fit bottom half of card and adhere.

6 Cut strip of Black Stripe. Wrap ribbon around Black Stripe; string small pumpkin tags on ribbon, tie bow, and adhere to card.

Haunted House

Designer: Nichol Magouirk

SUPPLIES

Rubber stamps: (Happy Halloween sentiment, Haunted House) *Hero Arts*

Dye ink: black, Memories, *Stewart Superior Corp.*

Pigment ink: Moonlight White, Brillance, *Tsukineko*

Black window card: *me & my BIG ideas*

Textured cardstock: Cantaloupe, *Bazzill Basics Paper*

Buttons: (orange, white) *Making Memories*

Ribbon: *me & my BIG ideas*

Watercolor crayons: *Lyra*

Other: scissors, adhesive, paintbrush

Finished size: 4" x 5½"

INSTRUCTIONS

❶ Cut square of Cantaloupe cardstock to fit inside card window.

❷ Stamp Haunted House with black on square.

❸ Color image with watercolor crayons; blend with damp paintbrush and let dry.

❹ Adhere stamped image inside card to show through window.

❺ Stamp Happy Halloween sentiment with Moonlight White three times on card; let dry.

❻ Adhere ribbon and buttons around window to create frame.

Spooky Spider

Designer: Nichol Magouirk

SUPPLIES

Rubber stamps:
(Spider) *Hero Arts*
(Happy Halloween!) *Savvy Stamps*

Dye ink: Coal Black, Ancient Page, *Clearsnap*

Handmade paper: black, Paper Passport, *Provo Craft*

Spider web: *Crafts, Etc.*

Pearlized paint: Marigold, Radiant Pearls, *Angelwings*

Ribbon: orange gingham, *Impress Rubber Stamps*

Other: white cardstock, white textured cardstock, adhesive, scissors, make-up sponge

Finished size: 4¼" x 5½"

INSTRUCTIONS

❶ Make card from white cardstock.

❷ Cut black handmade paper to fit card front; wrap ribbon around paper, tie knot, and adhere to card.

❸ Adhere spider web to textured white cardstock.

❹ Stamp Spider with Coal Black below spider web. Paint eyes with pearlized paint; let dry.

❺ Stamp Happy Halloween! with Coal Black below spider.

❻ Cut out stamped image and ink edges with Coal Black; adhere to card.

Spirited Halloween Parties

Give your celebration more than a ghost of a chance at success with these fun invitations, games, and treat containers.

Happy Haunting Invitation

Designer: Patty Lennon

SUPPLIES

Cardstock: black, purple, white
Green library pocket: *Li'l Davis Designs*
Ghost cutout: *O'Scrap!*
Accents:
   Black mesh: *Magic Mesh*
   Orange snaps: *Making Memories*
   Silver eyelet: *Creative Imaginations*
   Black gingham ribbon: *Offray*
Black Chalk: *Craf-T Products*
Font: CK Fraternity, "Creative Clips & Fonts by Becky Higgins" CD, *Creating Keepsakes*
Eyelet-setting tools

Finished size 5" x 4"

INSTRUCTIONS

❶ Cover strip of purple cardstock with mesh and adhere to library pocket. Trim with narrow black cardstock strips along top and bottom edges.

❷ Attach four snaps to pocket; adhere ghost.

❸ Mat with black cardstock.

❹ Print invitation on white cardstock and trim to tag shape.

❺ Cut purple cardstock square; adhere to tag. Set eyelet. Tie with ribbon.

❻ Chalk edges of tag and insert in pocket.

Happy Haunting!

Please Join us for a Extra Spooky Costume Party and Hauntingly Fun Evening.

When: Saturday, October 30, 2004
Where: The Lennons' House
Time: 7:00 p.m.
Regrets only: 555-5555
Costumes are Required.

Please bring a fresh pumpkin for the carving contest.

Inside

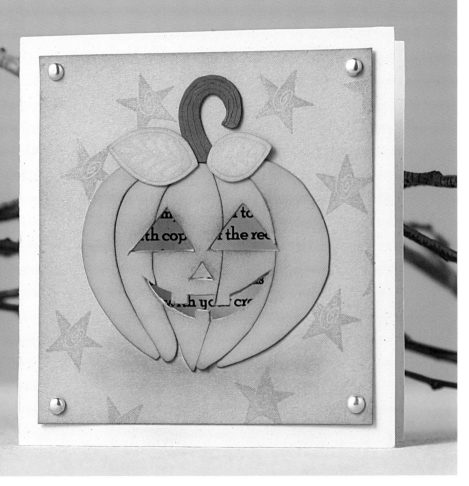

Pumpkin Carving Party

Designer: Nichole Heady

SUPPLIES

All supplies by Stampin' Up! unless otherwise noted.

Cardstock: Chocolate Chip, Naturals Ivory, Mellow Moss, Only Orange

Rubber stamps:

Star from Teeny Tinies set

Leaves from Tropical Blossoms set

Brown dye ink: Close to Cocoa

Pigment ink: Gold; Encore!, *Tsukineko*

Brads: Mini Deco Fasteners

Other: craft knife, cosmetic sponge

Finished size 4" square

INSTRUCTIONS

① Make card base from Naturals Ivory Naturals cardstock.

② Cut pieces, using pattern. Sponge pumpkin edges with brown ink. Stamp and cut out leaves. Make grooves in stem with craft knife.

③ Stamp stars on Mellow Moss cardstock square, using gold ink. Sponge cardstock edges with brown ink. Attach mini brads. Adhere square to card base.

④ Adhere pumpkin, stem, and leaves to card. Open card and lay flat.

⑤ Trace face pattern on pumpkin and cut out with craft knife, cutting completely through and card front. Sponge openings with brown ink.

⑥ Print invitation on Naturals Ivory cardstock. Trim, sponge edges with brown ink, and adhere to inside of card.

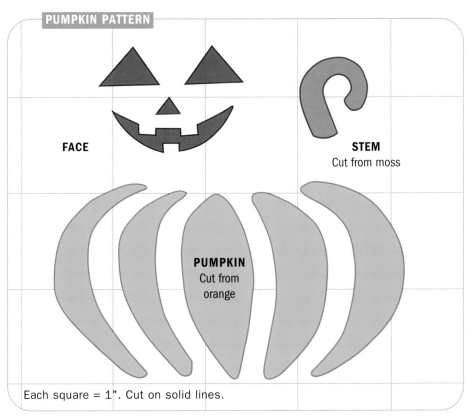

PUMPKIN PATTERN

FACE

STEM
Cut from moss

PUMPKIN
Cut from orange

Each square = 1". Cut on solid lines.

Spooky Fun and Games Party

Designer: Alice Golden

Invitation

SUPPLIES

White cardstock

Black textured cardstock: *Bazzill Basics Paper*

Accents:
    Mini envelope: *Impress Rubber Stamps*
    Black mini brads: *Limited Edition Rubberstamps*

Punches:
    9/16" circle punch: *McGill*
    Egg punch: All Night Media, *Plaid*
    Leaf punches: Paper Shapers, *EK Success*

Fonts:
    2Ps Flea Market, *www.twopeasinabucket.com*
    DesertDogHmk, *www.scrapvillage.com*

Dye ink: Orange; Brilliance, *Tsukineko*

1/8" orange grosgrain ribbon

Finished size 7¼" x 3½"

INSTRUCTIONS

1 Make card base with white cardstock. Print invitation on inside of card.

2 Print "we dare you. . ." on white cardstock. Trim to tag shape and fit to mini envelope. Sponge edges with orange ink and tie ribbon.

3 Create spooky eyes by punching circles, ovals, and leaves (trim off stems) from white cardstock and attaching mini brads for pupils. *Note: You can also punch small holes in eyes, and adhere to black cardstock for a similar effect.*

4 Adhere spooky eyes and mini envelope to black textured cardstock; trim. Adhere to card and place tag in envelope.

Invitation tag

A COMPUTER TIP

Using your computer to print out invitations makes this project go much faster. To make sure you get your wording positioned right, first print your text on plain white paper. Next, tape the paper you want printed directly over the text using low-tack tape. Finally, run the sheet through the printer again. This is a great way to use scraps of paper rather than running a whole sheet of cardstock or patterned paper through your printer.

Create a similar game for any special holiday or occasion by using different color combinations or words. Try C-U-P-I-D with red, white, pink, purple, and black cardstock for a Valentine's Day party, or P-A-R-T-Y using a birthday party's theme colors.

Turn a milk carton into a cute favor box by covering it with black cardstock, and adding spooky eyes, a tag, and some ribbon. Fill it with tasty Halloween treats.

Game

This game is played like BINGO, substituting colors for numbers.

SUPPLIES

Cardstock: green, yellow, white

Textured cardstock: black, orange, purple, *Bazzill Basics Paper*

Ghost stamp: *Savvy Stamps*

Dye ink:
Orange: Brilliance, *Tsukineko*
Coal Black permanent: Ancient Page, *Clearsnap*

Stickers:
Assorted alphabet
Border: Black & White Borders, *Me & My Big Ideas*
Halloween Kids: *Me & My Big Ideas*
Halloween: *PSX*
Jack-o'-Lantern: JoLee's by You, *EK Success*

Orange gingham ribbon: *Offray*

Punches:
1⅜" square punch: *Marvy Uchida*
1¼" circle: *McGill*

Other: thin cardboard, glass pebbles, fine-tip black marker, white acrylic paint, paintbrush, 25 wood discs

Finished size 9⅞" x 8½"

INSTRUCTIONS

❶ Create game board from cardboard. Cover with white cardstock.

❷ Accent with border stickers and ribbon. Spell "GHOST" with alphabet and Jack-o'-lantern stickers.

❸ Stamp ghost on white cardstock with black ink; ink edges with orange. Write "Free Space" using fine-tip marker. Punch out, using square punch, and adhere to center of game board.

❹ Punch 24 squares in various colors; arrange and adhere to board. *Note: Place only one of each color per column.*

❺ Create game board markers by adhering stickers to white cardstock, then punching or cutting to fit bottom of glass pebbles. Adhere to glass pebbles.

❻ Paint wood discs white. Punch five circles of each cardstock color, then adhere to back of discs. Add alphabet stickers to front. You'll have one disc for each letter/color combination (e.g., G/orange, H/yellow, etc.). The caller uses these discs to determine which squares to call out.

❼ Create additional game boards, alternating the arrangement of the color squares on each.

Wrapped Up in Halloween Fun Party

Designer: Julie Medeiros

Invitation

SUPPLIES

White cardstock

Envelope: *Ampad*

First-aid gauze: *Johnson & Johnson*

Accents:

Orange eyelet: *Making Memories*

Large wiggle eyes: *Fibre Craft*

Fonts:

Copperplate Gothic, *www.myfonts.com*

2Ps Vegetable Soup, *www.twopeasinabucket.com*

Adhesive dots: *Glue Dots International*

Other: brown ink, eyelet-setting tools, computer and printer

Finished size 4¾" x 4"

INSTRUCTIONS

❶ Seal envelope and cut an inch off side to create pocket.

❷ Wrap envelope with gauze, securing ends in back with adhesive dots. Ink edges of gauze. Adhere eyes with adhesive dots, tucking between layers of gauze. *Note: You can substitute strips of muslin or torn white paper for gauze.*

❸ To create text block to fit in envelope, click on "Insert" option in word processing software, then select "Text Box." Change background color to black and font to white; then change color of festive words to green or orange. Print invitation on white cardstock.

❹ Trim invitation. Add orange eyelet and tie with strip of gauze to make pull tag.

Inside invitation

Its time to get
WRAPPED UP
in the Halloween spirit...

Ask your
MUMMY
if you can
STUMBLE
over to the TOMB
at 1406 Rosedale St for a
MESMERIZING party
CREEP in at 6:00pm
as darkness falls
As the night
UNRAVELS,
we will play
GHOSTLY games
and dine on
FRIGHTENING foods

It will be a
SCREAM!

WORDING

Julie cleverly worded the invitation to her Halloween festivities. Adapt her ideas for your own Halloween gathering.

It's time to get
Wrapped Up
in the Halloween spirit. . .

Ask your
Mummy
If you can
Stumble
over to the Tomb
at [insert address] for a
Mesmerizing party.
Creep in at [insert time]
as darkness falls.
As the night
unravels,
we will play
Ghostly games
and dine on
Frightening foods.

It will be a
Scream!

Coffin Goodie Box

SUPPLIES

Cream cardstock

Wood-grain paper: *Pebbles Inc.*

Small rectangular gift box

Brown acrylic paint: *Plaid*

Alphabet stamps: *Hero Arts*

Accents:

  Black eyelets

  Faucet stickers: Fixer Upper;
  Nostalgiques, *EK Success*

Adhesive machine: *Xyron*

Other: black ink, chalk (optional), eyelet-setting tools, jute, paintbrush, matches, hole punch

Finished size 8¼" x 2" x 1"

INSTRUCTIONS

❶ Paint inside and outside of box and lid brown.

❷ Cut strips of woodgrain paper, and ink edges. Run through adhesive machine and adhere to box; fold excess inside box. Trim corners to fit neatly. Add strips to lid to create wood plank look. Set eyelets for nails at ends of boards.

❸ Join lid to box with two paper strip hinges. Place faucet stickers to create hinge look. *Note: You can also hand draw hinges or add real hinges.*

❹ Stamp "Open if you dare" on cream cardstock and burn edges. Punch holes, tie around box with jute and knot through hole.

Bonus Idea

CUPCAKES FROM THE CRYPT

Continue the mummy theme with your party treats by adding these cupcake toppers. Wrap people-shaped sticks (**Girls and Boys Something Sticks** from **Creative Hands**) with gauze. The wiggle eyes are a grand finishing touch, and the names they hold are especially fun for younger guests.

Give Thanks

Designer: Linda Beeson

SUPPLIES

Rubber stamps:
(Acorn) *Indigo Ink Studios*
(Four Block background) *Hero Arts*
(Grid) *A Stamp in the Hand Co.*
(Piccadilly Upper & Lower alphabets) *PSX*

Dye ink: Autumn Leaves, Kaleidacolor, *Tsukineko*

Textured cardstock: (white, Rust, Ivy) *Bazzill Basics Paper*

Other: copper embossing powder, adhesive, foam tape, scissors, embossing heat tool, hole punch, bone folder, ruler, ribbon

Finished size: 5½" square

CARD

❶ Make card from Rust cardstock. Score horizontal line 1" down from fold on each side.

❷ Punch two holes between fold and score lines; add ribbon.

FINISH

❶ Stamp Four Block background with Autumn Leaves on white cardstock. Cut out, ink edges, and mat with Ivy.

❷ Stamp Acorn with brown on white cardstock; emboss with copper. Cut out and adhere to upper left square with foam tape.

❸ Stamp "Give Thanks" with green in lower right square.

❹ Stamp Grid with Autumn Leaves on white cardstock. Trim, ink edges, and mat with Ivy.

❺ Adhere Four Blocks background to Grid, and Grid to card.

Leaf Collage

Designer: Laurie D'Ambrosio

SUPPLIES

Rubber stamps: (Leaves & Patterns, Happy Thanksgiving), *Hero Arts*

Chalk ink: (Sicilian Spice, Venetian Sunrise), Fresco, *Gary M. Burlin*

Cardstock: white, *Wausau*

Patterned paper: Orange Slush, *Carolee's Creations*

Adhesive: *Glue Dots International*

Pop-up dots: *Glue Dots International*

Chalk: *Craf-T Products* (red, orange, yellow, brown)

Decorative scissors: *Fiskars*

Other: waterproof ink (black, brown), tan paper, scissors, plastic wrap, cotton swab or make-up applicator

Finished size: 4¼" x 5½"

❶ Make card from white cardstock.

❷ Apply Venetian Sunrise to card front with crumpled plastic wrap. Repeat with Sicilian Spice.

❸ Stamp Leaves & Patterns with brown on white cardstock; chalk image.

❹ Cut out image with decorative scissors, mat with tan and Orange Slush. Trim with decorative scissors; adhere to card front with pop-up dots.

❺ Stamp Happy Thanksgiving with black on Orange Slush. Trim with decorative scissors; adhere to card.

Missing You This Thanksgiving

Designer: Gretchen Schmidt

SUPPLIES

Rubber stamps: (leaf, acorn from All Natural set) *Stampin' Up!*

Watermark ink: VersaMark, *Tsukineko*

Cardstock: (White, Terracotta, Cajun, Mustard, Maize) *Making Memories*

Color medium: (brown chalk) *Craf-T Products*

Accent: (metal frame) *Making Memories*

Font: (Think Small, Champagne) *www.two-peasinabucket.com*

Adhesive:
   (dots) *Glue Dots International;*
   double-sided tape

Tools: computer and printer, scissors, chalk applicator

Finished size: 5½" x 4¼"

INSTRUCTIONS

1. Make card from White cardstock.

2. Stamp Leaf at random on Terracotta and Mustard cardstock.

3. Print "Missing you this Thanksgiving" on stamped Mustard cardstock.

4. Adhere Cajun cardstock to center of card. Tear edges of stamped Terracotta and Mustard; adhere to card and trim to fit.

5. Stamp Acorn at random on Maize; chalk. Trim paper to fit behind metal frame; adhere to center of card.

6. Attach metal frame with dots.

Take Time for Kindness

Designer: Tresa Black

SUPPLIES

All supplies from Close To My Heart unless otherwise noted

Rubber stamps: (Grapevine, Stoneware Texture, Take Time...)

Dye ink: (Sunflower, Autumn Terracotta, Oak Brown, Tinted Embossing Pad)

Embossing powder: (gold) no source

Cardstock: (Ultra White, Pepperwood)

Accent: (beads) no source

Fasteners: (rust eyelets) no source

Fibers: (black) Waxy Flax, *Scrapworks*

Adhesive: (glue stick) no source

Tools: (eyelet-setting tools, scissors, heat tool, plastic container or plate) no source

Other: (bleach, paper towels, round sponge) no source

Finished size: 6" square

INSTRUCTIONS

1. Make card from Ultra White cardstock.

2. Apply Sunflower, Autumn Terracotta, and Oak Brown inks to front of card with round sponge. Use Stoneware Texture stamp to add speckles.

3. Fold paper towel into fourths, place in plastic container; pour on bleach to create pad.

4. Stamp Grapevine with bleach; tear right-hand edge of card.

5. Adhere 6" square Pepperwood cardstock to back of card front.

6. Stamp Take Time...; emboss.

7. Attach eyelets. String beads onto fibers, tying knots between beads. Tie to card front.

The Creative Thanksgiving Table

Celebrate, play games, and count your blessings with these fun table ideas.

Gratitude Table Ensemble

Designer: Wendy Sue Anderson

SUPPLIES

For all projects:

Patterned paper: Crazy Quilt, Yellow Striped; Life's Journey, *K&Company*

Sheer ribbons: Harvest, *Wal-Mart*

Other: adhesive dots, computer and printer

For cone centerpiece:

Ivory cardstock

Patterned paper: Black Gingham, Bow & Roses, Green Script, Red Striped, Travel Log, Travel Stickers; Life's Journey, *K&Company*

Cardboard cone: Angel, *Artifacts Inc.*

Sand dye ink: Memories, *Stewart Superior Corp.*

Small envelope template: Basic Round, *Scrap Pagerz*

Buttons: ladybug, autumn leaves, acorns; Dress It Up, *Jesse James & Co.*

Font: Heber, Journaling CD, *Chatterbox Inc.*

Decoupage adhesive: Mod Podge, *Plaid*

Other: black acrylic paint, excelsior moss, floral foam, paintbrush, wooden skewers, glue gun, glue stickers

For kid's activity book:

Ivory cardstock

Chipboard

Magnetic date stamp: *Making Memories*

1" loose-leaf binding rings

Stickers:
Rub-on letters; Cottage Architexture, *EK Success*

Black pebble letters: Domed Typewriter Keys; Life's Journey, *K&Company*

Label words: Fall; Real Life, *Pebbles Inc.*

Tag: Tags & Labels; Rebecca Sower Nostalgiques, *EK Success*

Accents:
Buttons: autumn leaves, acorn, lady bug; Dress It Up, *Jesse James & Co.* Autumn leaves, *Nature's Pressed*

Other: black thread, black permanent ink, computer and printer, sewing machine

For tags:

Patterned paper: Bow & Roses, Green Script, Red Striped, Travel Stickers; Life's Journey, *K&Company*

Round metal-rimmed tags: *Making Memories*

1/8" eyelets: Aluminum, *Making Memories*

Transparency sheet: *Apollo-Boone*

Font: Monument, Journaling CD, *Chatterbox Inc.*

Other: circle punch, eyelet-setting tools

Finished sizes:
Cone 7"
Mini envelopes 1³⁄₁₆" x 1½"
Wine glass tags 1½" diameter
Kid's activity book 7" x 5"

CONE & ENVELOPES

① Transfer cone pattern to Crazy Quilt paper and cut out.

② Cover cone with paper and adhere with decoupage adhesive. Paint edges.

③ Fill cone with floral foam and excelsior moss.

④ Create envelopes for each guest with small envelope template and patterned papers. Ink envelope edges. Hot glue envelopes to skewers.

⑤ Print names on cardstock, trim, ink edges and adhere to envelopes.

⑥ Cut ivory cardstock to fit inside each envelope. Ink edges.

⑦ Tie ribbons to skewers. Adhere buttons to envelopes with adhesive dots.

⑧ Arrange and insert skewers into cone.

DESIGNER NOTE

Wendy Sue thought it would be fun to create an interactive centerpiece that could become an ongoing tradition for the Thanksgiving feast. Have guests write down something that they are especially grateful for on slips of paper and put them in their personalized envelopes. The next year, everyone can look at what they wrote as they add something new, sharing with the group if they wish.

CONE PATTERN Enlarge 200%

CREATING PATTERNS FOR DIFFERENT SIZE CONES

Position the point of the cone in the lower left corner and along bottom edge of a 12" x 12" sheet of paper. Hold the point in place while you roll the cone to the left side of the paper. Hold a pencil next to cone opening with the lead on the paper and mark the arc while rolling. Cut along the arc. It may be necessary to do a little trimming after the paper is adhered.

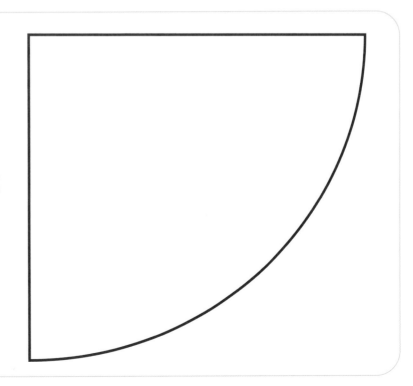

Kid's Thanksgiving Activity Books

INSTRUCTIONS

1. Cut front and back covers from chipboard.

2. Adhere quilt and yellow striped papers together. Trim to fit cover. Zigzag-stitch edges and adhere to cover. Tie bow in tag hole. Adhere leaf and tag.

3. Add rub-on letters for child's name and "FOR". Adhere "so" with pebble letters and "IS" and "THANKFUL" with label words. Add leaf and acorn buttons.

4. Print Thanksgiving-related words on ivory cardstock and cut to 7" x 5" for inside pages. Punch two ring holes in top.

5. Assemble with loose-leaf rings.

Wine Glass Tags

Different papers and words are used so that guests can easily identify their own glasses.

1. Punch patterned papers to fit tags.

2. Print "Thank You" in several languages on transparency sheet (see "Tag Ideas"). Trim to fit over punched paper.

3. Attach paper circle and transparency to tag with eyelet.

4. Tie ribbons through eyelets, leaving enough to tie around stem of glass.

ACTIVE CHILDREN

To keep the kids busy while the meal is being prepared, create these cute blessing books. The covers can be already decorated for the younger kids, while older ones can design their own. Print on the bottom corner of each page a word that describes something that the children might be thankful for. They can draw or write about why they are thankful for each item.

THANKFUL WORDS

Here are some words for the page in the Kid's Thanksgiving Activity Book.

Books, Church, Family, Food, Friends, Home, Pets, Teachers, Warm Clothes

MORE BOOK COVER IDEAS

See the photo for additional decorating ideas for the Activity Book cover. "Meagan's Blessings" has different patterned paper, tag, leaf, buttons, rub-ons, and raffia.

TAG IDEAS

Arigato, Danke, Gracias, Grazie, Mahalo, Merci, Thank You.

Find more thank you translations at www.freelang.net/expressions/thankyou.html

MORE WAYS TO USE TAGS

Decorate different items at the table with the tags. Fasten them to silverware, napkin rings, the centerpiece, tapered candles, gift or treat bags. See who can guess what the different languages are. The guest with the most correct answers wins a prize!

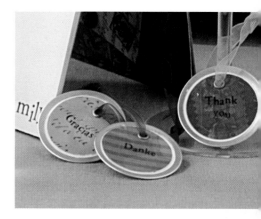

Blessing Mix

Designer: Stacy Croninger

Contents: Bugles, miniature pretzels, orange slices candy, salted peanuts, and candy corn.

SUPPLIES

Kraft cardstock

Paper scraps

Adhesives:
   Adhesive tabs; Vario tabs, *EK Success*
   Glue stick

Die cut: Super Scallop Tag (38-0946), Sizzix, *Provo Craft*

Die-cutting machine: Sizzix, *Provo Craft*

Rub-on words: "Give Thanks"

Other: raffia, clear cellophane bag, computer and printer, desired font

INSTRUCTIONS

1 Tear paper scraps into ½" strips.

2 Print Blessing Mix sentiment on cardstock. Trim to 4¼" x 5¼". On opposite side, apply two rows of adhesive tabs to back, and glue stick to edges.

3 Adhere torn scraps to cardstock, layering as desired. Add rub-on word.

4 Center die cut over poem and cut out.

5 Fill cellophane bag with snack mix. Tie closed with raffia and attach tag.

Tag Sentiment

BLESSING MIX

The Bugles are a symbol of the Cornucopia, a horn of plenty.

The Pretzels represent arms folded in thanks and prayer.

The Candy Corn reminds us that during the first winter, the pilgrims were allowed only five kernels of corn per day because food was so scarce.

The Fruit is a reminder that Thanksgiving is the celebration of the harvest.

The Peanuts represent seeds, the potential of the bounteous harvest for the next season if they are planted and well-tended.

STACY'S TIP

I'm constantly looking for quick and easy ideas for gifts, tags, and wraps. I'm also a pack rat who saves every paper scrap. So, this collaged scrap tag is a great solution for me. Try it with leftover Christmas wrap as well.

Snowmade Gifts and Greetings

Send winter warmth with a snowman's smile.

Winter

SURVIVAL KiT

It's just not funny
When your nose is runny;
You feel all soggy.
Hoarse and froggy.
Your throat is scratching;
The germs are hatching.
You know it's catching--
KERCHOOO!

--Kay Winters

Winter Survival Kit

Designer: Alice Golden

SUPPLIES

White paper

Patterned paper:
Lacy Blue Dots, *Carolee's Creations*
Purple Swirl Swatch, *Karen Foster Design*

Gallon-size paint can: *Home Depot*

Software program: "Creative Clips & Fonts by Becky Higgins" CD, *Creating Keepsakes*

Font: Holiday Leftovers, *www.fontdiner.com*

Poem: Runny Nose, *www.two-peasinabucket.com/peasoup.asp*

Dimensional adhesive: foam dots

Decorative-edge scissors: Deckle, *Fiskars*

Accents:
Alphabet stickers: Vintage, *Me & My Big Ideas*
Cardstock stickers: Snow Biz, *Snow Biz Tags and Borders, Doodlebug Design*
Bead chain: *Making Memories*
Silver eyelet

Other: eyelet-setting tools, double-sided tape or adhesive machine

Finished size 7¾" x 6½"

LABEL

❶ Trim Lacy Blue Dots paper to fit front of can.

❷ Tear strips of white paper to make snowdrifts. Adhere cardstock stickers and snowdrifts (see photo). *Note: Adhere one snowman cardstock sticker with dimensional adhesive.* Mat with Purple Swirl Swatch paper.

❸ Spell "SURVIVAL KIT" with alphabet stickers.

❹ Adhere label to paint can with double-sided tape or run label through adhesive machine.

LID

❶ Create round text box (approx. 4¾") in software program and type "Runny Nose" poem inside. Print on Lacy Blue Dots paper and cut out.

❷ Add cardstock stickers; mat with Purple Swirl Swatch paper trimmed with decorative edge scissors.

❸ Adhere to lid with double-sided tape or run through adhesive machine.

TAG

❶ Press two cardstock tag stickers together, back to back, to create tag.

❷ Add "to:" and "from:" and other desired stickers.

❸ Set eyelet through top and attach to paint can handle with bead chain.

WINTER SURVIVAL SUPPLIES

Fill the can with "get well" supplies to help someone survive winter: chicken soup, a small bottle of orange juice, hot cocoa packets, a cellophane bag filled with mini marshmallows, herbal tea bags, a small jar of honey, cough drops, lip balm, and facial tissues.

A TIP FROM ALICE

Cut out the cardstock stickers with the backing attached so you can experiment with different arrangements before adhering the stickers.

Bonus Idea

Decorate a paint can filled with gifts for any occasion. Fill it with baby items for a shower, craft supplies for a child's birthday, body care products for Mother's Day, or sports tickets, golf balls, and a TV Guide for Father's Day. Fill quart-size cans with holiday treats for the neighbors.

Snowman Soup

Designer: Stacy Hoppins

SUPPLIES

White cardstock

Patterned paper: Twilight Faded Dots; Snip Its, *Pebbles Inc.*

Vellum

Snowflake patterned cellophane bag

Snowman accent: Snow Wear; Fresh Cuts, *EK Success*

Light blue eyelets, twine: *Making Memories*

Vellum tape: *3M*

Font: CK Sassy, "Fresh Fonts" CD, *Creating Keepsakes*

Soup ingredients: single serving package of hot cocoa mix, mini marshmallows in resealable bag, chocolate kisses, candy cane

Eyelet-setting tools

Finished size 8" x 4¼"

INSTRUCTIONS

❶ Cut 6" x 4¼" rectangle of patterned paper to make bag topper.

❷ Tear three vellum strips to form snowdrifts (see photo). Adhere one to bottom of bag topper with vellum tape. Adhere snowman accent and remaining snowdrifts.

❸ Print "Snowman Soup" poem on white cardstock with blue ink. Trim and adhere to bag topper.

❹ Fill cellophane bag with Snowman Soup ingredients. Fold top of bag closed.

❺ Score and fold bag topper ¾" from top edge. Place over cellophane bag. Punch two holes through all layers. Unfold and set eyelets through front layer of bag topper.

❻ Replace topper on bag, thread twine through holes, and tie closed.

Was told you've been real good this year, Always glad to hear it With freezing weather drawing near You'll need to warm the spirit So here's a little Snowman Soup Complete with stirring stick Add hot water, sip it slow It's sure to do the trick!

Bonus Idea

Save time—mat the poem with a colored tag and tie it to a holiday mug filled with the Snowman Soup ingredients.

Glitter Snow Tags

Designer: Janelle Clark

SUPPLIES

Cardstock:
  Light blue, *American Crafts*
  White

Rubber stamp: snowman gift tag (from Holiday Woodcuts set), *Stampin' Up!*

Dye ink: Aurora (pink), Mist (light green); Ancient Page Petal Point, *Clearsnap*

Glassine pocket: *SilverCrow Creations*

Accents:
  Fibers
  Silver eyelets
  Glitter

Other: eyelet-setting tools, adhesive, black pen

Finished size 2¾" x 2½"

INSTRUCTIONS

❶ Stamp snowman on white cardstock; cut out, leaving ⅛" border. Write recipient's name with black pen. Mat with light blue cardstock and place in pocket.

❷ Fill pocket with glitter.

❸ Seal pocket with adhesive to prevent glitter from falling out.

❹ Set two eyelets in top of pocket; thread fibers through and knot.

Snowflake Stationery Set

Designer: Valinda Hatch

SUPPLIES

Rubber stamp: Large Snowflake, *Rubbermoon Stamps*

Foam stamps: Snowflakes, *Anita's Fabric Stamps*

Pigment ink: (light blue, medium blue, dark blue) Paintbox Brights, ColorBox, *Clearsnap*

Embossing powder: Suze Weinberg's Ultra Thick Embossing Enamel, *Ranger Industries*

Chalk: blue, *Craf-T Products*

Brads: Boardwalk Blue, *Lasting Impressions for Paper*

Other: cardstock (white, light blue, dark blue), adhesive, embossing heat tool, scissors, cotton swab or make-up applicator, ruler, pencil

Finished sizes:
Stationery: 6" x 8"
Card: 5½" x 4"
Gift card: 2½" square

STATIONERY

① Cut white cardstock to 6" x 8".

② Stamp Large Snowflake with light blue and dark blue in bottom corner. *Note: Apply light blue ink to stamp first then dark blue for two-tone coloring. Emboss.*

③ Stamp snowflakes with medium blue and dark blue on cardstock; emboss.

④ Apply chalk around snowflakes; attach brads to centers.

CARD

① Make card from white cardstock.

② Stamp Large Snowflake with light blue and dark blue on white cardstock; emboss.

③ Attach brad to snowflake center; mat with light blue and dark blue cardstock.

④ Adhere to card front.

GIFT CARD

① Make card from white cardstock.

② Stamp Snowflakes with dark blue on white cardstock. Stamp Snowflakes with medium blue over dark blue snowflake. *Note: Rotate stamp to create unique snowflake image.*

③ Mat with light blue and dark blue cardstock; adhere to card front.

Bonus Ideas

■ Emboss the double-stamped snowflake on your gift card, add a brad, and hand-write "glisten!" or "sparkle!"

■ Stamp snowflakes of various sizes in a vertical row. Cut out boots, a top hat, and a carrot nose from black and orange cardstock to create a snow friend to send on your stationery and cards.

Metallic Menorah Gift Bag & Dreidel Card

Designer: Anne Heyen

SUPPLIES

FOR ALL:

Embossed stickers: Hanukkah, Hanukkah Border, *Sandylion*

FOR BAG:

Silver metallic cardstock: *Canson*

Patterned paper: silver star, dreidel poem, *Sandylion*

Clear acrylic gift bag with card: *A.C. Moore*

Scallop square punch: *Marvy Uchida*

FOR CARD:

Blue window card: Paper Bliss, *Westrim Crafts*

Accents:
　Metal-rimmed vellum tag, silver eyelets: *Making Memories*
　Silver fibers: Angel Wings Set; *Rubba Dub Dub*

Other: craft knife, cutting mat, eyelet-setting tools, adhesive dots

Finished sizes:
　bag 9" x 7½",
　card 7¼" x 4¾"

BAG

❶ Punch scalloped square from silver star paper. Adhere to card (attached to bag handle). Adhere Star of David sticker.

❷ Cut 4¾" x 6" piece of dreidel poem paper. Adhere to 7" x 6¼" piece of silver star paper.

❸ Add menorah, ribbon border, "Happy Hanukkah," and mini star stickers to piece (see photo).

❹ Mat paper piece with cardstock and adhere to bag.

CARD

❶ Arrange ribbon border stickers around window on front of card. Add photo corner stickers to corners.

❷ Adhere dreidel sticker to each side of tag.

❸ Set eyelets through top and bottom of tag. Knot fibers through eyelets.

❹ Open card and place tag in center of window. Adhere end of fibers to top and bottom of window, using adhesive dots.

❺ Repeat step 1 on inside of window, hiding fiber ends under stickers.

A TIP FROM ANNE

Gift bags often come with cards attached to the handles. Dress up the cards with simple embellishments, rather than creating your own cards from scratch.

Bonus Idea

Make a card without a window. Just attach the dreidel tag accent in the center of the frame.

Hanukkah Candles Box & Card

Designer: Nicole Keller

SUPPLIES

Cardstock: light blue, white

Textured cardstock: dark blue, yellow, *Bazzill Basics Paper*

Mosaic square card: Paper Reflections, *DMD, Inc.*

Oval tag die: Sizzlits; Sizzix, *Provo Craft*

Die-cutting machine: Sizzix, *Provo Craft*

Punches:
    Candle: *EK Success*
    1" circle: *Family Treasures*

Chalk ink: Prussian Blue; ColorBox, *Clearsnap*

Font: 2Ps Arizona, *www.twopeasinabucket.com*

Accents:
    Silver brads: *Making Memories*
    Blue fiber: Adornments, *EK Success*

Other: stipple brush or sponge, ⅛" hole punch

Finished sizes:
    box 1½" x 2½" x 1½"
    card 4¾" square

BOX

❶ Cut out box, using pattern. Sponge with ink and assemble.

❷ Punch four 1" circles from dark blue cardstock and adhere one to each side of box.

❸ Punch four candles each from light blue and yellow cardstock. Trim flames from yellow candles. Adhere light blue candles to circles, and add yellow flames.

❹ Print "HAPPY HANUKKAH" on white cardstock. Die-cut into oval and mat with dark blue cardstock. Punch hole and tie to box with fiber.

CARD

❶ Sponge card with ink.

❷ Adhere dark blue cardstock square inside front of card.

❸ Punch nine candles each from light blue and yellow cardstock. Trim flames from yellow candles. Adhere light blue candles to windows, and add yellow flames.

❹ Print "HAPPY HANUKKAH" on white cardstock; trim and attach to card with brads.

Bonus Idea

Make a Christmas card with holly punch-outs.

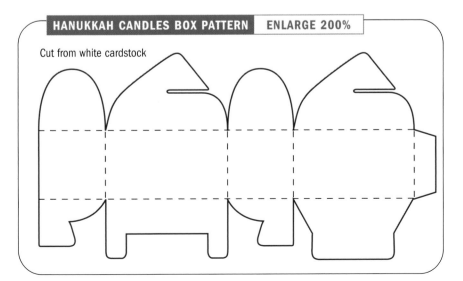

HANUKKAH CANDLES BOX PATTERN   **ENLARGE 200%**

Cut from white cardstock

Majestic Menorah

Designer: Ann Morgenstern

SUPPLIES

All supplies from Stampin' Up! unless otherwise noted.

Rubber stamps: (Happy Hanukkah!, menorah)

Dye ink: (Silver)

Watermark ink: VersaMark, *Tsukineko*

Cardstock: (Night of Navy, Bliss Blue)

Accent: (jump ring) no source

Fibers: (navy organza ribbon, silver cord) no source

Shrink plastic sheet

Adhesive

Tools: (scissors, oven, baking sheet, rectangle punch, hole punch) no source

Finished size: 4¼" x 5½"

INSTRUCTIONS

❶ Make card from Bliss Blue cardstock. Mat with Night of Navy cardstock.

❷ Stamp Happy Hanukkah! randomly on front of card with watermark ink.

❸ Punch rectangle at top center of card.

❹ Stamp menorah with Silver ink on shrink plastic and cut out; punch hole at top and bake according to manufacturer's instructions. Let cool.

❺ Attach jump ring to shrink plastic charm; attach to window on card front.

❻ Wrap ribbon and silver cord around fold; tie bow.

Happy Hanukkah

Designer: Nicole Keller

SUPPLIES

Rubber stamp: (One Candle) *Hero Arts*

Pigment ink: (Graphite Black) Brilliance, *Tsukineko*

Cardstock: (white, yellow, navy, blue-gray)

Textured cardstock: (Baby Blue) *Bazzill Basics Paper*

Vellum

Accent: (metal S-clip) *7gypsies*

Fibers: (blue ribbon)

Font: (CK Cosmopolitan) "Creative Clips & Fonts" CD, *Creating Keepsakes*

Adhesive

Tools: computer and printer, wire cutters

Other: silver wire

Finished size: 6" x 3½"

INSTRUCTIONS

❶ Make card from Baby Blue cardstock.

❷ Stamp One Candle nine times on white, blue-gray, and yellow cardstock.

❸ Cut flames from yellow, and candles from blue-gray. Adhere to corresponding candle parts on white.

❹ Mat stamped image with navy cardstock.

❺ Print "Happy Hanukkah" on vellum; attach S-clip with wire; adhere to card front.

❻ Wrap ribbon around card; adhere. Adhere stamped image over ribbon.

Happy Chanukah

Designer: Anne Heyen

SUPPLIES

Fibers: *Rubba Dub Dub*

Watercolor pencils: *Derwent*

Tag: *DMD Industries*

Chalk: *Craft-T Products*

Vellum: *Paper Adventures*

Patterned paper: *Colors by Design*

Eyelet: *doodlebug design*

Font: Peppermint Tea, *Two Peas in a Bucket*

Clear embossing powder: *Ranger Industries*

Finished size: 3¼" x 6¼"

Shalom

Designer: Allison Strine

SUPPLIES

Tag: *Making Memories*

Shalom sticker: *Mrs. Grossman's*

Blue and ivory textured paper: *Artistic Scrapper*

Star of David punch: *The Punch Bunch*

Peace rubber stamp: *Stampington & Company*

Texture rubber stamp: *Junque*

Ink: Brilliance, *Tsukineko*

Other: silver pen, vellum, eyelet, silver fibers, blue and white cardstock

Finished size: 6½" x 5"

Menorah

Designer: Allison Strine

SUPPLIES

Rubber stamps:
  (Menorah) *Stamp Oasis*
  (Boxed alphabet) *Wordsworth*

Dye ink: (Lapis Blue, Azalea, Coral Red, Amethyst) Ancient Page, *Clearsnap*

Pigment ink: black, ColorBox, *Clearsnap*

Embossing powder: Claret, Stamp-n-Stuff, *Mark Enterprises*

Patterned paper: Penciled Violet Solid, *Wordsworth*

Card template: Wild Card Z012, *Wordsworth*

Other: gold cardstock, vellum, embossing heat tool, craft knife, ruler, scissors, adhesive

Finished size: 5½" square

INSTRUCTIONS

❶ Make card from template and gold cardstock.

❷ Stamp Menorah with black; emboss.

❸ Trace card template on back of Penciled Violet Solid; cut slightly smaller and adhere to card front.

❹ Stamp "happy hanukkah" with various colors on vellum. *Note: Ink just the letter portion of the stamp using a corner of the ink pad.*

❺ Tear and adhere inside card through frame.

Button Menorah

Designer: Allison Strine

SUPPLIES

Patterned cardstock: Blue Box, *Wordsworth*
Adhesive: *Glue Dots International*
Other: buttons (red, orange, yellow), blue cardstock, metal accent, blue thread, sewing machine, scissors

Finished size: 6½" x 5"

INSTRUCTIONS

1 Make card from blue cardstock.

2 Cut square of Blue Box to fit card; zigzag-stitch to card front.

3 Cut nine rectangles of blue cardstock. *Note: Angle sides and ends of rectangles.*

4 Adhere rectangles to card front; adhere buttons above rectangles. Adhere metal accent to middle candle.

Designer: Anne Heyen

SUPPLIES

Patterned paper: *KI Memories*
Tile stickers: blue, Tile's Play, *EK Success*
Instant accent: Star of David, Jolee's By You, *EK Success*
Alphabet stickers: *Mrs. Grossman's*
Adhesive: *Glue Dots International*
Card: white, *DMD Industries*
Other: scissors, blue cardstock

Finished size: 7" x 5"

INSTRUCTIONS

1 Cut blue cardstock fit card front; adhere.

2 Cut patterned paper slightly smaller; adhere to card.

3 Place tile stickers in top left corner; attach Star of David accent to center of tiles.

4 Spell "shalom" with alphabet stickers.

Party on!

Have fun with a holiday cookie swap.

Cookie Swap Party Ensemble

Designer: Alisa Bangerter

SUPPLIES

FOR ALL:

Paper-thin cork: *Magic Scraps*

Brown chalk: *Craft-T Products*

Narrow white rickrack: *Wrights*

Red gingham ribbon: *Offray*

FOR RECIPE BOOK:

Tan cardstock

White paper

Kraft tissue paper: *DMD, Inc.*

Foam alphabet stamps: "c", "o", Philadelphia lowercase, *Making Memories*

Round concho: *Scrapworks*

"K" metal sticker

"I" wood letter: *Walnut Hollow*

"E" pebble sticker: Poem Stone Upper Case Clear, *Creative Imaginations*

"S" alphabet sticker: Sonnets Collection, *Creative Imaginations*

Accents:
Large red button: *Making Memories*
Small red buttons: *Lasting Impressions*
White rickrack: *Wrights*
Black seed beads: *Darice*
Round metal-rimmed tag: *Making Memories*

Spiral Clips: Round, square, *Scrapworks*

Permanent ink: black, red

"Christmas Cookies" poem: Author Bobbi Katz, ww.twopeasinabucket.com /peasoup.asp

Ribbons: black gingham, brown plaid, red grosgrain, tan net: *Offray*

Cookie Time!

Clitter, clatter
Baking tins,
Cookie cutters,
Rolling pin.
Christmas cookies,
Let's begin!

Sugar, flour, eggs, & butter,
Mixing bowls & a wooden spoon.
Round & round we turn the batter.
We'll have dough to roll out soon.

Cut the cookies with the cutters-
Diamond, circle, crescent moon.
Pop them all into the oven.

GINGERBREAD COOKIES

2/3 cup margarine	1 teaspoon salt
1/2 cup granulated sugar	1 teaspoon ground ginger
1/2 cup brown sugar	1 teaspoon ground cloves
1 egg	1 teaspoon ground cinnamon
1/4 cup molasses	2 cups flour
1 teaspoon baking soda	

Cream together margarine and sugars. Add egg, molasses, soda, salt, and spices. Stir in the flour and mix well. Let dough chill in refrigerator for several hours. Roll dough out onto a lightly floured surface and using cookie cutters, cut shapes. Place cookies onto a greased baking sheet and bake at 375 degrees for 10 minutes.

Other: adhesive, computer and printer, fibers, hole punch, paper clips, small white tag

FOR GLASS PLATE:

Textured cardstock: black, red

Red tissue paper: *Heartland Paper Company*

12" glass plate: Indiana glass, *Lancaster Colony Corporation*

Punches:

Large hole: *Carl Manufacturing*

Small round: *McGill*

Folk heart: Paper Shapers, *EK Success*

White acrylic paint: *Delta*

Foam alphabet stamps: Misunderstood Uppercase, *Making Memories*

Decoupage adhesive: Collage Gel; Crafter's Pick, *API*

Wide white rickrack: *Wrights*

Other: cosmetic sponge, craft knife, foam adhesive dots, paintbrush, pencil, water-based varnish, needle, white thread

Finished sizes:
recipe book 3½" x 6½"
plate 12" diameter

Recipe Book

BOOK

❶ Cut 12 cardstock pieces to 3½" x 6½". Have spiral-bound into book at local copy shop.

❷ Tear ¼" off right side of each page. Chalk around each page with brown.

COVER

❶ Crumple tissue strip, smooth, and adhere across bottom of front cover. Adhere beads.

❷ Chalk edges of small tag. Cut small gingerbread woman, using pattern on p. 251. Embellish with beads, buttons, and rickrack; adhere to tag. Tie tag to binding.

❸ Tie ribbons and fibers along binding.

"COOKIES" TITLE

❶ Stamp "C" with foam stamp and red ink on kraft cardstock. Trim, leaving cardstock showing around edges and adhere with foam adhesive dots.

❷ Wrap red gingham ribbon around concho for first "O."

❸ Cut narrow tag from cardstock and chalk edges with brown. Punch hole and tie rickrack. Stamp "O" with foam stamp and black ink; adhere.

❹ Cut abstract shape from thin cork and chalk edges with brown. Adhere to cover and adhere metal "K."

❺ Adhere "I." Tie fiber through large button and adhere.

❻ Apply letter pebble "E" to metal-rimmed tag, add fiber, and adhere.

❼ Adhere "S" sticker.

INSIDE

❶ Print poem on white paper (see photo); tear and chalk edges. Adhere poem to inside cover and embellish with buttons.

❷ Print recipes on white paper; trim. Attach recipes to pages with two clips each.

Plate

❶ Cut large gingerbread woman and two hearts from cork, using patterns. Chalk edges with brown. From cardstock, punch red heart cheeks and buttons, and black eyes. Stitch white thread through buttons. Embellish gingerbread woman and hearts with narrow rickrack, ribbon, and punched shapes.

❷ Brush decoupage adhesive on plate back. Press gingerbread woman and hearts into adhesive, centering carefully. Adhere wide rickrack around plate rim and let dry.

❸ Crumple and smooth large piece of tissue paper; trim a bit larger than plate. Lay plate on tissue and mark where to stamp letters.

❹ Stamp letters on tissue, using foam stamps and white paint; let dry.

❺ Brush decoupage adhesive over entire plate back. Press stamped tissue to plate back; smooth out air bubbles and let dry.

❻ Trim excess tissue from plate.

❼ Brush varnish on plate back to seal.

A TIP FROM ALISA

To clean plate, wipe top with a damp cloth. Never immerse in water.

LOCATING LYRICS

Can't find the right phrases to include with your creations? Solve this quandary with the Web. Countless poems, lyrics, and quotes can be found in cyberspace. Visit a search engine and type phrases such as "cookie poem" or "holiday quotes", and you'll be amazed at the exciting expressions you'll find.

Bonus Ideas

- In addition to bringing cookies to a swap, ask each guest to bring a copy of her recipe for each attendee and have a recipe swap as well.

- Make tabbed, index card shaped invitations from tan cardstock. Stamp "You're Invited" on the tab.

- A set of matching recipe cards makes an appreciated party favor. Print card information on white cardstock and cut to desired size. Make a tan envelope for the cards and embellish with rickrack and ribbon.

PATTERNS

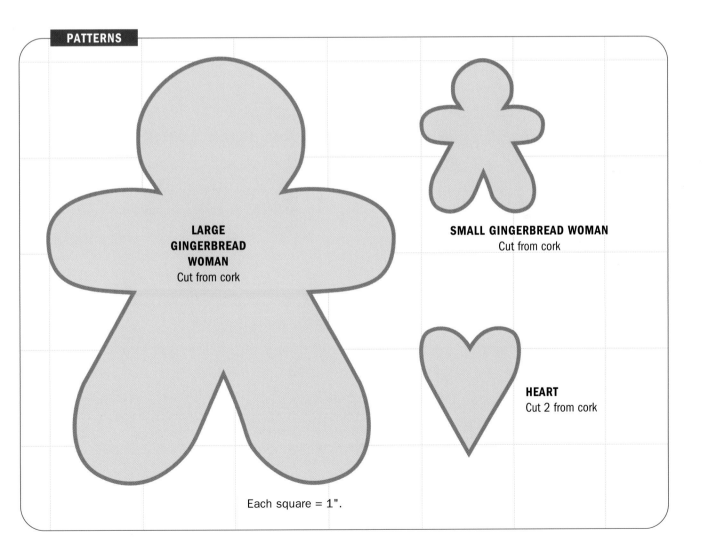

LARGE GINGERBREAD WOMAN
Cut from cork

SMALL GINGERBREAD WOMAN
Cut from cork

HEART
Cut 2 from cork

Each square = 1".

Warm the hearts of your loved ones with handmade party items.

Happy Holly-days Party

Designer: Lori Bergmann

SUPPLIES

Rubber stamps:
(holly leaf) Christmas Foliage, *Stampin' Up!*

(Holly Swirl) Holiday Quad Cube, *Stampendous!*

Cardstock: red, *Bazzill Basics Paper*

Paper: (Celery, Spinach) Velvet, *K&Company*

Patterned paper: holly, Old Christmas Days assortment, *Provo Craft*

Vellum: *WorldWin*

Circle template: Coluzzle, *Provo Craft*

Fonts:
(2Peas Beautiful) *twopeasinabucket.com*

(PC Licorice) HugWare, *Provo Craft*

Fine-tip pen: red, *EK Success*

Snaps: Tulip Red, Flat Head, *Stamp Doctor*

Adhesive: (dots, strip) *Glue Dots International*

Acrylic paint:
(Light Ivory, Metallic 14K Gold) Ceramcoat, *Delta*

(Cranberry) Adirondack, *Ranger Industries*

Varnish: iridescent gold, Ceramcoat, *Delta*

Sealer: *Delta*

Other: paper maché box, gold tissue paper, empty film canister or cardboard cylinder, small gifts or candies for party favor, misting bottle filled with water, ribbon, paintbrush, palette, sponge, eyelet-setting tools, scissors, ruler, adhesive, vellum adhesive, computer and printer, iron

Finished size
Invitation: 6" square
Gift box: 2¼" x 2¼" x 1½"
Party favor: 7" x 1"

Invitation

MAKE INVITATION

❶ Cut 6" square of cardstock; trim and adhere slightly smaller square of patterned paper to front.

❷ Print party details on vellum; let dry. Cut with circle template. Color "Christmas Party!" with pen.

❸ Cut another circle from vellum; adhere behind printed circle with vellum adhesive. Adhere to invitation.

STAMP HOLLY LEAVES

Read "Heat-Stamping Tips" before you begin.

❶ To heat stamp holly leaf, mist textured side of velvet paper with water. Place textured side down over holly leaf stamp and press with hot iron for 5–10 seconds.

❷ Cut out and adhere to invitation with adhesive dot.

❸ Repeat steps 1–2 to create wreath.

❹ Add snaps and ribbon.

GIFT BOX

Let paint dry between coats.

❶ Coat paper maché box and lid with sealer; let dry.

❷ Paint with 2–3 coats of Light Ivory. Apply one coat of varnish.

❸ Stamp Holly Swirl on lid with Metallic 14K Gold.

❹ Dot Cranberry paint on sides of lid.

❺ Cover box with patterned paper.

❻ Accent lid with holly leaves and snap.

PARTY FAVOR

❶ Place small gifts or candies in film canister or cardboard cylinder.

❷ Wrap with gold tissue paper; tie ends closed with ribbon.

❸ Cut strip of cardstock to same width as canister; adhere slightly narrower piece of patterned paper to center. Wrap around favor and adhere ends with adhesive strips.

HEAT-STAMPING TIPS

- Test some samples first to determine which temperature works best.

- Do not move the iron while pressing.

- Do not place the steam holes on the stamp or they may create circles on the design.

- Cut out each leaf after heat-stamping. Each time you heat-stamp an image, any previously stamped images on the paper will fade as the paper reheats.

Bonus Ideas

- No holly-days party would be complete without matching place cards and napkin rings!

- Add extra flair to the party favors by cutting the edges of the tissue paper with decorative-edge scissors or layering several colors of tissue paper.

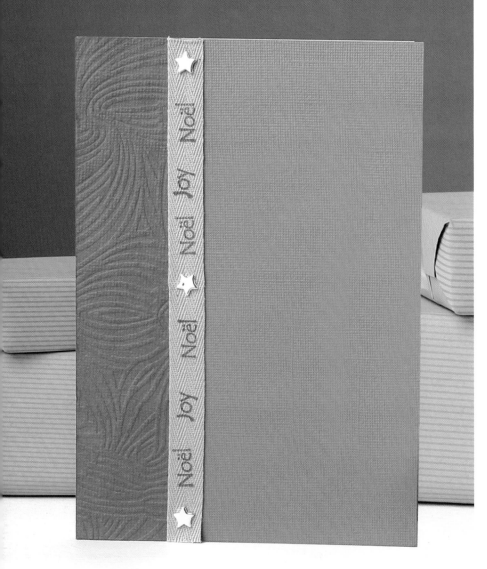

Joy Noel

Designer: Sande Krieger

SUPPLIES

Rubber stamps: (Noel, Joy) *Hero Arts*
Pigment ink: Blazing Red, StazOn, *Tsukineko*
Embossed paper: red, *Provo Craft*
Other: cardstock (green, cream), star brads, twill ribbon, adhesive, scissors

Finished size: 7" x 5"

❶ Make card from cream cardstock.

❷ Cut green cardstock to fit card front; adhere.

❸ Cut strip of red handmade paper; adhere to card front along fold.

❹ Stamp Noel and Joy on twill ribbon; cut to fit card and adhere to seam.

❺ Attach star brads to card front.

Simple Sentiments

Pick an appropriate Christmas wish for your card:

Christmas is the time to remember that we are all in the world together.

What is **Christmas?**
It is belief in the **past,**
courage for the **present,**
and hope for the **future.**
—*Anes M. Pharo*

May you have
The gladness of Christmas
which is hope;

The spirit of Christmas
which is peace;

The heart of Christmas
which is love.
—*Ada V. Hendricks*

But not alone at Christmastime
comes holiday and cheer,
for one who loves a little child
has Christmas all the year.
—*Florence Evelyn Dratt*

*Believe in Santa
& charge cards!*

—*www.craftsayings.com*
Set in Dorchester Script, Adobe

Even when it's cold outside
our memories keep us warm.

Christmas calories don't count!

Think of Christmas,
Think of snow,
Think of sleigh bells,
Ho, ho, ho!

Create quick & easy holiday wishes for Christmas with these unique stamped designs.

Thumbprint Reindeer

Designer: Tresa Black

SUPPLIES

All supplies from Close To My Heart unless otherwise noted.

Rubber stamps: stars & swirls from Sun, Moon & Stars set, Merry Christmas from Merry Christmas Blocks set

Dye ink: Oak Brown, Cranberry

Cardstock: white, black, Cranberry

Pen: black, My Legacy Writers

Other: (red glitter, adhesive, scissors, computer with printer, font, ruler) no source

Finished size: 8½" x 4"

❶ Make card from white cardstock.

❷ Stamp Merry Christmas and stars & swirls with Cranberry on Cranberry cardstock; mat with black and adhere to card front.

❸ Print names on white cardstock; cut into 1½" x 1¾" rectangles. *Note: Center name at bottom of rectangle.*

❹ Stamp child's fingerprint with Oak Brown on each rectangle.

❺ Draw antlers, ears, and eyes on each fingerprint; adhere glitter for noses.

❻ Adhere rectangles to black cardstock strip; trim and mount on card front.

Christmas Toys

Designer: Cheryl McMurray

SUPPLIES

Pre-painted wood shapes: Mini Carefree Collectibles, *Provo Craft*

Cellophane: *Stampin' Up!*

Font: CK Handprint, "The Best of Creative Lettering" CD Combo, *Creating Keepsakes*

Other: yellow gold cardstock; red speckled, green polka dot, and purple speckled patterned paper

Finished size: 4⅝" x 6¾"

Bonus Idea

You can easily customize this card for people of all ages—just substitute other images for toys. Try fashion images for ladies, cars or tools for men.

Have a Sweet Christmas

Designer: Cheryl McMurray

SUPPLIES

Patterned paper: The Robin's Nest

Square punch: *Marvy Uchida*

Scallop edge scissors: *Fiskars*

Alphabet stickers: Sticko, *EK Success*

Other: peppermint candies, white and black cardstock

Finished size: 7⅜" x 4⅝"

Elegant Candy Canes

Designer: Kathleen Paneitz

SUPPLIES

Font: Bickley Script, downloaded from the Web

Silver metallic paper: Canford, *Daler-Rowney*

Red and clear beads: Blue Moon Beads, *Elizabeth Ward & Co.*

White wire: *Artistic Wire*

Red chalk: *Craf-T Products*

Red pen: ZIG Writer, *EK Success*

Other: silver cord, red and white cardstock, silver eyelets, red ribbon, white gift bag

Finished Sizes:
    Bag: 5¼" x 8¼"
    Card: 4" x 5"

INSTRUCTIONS

❶ To make candy cane, poke small hole in white cardstock; thread wire through and adhere in back.

❷ String beads onto wire.

❸ Poke hole in cardstock; thread wire through and adhere in back.

❹ Tack candy cane down with small wire lengths.

Stamped Season's Greetings

Designer: Linda Beeson

SUPPLIES

Ink pads: Cosmic Copper and Galaxy Gold, Brilliance, *Tsukineko*

Chalk finish ink pad: Tuscan Earth, Fresco, *Stampa Rosa*

Crackle background rubber stamp: *Paper Inspirations*

Vine background rubber stamp: *Hero Arts*

Stamps: (Holly and sentiment) *Printworks*

Gold embossing powder: *Printworks*

Crackle patterned paper: *Debbie Mumm*

Fibers: *On The Surface*

Metal tag: *Making Memories*

Ribbon: *Impress Rubber Stamps*

Adhesive dots: *Glue Dots International*

Other: beige, cranberry textured, light green, and white cardstock

Finished size: 4¼" x 5⅜"

Peace On Earth

Designer: Diane L. Layland

SUPPLIES

Angel rubber stamp: *PSX*

Sentiment rubber stamps: *Hero Arts*

Gold cardstock: *Stampin' Up!*

Other: white mulberry paper, white card-stock, white card, gold thread, gold embossing powder, gold ink pad

Finished size: 4¼" x 5⅜"

Christmas Tree

Designer: Jane Marino

SUPPLIES

Rubber stamps: (Jazzy Tree) *Paper Inspirations*; (Happy Holidays) *PrintWorks*

Watermark ink: VersaMark, *Tsukineko*

Embossing powder: (gold)

Cardstock: (cream, gold metallic)

Adhesive: red glitter glue, double-sided tape

Tools: scissors, heat tool

Finished size: 5" x 7"

INSTRUCTIONS

❶ Make card from cream cardstock.

❷ Stamp Jazzy Tree on cream cardstock; emboss. Accent with glitter glue.

❸ Cut out and mat stamped image with gold metallic cardstock; adhere to card front.

❹ Stamp Happy Holidays under stamped tree; emboss.

Bonus Idea

Make a matching envelope by embossing a partially stamped tree on the front. Make sure you leave plenty of room for the sender's and recipient's addresses.

Wonderful Time Of The Year

Designer: Kathleen Paneitz

SUPPLIES

Rubber stamp:
   (Clock) *Magenta Rubber Stamps*
   (Christmas Definition) *Hero Arts*

Pigment ink: (Raspberry, Green Tea) VersaColor, *Tsukineko*

Cardstock: (cream)

Textured cardstock: (Ivy, Crimson) *Bazzill Basics Paper*

Paper accents: (tag) *Avery Dennison*

Fastener: (pewter tree brad) *Creative Impressions*

Fibers: (green gingham ribbon) *Offray*

Font: (2P Typo) www.twopeasinabucket.com

Adhesive

Tools:
   (tag punch) Paper Shapers, *EK Success*
   scissors, computer and printer

Other: bleach, paper towels, plastic container

Finished size: 5" x 4¾"

INSTRUCTIONS

❶ Make card from Crimson cardstock.

❷ To make bleach stamp pad, fold paper towel in fourths and place in plastic container; pour on bleach.

❸ Stamp Clock with bleach on card front.

❹ Stamp Christmas Definition with Raspberry on tag; ink edges with Green Tea.

❺ Print "it's the most wonderful time of the year" on cream cardstock; punch out with tag punch. Ink edges with Green Tea.

❻ Attach tree brad to cream cardstock; cut out and ink edges with Green Tea. Mat with Ivy cardstock; tear one edge and adhere to stamped tag.

❼ Adhere tags to card front; add ribbon.

Bonus Idea

Make this card for the New Year. Use black and silver papers, and the clock stamp. Print "Happy New Year" or another related saying or definition on the tags.

Embossed Tree

Designer: Gretchen Schmidt

SUPPLIES

Rubber stamps:
(tree) Bitty Bolds set, *Stampin' Up!*
(It's My Type medium alphabet) *Ma Vinci's Reliquary*

Dye ink: Christmas Green, Real Red) *Stampabilities*

Watermark ink: VersaMark, *Tsukineko*

Embossing powder: clear, *Mark Enterprises*

Photo corners: (black, brown) *Canson*

Other: cardstock (red, green, cream), embossing heat tool, facial tissues, adhesive, scissors

Finished size: 4¼" x 5½"

❶ Make cards from red and green cardstock.

❷ Stamp tree with watermark on cream cardstock; emboss. Apply Real Red over embossed image with facial tissue; repeat for second card with Christmas Green.

❸ Stamp "Joy" with Real Red and "Noel" with Christmas Green at bottom of embossed images. *Note: Stamp in same color as applied to embossed image.*

❹ Attach stamped images to front of cards with photo corners.

❺ Stamp tree with watermark across bottom of each card.

Simple Sentiments

Add sweet messages of love to family members' holiday gifts:

You are the Christmas of my life, every day of my life.

To my Santa- from the Mrs.
Set in CK Tea Party

Winter is a time for frosty days and snowy nights— a time for home.

Softly as a new snow you crept into my life.

The happiest moments of my life have been the few which I have spent in the bosom of my family.
—Thomas Jefferson

Pretty Poinsettia Card

Designer: Laura Nicholas

SUPPLIES

Cardstock: cream, dark green, red,
DMD, Inc.

Pink chalk: Chalklets, EK Success

Accents:
   Yellow brads: Boxer Scrapbook
   Productions

   Printed ribbon: Holiday Happiness,
   Lavish Lines

Other: adhesive dots, scoring tool or
stylus

Finished size 5" square

INSTRUCTIONS

❶ Make card base from red cardstock.

❷ Cut two 4" squares of cream
cardstock and mat with dark green
cardstock. Adhere one to front and one
inside card.

❸ Tear five 3½" long petals and crease
centers with scoring tool or stylus. Chalk
petals to soften color. Adhere together,
slightly overlapping.

❹ Tear five 2½" long petals, crease
centers, apply chalk, and adhere

together. Add brads to middle. Adhere to
larger petals to make poinsettia.

❺ Tear three leaves, 3–4" long, from
dark green cardstock. Crease centers
and adhere behind poinsettia.

❻ Cut three 6" lengths of ribbon. Form
one into loop and adhere behind
poinsettia. Adhere other two lengths to
opposite side of poinsettia, so words
face same direction. Note: Position
ribbon so it looks like it is all one piece.

❼ Adhere poinsettia to card with
adhesive dots.

Bonus Ideas

Throw a
poinsettia party!
Place these lovely
paper flowers on
gift wrap, bags,
tags, place mats,
napkin rings, and
candle wraps.

A Picture's Worth...

Photos are memories made visible, in a form that can be shared. Share your warm memories by sending them as handmade greeting cards.

Noel Card

Designer: Tiffany Bodily

SUPPLIES

Cardstock:
  Deep red
  Avocado Gingham, *O'Scrap!*
White card and envelope: *Petersen-Arne*
Stickers:
  Heart, holly: Glad Tidings; Stick-Its, *O'Scrap!*
  Noel: Happy Holidays; Thoughts That Stick, *O'Scrap!*
Photo

Finished Size 5" x 7"

INSTRUCTIONS

❶ Cut red cardstock to fit card front and adhere. Cut gingham paper slightly smaller and adhere.

❷ Mat photo with red cardstock and adhere.

❸ Apply heart, holly, and Noel stickers.

The tag reads:

Love,
The
Deakins

The photo caption reads:

HO! HO! HO!

Ho Ho Ho
Digital Photo Card

Designer: Melissa Deakin

SUPPLIES

Cardstock: red, white

Digital photo

Font: 2Ps Renaissance,
www.twopeasinabucket.com

Photo imaging software: Adobe
Photoshop, *Adobe Systems Inc.*

Accents:

  Small tag: *Avery*

  Red embroidery floss: *DMC*

  Red gingham ribbon: *JoAnn Stores*

Other: computer and printer

Finished size 4½" x 6½"

INSTRUCTIONS

❶ Type "HO! HO! HO!" on photo with imaging software and print. *Note: Use white rub-on letters if photo software is not available.*

❷ Mat photo with red cardstock.

❸ Print sentiment on tag.

❹ Tie ribbon around matted photo. Tie tag to knot with floss.

❺ Make card base with white cardstock and adhere photo.

MELISSA'S TAG PRINTING TIP

First print the text on plain paper. Position the tag over the printed text and adhere with repositionable adhesive. Reprint text on the paper with the adhered tag. Remove the adhesive and the printed tag is complete.

Pet Greetings

Designer: Kathleen Paneitz

SUPPLIES

Cardstock: cream, red

Textured cardstock: Fawn, Ivy, *Bazzill Basics Paper*

Photo

Pigment ink: Green Tea; VersaColor, *Tsukineko*

Dye ink: Sepia; Archival, *Ranger Industries*

Accents:
   "'tis the season": Ribbon Words, *Making Memories*

   Round antique copper brad: Variety Pack 3, *Making Memories*

   Square metal-rimmed vellum tag: Tagged, *Making Memories*

Font: CK Stenography, "Fresh Fonts" CD, *Creating Keepsakes*

Punches:
   Mini paw punch: All Night Media, *Plaid*

   Square punch: Paper Shapers, *EK Success*

Other: computer and printer

Finished size 4½" x 5"

INSTRUCTIONS

❶ Make card base from Ivy cardstock.

❷ Mat photo with Fawn cardstock, leaving wider area on left side.

❸ Wrap ribbon around matted photo and secure with brad. Adhere to card base.

❹ Print holiday message on cream cardstock. Trim and ink edges with Sepia and adhere to card.

❺ Punch square from cream cardstock and ink edges with Green Tea.

❻ Punch paw from red cardstock and adhere to cream square.

❼ Adhere square to tag, and tag to card.

KATHLEEN'S TIP

Here's a simple way to apply adhesive to very small punch-outs: adhere double-sided photo tape to the back of the cardstock before punching. Punch through the taped cardstock. Peel off the tape backing and the tiny punch-outs will be ready to stick.

Happy Holidays

Designer: Alice Golden

SUPPLIES

Green floral patterned paper: Pine Bough Large Rose Solid, *Daisy D's Paper Company*

Striped no-fray crafting fabric: Knightsbridge Crimson; Fabrications, *K&Company*

Frame kit: Frame Basics, *Me and My Big Ideas*

Photo

Green printed twill ribbon: "Happy Holidays", *Making Memories*

Scarlet tacks: *Chatterbox*

Black solvent ink: StazOn, *Tsukineko* (optional)

Adhesive machine: *Xyron* (optional)

Other: double-sided adhesive tape, needle tool

Finished size 6½" square

INSTRUCTIONS

❶ Cover frame back with green paper, following manufacturer's instructions.

❷ Cover frame front with crafting fabric. *Note: It may be helpful to use an adhesive machine.*

❸ Adhere photo to frame front. Cover photo edges with twill ribbon (see photo). Adhere tacks to ribbon corners. *Note: Use a needle tool to hollow out a well for the shaft so the tack sits flat on the ribbon.*

❹ Assemble frame according to manufacturer's instructions. *Note: If desired, before frame assembly use black solvent ink to antique screw tops included in frame kit. Press each screw top on ink pad several times; let dry.*

Bonus Ideas

ONE MAKES MANY

Create new frame displays by changing one or more of the basic design elements.

■ Use real fabric, handmade paper, wrapping paper, or crumpled tissue paper to cover the unfinished frame.

■ Hot-glue buttons, rivets, or charms over screw tops for a more fanciful finish.

■ Adhere several smaller pictures for a mini photo collage.

■ Change the printed twill ribbon to match other holidays and events.

Cards Bearing Gifts

Combine beautiful designs with little treasures to create joyful surprises.

Charming Christmas Tree

Designer: Wendy Johnson

SUPPLIES

Cardstock: green, oatmeal, red, tan, *Bazzill Basics Paper*

Brown chalk: *Craf-T Products*

Font: Primary, "Art of Creative Lettering" CD, *Creating Keepsakes*

Accents:
  Silver charms
  Red brads: *Impress Rubber Stamps*
  White string

White embroidery floss: *DMC*

Needle

Finished size 7½" x 4¼"

INSTRUCTIONS

❶ Make card base from red cardstock.

❷ Cut oatmeal cardstock slightly smaller than card front; chalk edges.

❸ Print "Merry Christmas" on oatmeal cardstock and cut into small tag. Chalk edges and mat with red cardstock. Punch hole in top.

❹ Cut 6" x ½" strip of tan cardstock, tie tag around bottom with string, and adhere to oatmeal piece for tree trunk.

❺ Cut eight ½" wide strips of green cardstock. Trim one strip to ½" long. Cut each remaining strip approx. ½" longer than previous one. Adhere to trunk to create tree.

❻ Stitch charms to tree with embroidery floss. Add brads.

❼ Adhere oatmeal piece to card base.

Bonus Idea

The recipient can cut the charms off the card and add them to a bracelet. Choose charms that reflect her favorite activities, animals, flowers, and lifestyle.

Festive Earrings Card

Designer: Barbara Haché

SUPPLIES

Brown cardstock

12" x 12" double-sided cardstock: Red Pepper/Solar White; Duplex Sheets, *Neenah Paper*

Holly patterned paper: *Anna Griffin*

Vellum

Square punches: 2½", 2"

Brown chalk: Chalklets, *EK Success*

Green organza ribbon: *Offray*

Label maker, black tape: *Dymo*

Gold French hook ear wires, jump rings: *Michaels*

Christmas light charms

Other: bone folder, craft knife, paper piercing tool, needlenose pliers, sewing machine, gold thread

Finished size 8¼" x 4"

CARD

❶ Cut 8¼" x 11⅞" piece of red/white cardstock. Score and fold, positioning white side of cardstock on outside of card (see Figure a). Cover card front with holly paper, leaving a ¾" overhang.

❷ Cut slits (See Figure b). Adhere 6" length of ribbon inside front edge of card. Fold and adhere ¾" holly paper over ribbon end. Insert a second 6" length of ribbon through opposite slit; knot end inside card to secure.

❸ Punch 2" square window in inner flap. Punch 2½" window in front flap, centered over inner window (see Figure c and "A Tip from Barbara").

❹ Chalk edges of front window and card.

❺ Print "MERRY CHRISTMAS" with label maker and adhere to card.

❻ To make earrings, connect bulb charms to ear wires with jump rings, using needlenose pliers. Pierce two holes in white cardstock above small window and insert earrings (see Figure d).

❼ Tie card closed.

ENVELOPE

❶ Cut two pieces of vellum slightly larger than card. Machine-stitch together along side and bottom edges.

❷ Punch 2½" square of holly paper and mat with brown cardstock. Adhere to envelope, aligned over window of card.

A TIP FROM BARBARA

After punching the 2" window in the back flap, fold the card closed, with the back flap on top, and trace the window onto the front flap. Open the card and place the 2½" square punch upside down on the front flap and use the traced window as a guide to punch the larger hole.

Bonus Idea

Hang a Christmas charm, magnet, or small ornament from the card window.

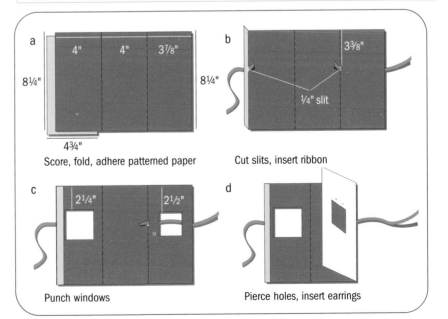

a 8¼" 4" 4" 3⅞" 4¾"
Score, fold, adhere patterned paper

b 8¼" 3⅜" ¼" slit
Cut slits, insert ribbon

c 2¼" 2½"
Punch windows

d
Pierce holes, insert earrings

Christmas Gift Card Holder

Designer: Dawn Brookey

SUPPLIES

Green cardstock

Patterned paper: Green Stripe, Holiday Images, Red Patchwork, *K&Company*

Accents:

Burgundy organza ribbon, gold spiral clip, silver decorative brads, "merry christmas" eyelet: *Making Memories*

"Dec 25" tag sticker: *Pebbles Inc.*

Silver jump ring: *Westrim Crafts*

Other: gift card, hole punch, eyelet-setting tools

Finished size 7" x 4½"

INSTRUCTIONS

❶ Make card base from cardstock.

❷ Cut Green Stripe paper to fit card front. Cut strip of Red Patchwork paper and attach to top with brads. Set eyelet below strip. Adhere striped piece to card.

❸ Cut 4½" x 3" piece of Red Patchwork paper. Adhere cardstock strip to top and Holiday Images paper to center. Tie ribbon around piece.

❹ Mount sticker on cardstock, punch hole through top, and attach to ribbon with jump ring. Slip gift card under ribbon and secure with clip. Adhere piece to card.

Bonus Ideas

- Change the colors and message to make gift card holders for birthdays, weddings, and baby showers.

- Gift cards come in so many attractive colors and designs—why not create your gift card holder to match?

Simple Sentiments

No Christmas card is complete without a funny, inspiring, or clever quip:

*Love is the light of Christmas
At Christmas play and make
good cheer For Christmas comes
but once a year.*

—Thomas Tusser

*I will honor Christmas in my heart,
and try to keep it all the year.*

—Charles Dickens

May peace and plenty be
the first to lift the latch
on your door,
And happiness
be guided to your home by
the candle of Christmas!

—*An Irish Blessing*
Set in Life Roman by Adobe Systems, Inc.

*Christmas waves a magic wand over this
world, and behold, everything is softer and
more beautiful.*

—*Norman Vincent Peale*
Set in Sanvito Roman by Adobe Systems. Inc.

*Christmas begins about the first of
December with an office party and ends
when you finally realize what you spent,
around April fifteenth of the next year.*

—P.J. O'Rourke

*I wish we could put up some of the
Christmas spirit in jars and open a jar
of it every month.*

—Harlan Miller

*Winter is a time to gather
golden moments and enjoy
every idle hour.*

—John Boswell

Fluttering flakes a Christmas makes.

Special Delivery

Designer: Michelle Tardie

SUPPLIES

Black cardstock: *Bazzill Basics Paper*

Patterned paper:
  Brushed Red, *Creative Imaginations*
  Cabin Plaid (double-sided),
  Chatterbox Inc.

Stickers:
  Clear epoxy Postage Pals, circle;
  Creative Imaginations
  Vellum holly, *Provo Craft*
  Black alphabet; Shotz, *Creative
  Imaginations*

Dimensional adhesive: foam squares,
3M

Movie tickets, gift card, or money

Finished size 4" x 6"

INSTRUCTIONS

❶ Make card base from cardstock. Adhere Cabin Plaid paper to front.

❷ Cut 2" wide strip of Brushed Red paper; tear and slightly curl top edge. Spell "Delivery!" with alphabet stickers; adhere "25 DEC" epoxy sticker. Adhere strip to bottom of card with dimensional adhesive.

❸ Adhere round "SANTA CLAUS" and cancellation line epoxy stickers to Brushed Red paper and cut out. Adhere to top of card with dimensional adhesive.

❹ Cut 4" x 6" piece of Brushed Red paper and adhere inside card. Cut 2½" x 6" piece of Cabin Plaid paper; cut triangle from center top. Apply dimensional adhesive along bottom and side edges and adhere inside card for pocket.

❺ Adhere holly sticker to reverse side of Cabin Plaid paper; place epoxy circle over it and trim. Adhere to pocket with dimensional adhesive.

❻ Place movie tickets, gift card, or money in pocket.

Inside

Holiday Tea

Designer: Toni Armstrong

SUPPLIES

Patterned paper: Hydrangea Word Print; Sonnets, *Creative Imaginations*

Vellum

White card

Pocket template: 1-P, *Deluxe Designs*

Tea bag: Earl Grey, *Tazo Tea*

Accents:
Merry Christmas rub-on, silver fibers, snowflake plaque: *Making Memories*

Snowflake buttons: *Doodlebug Design*

Epoxy snowflake sticker: *Creative Imaginations*

Other: craft knife, vellum adhesive, metal adhesive

Finished size 6½" x 5"

INSTRUCTIONS

❶ Cut patterned paper slightly smaller than card; adhere.

❷ Cut pocket from vellum, using template. Assemble with vellum adhesive.

❸ Add rub-on greeting to bottom of pocket. Wrap with fibers, adhering ends in back. Adhere button and plaque with metal adhesive.

❹ Adhere pocket to card. Adhere tea bag in top of pocket.

❺ Add epoxy sticker and button.

Bonus Ideas

■ Include an invitation inside the card for the recipient to join you for tea to calm her post-holiday nerves.

■ Tea bag wrappers come in different colors—adapt the design of your card to match!

■ Instead of a tea bag, include a gift card, miniature candy bar, photo, or hand-made coupon.

Grandma's Mini Album

Designer: Melissa Deakin

SUPPLIES

Card:

Red embossed cardstock: *K&Company*

Vellum: *Stampin' Up!*

Fonts:

Scriptina, *www.scrapvillage.com*

Century Gothic, Georgia, *Microsoft*

Adhesive dots: *Glue Dots International*

Accents:

Poinsettia: Jolee's by You, *EK Success*

Red satin ribbon: *May Arts*

Gold brads

Album:

Light green textured cardstock

Paper: Breeze, Olive, *KI Memories*

Polka dot paper: Poolside Rhinestone, *KI Memories*

Mini album: Sage, *KOLO*

Green polka dot ribbon

Punches:

Flower, ⅛" circle, *EK Success*

Corner rounder: *Marvy Uchida*

Fonts:

Scriptina, *www.scrapvillage.com*

Tempus Sans ITC, *Microsoft*

Photos

Finished sizes:

card 5" square,

mini-album 2½" square

CARD

❶ Make card base with cardstock.

❷ Print text on vellum and trim to 2¾" x 5". Attach to card with brads to make pocket.

❸ Adhere poinsettia to pocket.

❹ Tie ribbon into bow and adhere to top of card.

ALBUM

❶ Print "joy" on cardstock with white ink; trim to 1¾" square. Adhere behind window of mini album.

❷ Print quotation on desired paper and trim to fit album page. Adhere other papers and punched shapes as desired. Round corners with corner rounder and adhere inside album.

❸ Round corners of photo and adhere to facing page.

❹ Repeat steps 2–3 to finish remaining pages.

❺ Replace ribbon ties with polka dot ribbon.

❻ Insert into pocket of card.

TIPS FROM MELISSA

■ Use coordinating papers to make your album cohesive and pleasing to the eye.

■ A great resource for inspirational quotations is *Quote, Unquote,* published by Autumn Leaves.

Bonus Ideas

Mini albums are fun to make! Create one for new parents, filled with photos of their baby. Or, fill one with pictures of your children and leave it on your desk at work for others to admire.

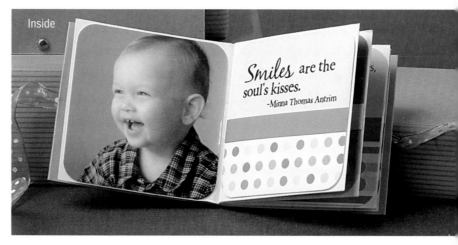

Handmade Holiday Gifts

Try our pattern (center) or create your own fun variations.

Crazy Quilted Paper Stockings

Designer: Sharon Soneff

SUPPLIES

Green oversized heavy paper: *Canson*

Patterned paper:
Muted reds: Cranberry & Moss Damask, Filigree, Heavy Damask, Leaf Damask, Vine Stripe; Historical Cranberry; Sonnets, *Creative Imaginations*

Soft greens: Dark Damask, Fleur-de-Lis; Historical Moss; Sonnets, *Creative Imaginations*

Accents:
Tassel, trims: Cranberry, Moss; Sonnets, *Creative Imaginations*,

Green trim, red trim, red velvet ribbon: *Wrights*

Brown faux fur: *Denver Fabrics*

Maroon thread: *Coats & Clark*

Other: glue gun, glue sticks, repositionable adhesive dots, sewing machine

Finished size 20½" x 9"

Simple
or extravagant,

Extra large or small,

Gifts that come
from hands and
heart

Bring pleasure
to us all.

INSTRUCTIONS

❶ Cut two stockings from oversized green paper and patches from patterned papers, using pattern.

❷ Arrange and adhere patches to stocking with repositionable adhesive. *Note: Begin the patchwork 4" below the stocking top.* Hot-glue strips of ribbon and trim over seams.

❸ Adhere edges of decorated stocking to plain stocking with repositionable adhesive. Straight stitch around stocking; leave top open.

❹ Hot-glue ribbon loop to stocking back.

❺ Cut 4" fur strip and hot-glue around stocking top, placing seam in the back. Hot-glue tassel to cuff base.

Bonus Ideas

- Make miniature stockings for tree ornaments.
- Hang the stockings on the stair rail.
- Use a stocking as a unique wrap for home-baked cookies.
- Hang a favor-filled stocking on the back of every chair at the table for Christmas dinner.

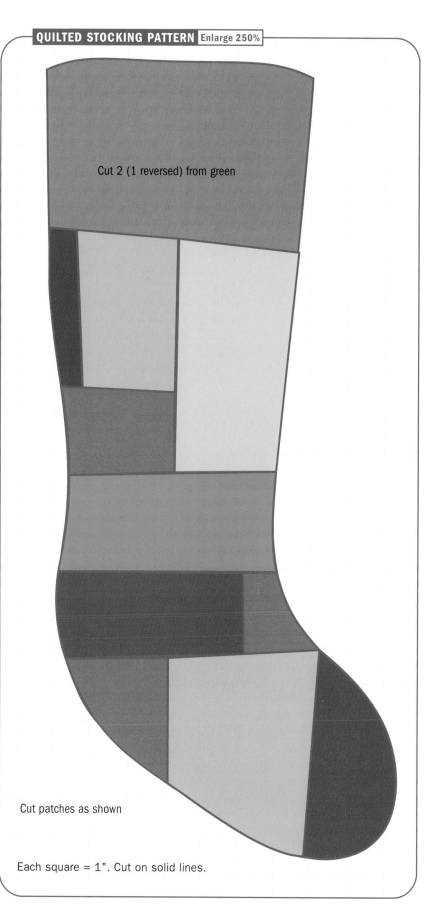

QUILTED STOCKING PATTERN Enlarge 250%

Cut 2 (1 reversed) from green

Cut patches as shown

Each square = 1". Cut on solid lines.

Jingle Bells CD Holder

Designer: Nichol Magouirk

SUPPLIES

Antique white paper

Olive crackled patterned paper: Crackle Collection, *Creative Imaginations*

Cardboard CD pocket blank: Single Slant Journal, *Pinecone Press*

Musical transparency sheet: Narratives, *Creative Imaginations*

Clear number stickers: Thoughtz; Art Warehouse, *Creative Imaginations*

Rub-ons:
   Numbers: *Li'l Davis Design*
   "jingle all the way": Christmas: Simply Stated, *Making Memories*

Ribbons:
   Lime green, red: *SEI*
   Black organza, red/white stitching, *Making Memories*
   Gingham: black, red; *Impress Rubber Stamps*

Spray adhesive: Scrappers Mount, *Creative Imaginations*

Foam lowercase letter stamps: Philadelphia, *Making Memories*

Acrylic paint: Childhood (red), Cityscape

(white): Scrapbook Colors, *Making Memories*

Other: awl, computer and printer, font, light brown chalk, paintbrush, paper towel, red thread, sewing machine, small jingle bells

Finished size 5" square

INSTRUCTIONS

❶ Adhere red ribbon ties to CD holder (see photo).

❷ Trace CD blank on patterned paper and cut out. Adhere Olive paper to the CD blank, using spray adhesive.

❸ Zigzag-stitch along notched edge. Fold and assemble CD holder according to manufacturer's instructions.

❹ Paint back of transparency with white paint and wipe some off around edges with paper towel. Let dry.

❺ Stamp "Jingle Bells" on transparency front with red paint. Let dry.

❻ Adhere transparency to front cover of CD holder. Open holder and zigzag-stitch around entire holder.

❼ Apply clear number sticker to front cover.

❽ Make holes in spine with awl, thread ribbons through and tie with bells.

❾ Rub-on "jingle all the way" on inside of holder.

❿ Apply number rub-on strip along right edge.

⓫ Print song list on antique white paper; cut out titles, chalk edges, and adhere inside holder.

⓬ Burn songs listed to CD and slip in holder.

Inside

Here We Go A Caroling!

Designer: Michelle Tardie

SUPPLIES

Olive cardstock

Gingham paper: Scarlet Checks; Rec Room, *Chatterbox*

Mini album: *DMD, Inc.*

Cut-outs: tree, heart, ornament, Merry Christmas; Embossibles, *We R Memory Keepers*

Black rub-on alphabet: Providence; Simply Stated, *Making Memories*

Black alphabet stickers: Vintage Alpha Large; Scrappychic, *Me and My Big Ideas*

Font: Times New Roman, *Microsoft*

Vanilla fabric: Hemp; Artistic Scrapper, *Creative Imaginations*

Adhesives:
Mini adhesive dots, *Glue Dots International*
Double-sided foam tape; Scotch Mounting; *3M*

Christmas carols: *www.christmas-carols.net*

Other: paper trimmer, sandpaper, twine

Finished size 3¾" square

COVER

❶ Adhere gingham paper to cover, trim to fit, and lightly sand edges.

❷ Cut fabric rectangle, fray, and adhere to cover with adhesive dots.

❸ Cut out tree and spell "CAROLS . . ." with rub-on letters. Wrap length of twine around tree and tie in front. Adhere tree to cover with foam tape.

INSIDE PAGE

❶ Cut cardstock to fit and adhere to left page. Lightly sand paper edges.

❷ Write carol title with alphabet stickers and embellish with cut-out.

❸ Print carol on back of patterned paper, trim, fold in half, and adhere to right page. Embellish with ornament cut-out.

TIPS FROM MICHELLE

■ Paint the backs of cut-outs that are larger than the album page with compatible colors.

■ Sand each inside page to give the album a more consistent look. This also hides any mis-cuts.

■ Remove unused pages to make the book lie flatter.

■ Instead of a distressed look, decorate the album with hymns, songs, and elegant embellishments.

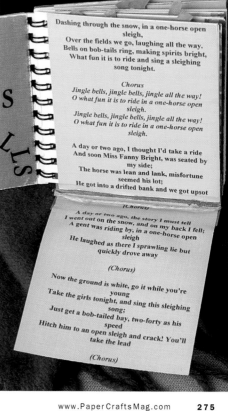

Fold out carol page

Dashing through the snow, in a one-horse open sleigh,
Over the fields we go, laughing all the way.
Bells on bob-tails ring, making spirits bright,
What fun it is to ride and sing a sleighing song tonight.

Chorus
Jingle bells, jingle bells, jingle all the way!
O what fun it is to ride in a one-horse open sleigh.
Jingle bells, jingle bells, jingle all the way!
O what fun it is to ride in a one-horse open sleigh.

A day or two ago, I thought I'd take a ride
And soon Miss Fanny Bright, was seated by my side;
The horse was lean and lank, misfortune seemed his lot;
He got into a drifted bank and we got upset

(Chorus)
A day or two ago, the story I must tell
I went out on the snow, and on my back I fell;
A gent was riding by, in a one-horse open sleigh
He laughed as there I sprawling lie but quickly drove away

(Chorus)

Now the ground is white, go it while you're young
Take the girls tonight, and sing this sleighing song;
Just get a bob-tailed bay, two-forty as his speed
Hitch him to an open sleigh and crack! You'll take the lead

(Chorus)

Inside

INSTRUCTIONS

❶ Pierce hole through top of CD (see "How to Pierce a CD," page 277).

❷ Cut 2 circles from paper, using CD as template.

❸ Adhere circles to both sides of CD, marking position of hole on circle; pierce hole.

❹ Ink edges of file folders. Apply year rub-ons to top tabs. Adhere "Naughty" and "Nice" labels.

❺ Lightly sand photo edges and staple to corresponding folder. Adhere one to each side of CD.

❻ Insert jump ring through hole and attach beaded chain for hanger.

Naughty or Nice?

Designer: Alice Golden

SUPPLIES

Patterned paper: Crinkled Christmas; Rebecca Sower, *EK Success*

Mini CDs: *Memorex*

2 small photos (to represent "naughty" and "nice")

Dye ink: Old Paper; Distress Ink, *Ranger Industries*

Accents:
  Mini file folders: Paper Reflections, *DMD, Inc.*

  Stickers: Naughty, Nice; Real Life, *Pebbles Inc.*

  Rub-ons: Dates & Numbers; Office Collection, *Autumn Leaves*

  Silver beaded chain: *Making Memories*

  Silver jump ring

Other: needle tool or awl, heat tool, heat-proof surface (such as aluminum foil-covered cardboard), stapler, fine sandpaper

Finished size 3¼" round

❶ Place CD on heat-proof surface and warm with heat tool for 5–10 seconds until it starts to soften.

❷ Immediately pierce hole through top of CD with needle tool. *Note: You may need to apply pressure and twist needle tool through CD. If CD isn't soft enough, reheat and try again. Be careful not to overheat CD or it may melt or warp.*

Victorian Trio

Designer: Alice Golden

SUPPLIES

Patterned paper: Holiday Stripe, Holiday Traditions, *K&Company*

Mini CDs: *Memorex*

Watermark ink: Versamark, *Tsukineko*

Embossing powder: Gold; Ultra Thick Embossing Enamel, *Ranger Industries*

Gold metallic rub-on finish: *Craf-T Products*

Dimensional adhesive: foam tape

Accents:
   Embossed stickers: Holiday Images, Holiday Flowers, *K&Company*

   Gold metallic thread: *Hirschberg Schutz*

   Red satin ribbon

Other: needle tool or awl, heat tool, heat-proof surface (such as aluminum foil-covered cardboard)

Finished size 3¼" round

INSTRUCTIONS

❶ Pierce hole through top of CD (see "How to Pierce a CD").

❷ Cut circle from each paper, using CD as template. Adhere Holiday Stripe circle to front of CD and Holiday Traditions circle to back, marking position of hole on circle; pierce hole.

❸ Ink rim of CD and heat-emboss.

❹ Decorate CD with stickers, using dimensional adhesive to adhere some stickers. *Note: For Joy ornament, cut out bells and pierce holes through top. String with gold thread. Highlight stickers with rub-on finish.*

❺ Adhere red bow to top of each ornament. String thread through top hole for hanger.

Bonus Ideas

■ Fasten several CDs together with ribbon, beaded chain, or wire to make a garland.

■ Use a photo from a favorite vacation on the front of the CD, and a list of memories on the back.

INSTRUCTIONS

❶ Cut stocking pieces, using pattern. Stamp with stars.

❷ Cut toe and heel pieces, using pattern. Adhere gold toe and heel to stocking pieces and machine-stitch inside edges. Adhere velvet toe and heel pieces.

❸ Apply heavy-duty adhesive along side and bottom edges of stocking pieces and adhere together. When dry, gently stuff with cotton batting.

❹ Cut 1½" x 5½" strip of velvet paper; machine-stitch bottom edge. Fold in half widthwise to form stocking cuff. Adhere alphabet sticker to front of cuff for monogram. Punch five holes along front edge with needle tool, and attach jingle bells with thread.

❺ Adhere side edges of cuff together; attach ribbon hanging loop to inside back. Place cuff over top of stocking and adhere to stocking.

❻ Line stocking edges with gold paint pen.

A TIP FROM ALICE

Add a tiny drop of glue to the end of the stitching to keep it in place.

Bonus Ideas

- Make a stocking for each family member—tuck a gift card, tickets, jewelry, or money and a mini candy cane inside, then hang the stockings on your tree as a Christmas morning surprise.

- Use stockings as party favors or place cards for a holiday meal.

- Create only the front side of the stocking and attach it to a card or scrapbook page.

Monogrammed Stocking

Designer: Alice Golden

SUPPLIES

Patterned paper: Royal Christmas, *PSX*

Gold metallic paper: Earthtone Metals, *Hanko Designs*

Velvet paper: Wine, *SEI*

Rubber stamps:
    Antique Alphabet set: All Night Media, *Plaid*
    Star trio

Gold pigment ink: *Anna Griffin*

Accents:
    Alphabet stickers: Holiday Traditions, *K&Company*
    Gold organdy ribbon: *Michaels*
    Gold mini jingle bells: *Westrim Crafts*
    Gold thread

Other: fine-tip gold paint pen, needle tool, sewing machine, heavy-duty adhesive, cotton batting

Finished size 5¼" x 3½"

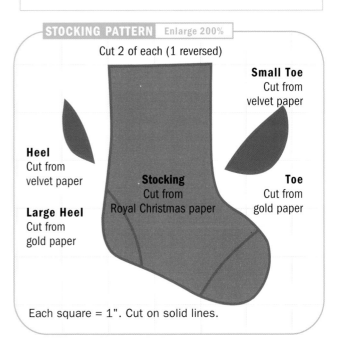

STOCKING PATTERN Enlarge 200%

Cut 2 of each (1 reversed)

Small Toe
Cut from velvet paper

Heel
Cut from velvet paper

Stocking
Cut from Royal Christmas paper

Toe
Cut from gold paper

Large Heel
Cut from gold paper

Each square = 1". Cut on solid lines.

Back

Child Star

Designer: Alice Golden

SUPPLIES

Paper maché star ornament

Pink paper: *Anna Griffin*

Patterned paper:
  Pink Toile, *Anna Griffin*
  Strawberry Delight, *Paper Adventures*
  Rose Water Color Dots, *The Paper Patch*

Rubber stamp: Holiday Print background, *Stampin' Up!*

Pigment ink: Champagne; Encore!, *Tsukineko*

Photo of child (1¾" x 1¼")

Transparency film

Gesso: *Liquitex*

Pink acrylic paint: Folk Art, *Plaid*

Adhesive: decoupage, metal

Assorted fonts

Accents:
  Negative strip: Narratives; Karen Russell, *Creative Imaginations*
  Alphabet charms, metal number (for child's age): *Making Memories*

Silver ribbon: *Jo-Ann Stores*

Silver brads: *Lasting Impressions for Paper*

Silver cord

Other: paintbrushes, stapler, fine sandpaper, craft knife, piercing tool

Finished size 4¾" x 4¾" x ½"

PREPARE

❶ Paint ornament with gesso; let dry. Paint sides pink.

❷ Paint alphabet charms and metal number pink; let dry. Sand, leaving paint only in recessed areas.

❸ Stamp pink paper with Holiday Print, using Champagne ink.

❹ Tear patterned and stamped paper into pieces (see figure a).

❺ Coat each piece with decoupage adhesive and layer on front of ornament, letting paper protrude over edges. Apply coat of decoupage adhesive over paper; let dry until tacky. Trim paper from edges with craft knife.

❻ Repeat step 4 to cover back of ornament. *Note: Proceed to "Embellish" steps 1–2 while adhesive is still tacky.*

EMBELLISH

❶ On transparency film, print "FA-VORITE" and list of child's favorite toy, food, bedtime story, song, and color. Place on back of ornament. Pierce holes in corners and push brads through.

❷ Cut one negative sleeve from strip and insert photo. Staple to front of ornament. Adhere metal number and alphabet charms to spell baby's name, using metal adhesive.

❸ Adhere ribbon around sides of ornament. Remove hanger from ornament and replace with silver cord; secure with craft glue.

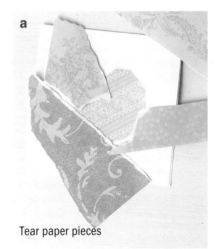

a

Tear paper pieces

Bonus Idea

Create a personalized ornament for each of your children during every year of their childhood. Give the ornaments to the grandparents each Christmas—they'll look forward to them all year long!

Hanging Frame Trio

Designer: Nicole Keller

SUPPLIES

All supplies from Anna Griffin unless otherwise noted.

Cream cardstock

Patterned paper: Holly Botanical, Poinsettia, *Striped Fabric*

Red paper

Cardboard: (no source)

Brown ink

Red satin bows

Photo corners: Clear, *Pioneer Photo Albums*

Red ribbon

Photos: 3½" x 5"

Other: (glue gun, glue sticks, sponge) no source

Finished size 7" x 9" each frame

INSTRUCTIONS

❶ Cut three frame bases from corrugated cardboard. Cover each piece with Striped Fabric paper. Wrap and adhere edges to back. *Note: Make sure stripes on each frame are aligned for a professional appearance.*

❷ Cut three pieces cream cardstock to 6" x 8" and adhere to backs for finished look.

❸ Gently age bows and ribbon corners, using ink and sponge. Let dry.

❹ Adhere bows to center bottom of two frames (see photo), and adhere bow ends to frame below.

❺ Adhere bow to top of top frame. Trim ends and use trimmed piece to create hanging loop. Adhere loop to back of top frame.

❻ Cut three pieces Holly paper to 5½" x 7¾"; center and adhere to frames.

❼ Cut three pieces thin cardboard to 5" x 7" and cover with Poinsettia paper. Wrap and adhere edges to back; adhere ribbon photo corners. Center and adhere to Holly paper.

❽ Mat pictures with red paper, using clear photo corners.

❾ Adhere matted pictures to center of Poinsettia paper.

A TIP FROM NICOLE

Colors of your project components don't quite match? Use stamping inks and sponges to harmonize your papers, ribbons, and embellishments.

Bonus Ideas

Adapt this project for other occasions with differing ribbon colors and patterned papers.

- Decorate a baby's room with coordinating colors, birth picture, announcement, and baby's statistics.

- Adhere meaningful words, phrases, or poems instead of photos. For example: Peace, Hope, Joy.

May your days be happy,
your heart be light,
your Christmas merry,
and the New Year bright!

Heart Be Light Candle

Designer: Heather Erickson

SUPPLIES

Tan textured cardstock: Harvest, *Bazzill Basics Paper*

Patterned paper: Red Diamonds, *K&Company*

Vellum

White pillar candle

Font: CK Extra, "Fresh Fonts" CD, *Creating Keepsakes*

Accents:
   Sage green silk ribbon, *Offray*
   Green button
   White thread

Other: 1/16" hole punch, needle, vellum adhesive, glue stick

Finished size 6" x 3¼"

INSTRUCTIONS

❶ Cut 4¼" wide strip of cardstock to wrap around candle. Adhere 3" wide strip of patterned paper to center.

❷ Adhere ribbon over top and bottom edges of patterned paper, using glue stick.

❸ Stitch button to top front of piece with white thread.

❹ Wrap piece around candle and adhere ends in back. Cover seam with piece of patterned paper.

❺ Print poem on vellum and trim. Mat with cardstock, using vellum adhesive, and punch holes in top corners to make sign. Thread string through holes to create hanger, adhering ends behind cardstock. Adhere button to candle and hang sign on button.

"Just Popping By" Tag

Designer: Alisa Bangerter

SUPPLIES

Cardstock: Black, Cardinal, *Bazzill Basics Paper*

Textured cardstock: Malt, Sunflower, *Bazzill Basics Paper*

Bag of popcorn

Lettering template: *Pebbles Inc.*

Fonts: CK Wanted, CK Constitution, "Fresh Fonts" CD, *Creating Keepsakes*

Chalk: black, brown, *Craf-T Products*

Acrylic paint: green, yellow, *Delta*

Walnut ink: *Postmodern Design*

Dimensional adhesive: foam squares, *Making Memories*

Accents:
   Yellow mesh: Maruyama Paper, *Magenta*
   Popcorn die cuts: Ellison, *Provo Craft*
   Brass wire: *Artistic Wire*
   Gingham ribbon: green, red, *Offray*
   Black buttons: *Making Memories*
   Red paper clips
   Raffia

Other: black thread, needle, circle punches (¼", ½"), craft knife, paintbrush, small dowel

Finished size 6¾" x 4"

PREPARE TAG

❶ Cut tag from Malt cardstock. Apply yellow paint to edges, using dry paintbrush; let dry. Chalk edges with black. Adhere mesh to tag.

❷ Brush edges of ribbon with diluted walnut ink. Wrap green ribbon around top of tag, adhering edges in back. Wrap red ribbon around bottom, knotting ends in front. Stitch black thread through button and adhere over knot.

❸ Punch ½" circle from Black cardstock. Adhere to top of tag and punch ¼" hole through center. Add raffia.

DECORATE TAG

❶ Print "Just," "by," and "with a" on Sunflower cardstock. Stitch around words and tear edges; chalk with brown and black. Adhere to tag (see photo).

❷ Cut letters to spell "Holiday" from black cardstock, using template. Adhere to tag.

❸ Print "POPPING" and "HI" on Sunflower cardstock. Cut out, leaving small border. Mat "POPPING" with Cardinal cardstock and chalk edges with brown. Dry brush edges of "HI" with green paint. Adhere letters, overlapping, to tag with dimensional adhesive.

❹ Wrap three lengths of wire around dowel to curl. Chalk popcorn die cuts with brown. Adhere each die cut, plus the end of one wire length, to tag with dimensional adhesive. Adhere other ends of wire lengths under letters.

❺ Add button and paper clips.

❻ Attach to popcorn bag.

Santa Chex His List Tag

Designer: Gretchen Schmidt

SUPPLIES

Cardstock: black, blue, oatmeal, red, *Making Memories*

Alphabet rubber stamps:
It's My Type (for "chex"), *Ma Vinci's Reliquary*
Buttons Uppercase (for "twice"), *PSX*

Watermark ink: Versamark, *Tsukineko*

Embossing powder: Rich Red, *Ranger Industries*

Fonts:
Harting, *www.dafont.com*
2Ps Typo, *www.twopeasinabucket.com*

Hole punch: *McGill*

Label maker and blue tape: *Dymo*

Adhesive dots: *Glue Dots International*

Adhesive: Diamond Glaze, *JudiKins*

Accents:
Red ribbon, ribbon charm: *Making Memories*
Silver washer eyelet: *Creative Impressions*
Alphabet beads: *Darice*

Other: eyelet-setting tools, heat tool, glass jar, Chex mix ingredients (see "The Original Chex Party Mix")

Finished size 5¼" x 2¾"

INSTRUCTIONS

❶ Print the sentiment on oatmeal cardstock (see "How to Print Sentiment") Leave ¾" space between "Santa" and "his" for "chex."

❷ Stamp and heat-emboss "chex." Add desired words with stamps, labels, and alphabet beads.

❸ Cut tag from red cardstock and adhere printed piece.

❹ Tear top edge of blue cardstock and adhere to bottom of tag. Cut thin strip of black cardstock, weave through ribbon charm, and adhere over torn piece.

❺ Cut small square of blue cardstock and adhere to top of tag. Set eyelet through square and add ribbon.

❻ Attach to jar of Chex mix.

HOW TO PRINT SENTIMENT

❶ Create a 4¾" x 2½" text box in a word processing program.

❷ Type the sentiment in desired fonts.

❸ Change the color of the words you do not want to print to white. This will allow space for the words on the cardstock without altering the position of the other text.

❹ Print the sentiment on cardstock and trim.

TIME-SAVING TIP

Print the sentiment in assorted fonts and colors instead of using stamps, labels, and alphabet beads.

THE ORIGINAL CHEX PARTY MIX

1 c. mixed nuts

1 c. pretzels

1 c. garlic-flavored bite-size bagel chips or regular-size bagel chips, broken into 1" pieces

3 c. each Corn, Rice, and Wheat Chex cereal, *General Mills*

6 tbsp. margarine or butter*

2 tbsp. Worcestershire sauce

¾ tsp. garlic powder

1½ tsp. seasoned salt

½ tsp. onion powder

*Do not use spread or tub products.

Heat oven to 250°. Melt margarine in large roasting pan in oven. Stir in seasonings. Gradually stir in remaining ingredients until evenly coated. Bake 1 hour, stirring every 15 minutes. Spread on paper towels to cool. Store in airtight container. Makes 12 c.

You'll find this and more mouth-watering Chex mix recipes at www.chex.com/recipes.

Christmas Gone Postal Tag

Designer: Kathleen Paneitz

SUPPLIES

Rubber stamps:
  (Christmas Definition, First Class Mark Stamp) *Hero Arts*
  (Paris Post Mark) *Stampabilities*

Dye ink: Sepia, Archival Ink, *Ranger Industries*

Cardstock: Chiffon, *Bazzill Basics Paper*

Patterned paper: Postal, *Magenta Rubber Stamps*

Small tag: *Avery Dennison*

Brad: gold star, *Impress Rubber Stamps*

Eyelet: gold star, *Stamp Doctor*

Ribbon: *Offray*

Punch: ⅝" circle, *Family Treasures*

Other: cardstock (brown, cream), eyelet-setting tools, scissors, ruler, adhesive, cosmetic sponge, cotton ball

Finished size: 2½" x 4¾"

INSTRUCTIONS

❶ Cut tag from cream cardstock; cover with Chiffon. Tear patterned paper and adhere to right side of tag.

❷ Stamp First Class Mark Stamp on top left, and Paris Post Mark on bottom of tag.

❸ Ink tag edges. Randomly daub tag with ink, using cotton ball.

❹ Stamp definition on small tag; ink edges. Tie ribbon through hole and adhere to large tag. Add brad.

❺ Punch circle from brown cardstock and adhere to top of tag; set eyelet.

STAMP SOURCES

The First Class Mark Stamp and Christmas Definition stamps from Hero Arts have been discontinued. If you can't find the stamps, substitute the images as follows:

❶ Print Christmas definition on cardstock with your printer, and cut into tag shape.

❷ Use a different postal rubber stamp. You'll find several to choose from at Limited Edition Rubberstamps (877/9-STAMPS, *www.limitededitionrs.com*).

Sing Noel Tag

Designer: Linda Beeson

SUPPLIES

Rubber stamps:
  (NOEL) *Art Impressions*
  (Music Pattern) *Penny Black*
  (Holly leaves) *PrintWorks*

Pigment ink:
  (green) ColorBox, *Clearsnap*
  (Galaxy Gold) Brilliance, *Tsukineko*

Embossing powder: clear, *Stamp LaJolla*

Stickers: round epoxy, Page Pebbles, *Making Memories*

Other: cardstock (red, white), ribbon, red eyelet, ½" circle punch, scissors, ruler, adhesive, embossing heat tool, dimensional adhesive, eyelet-setting tools

Finished size: 2¾" x 4¾"

❶ Stamp music on white cardstock with Galaxy Gold; emboss. Randomly stamp holly image over music with green. Cut into tag; mat with red cardstock.

❷ Punch circles from red cardstock; adhere to card as holly berries. Adhere stickers over circles.

❸ Stamp Noel on white cardstock with green; emboss. Trim and mat with red cardstock; adhere to tag with dimensional adhesive.

❹ Set eyelet through tag and add ribbon.

Symbols of the Season Gift Bag

Design: Cindy Schow

SUPPLIES

Acrylic stamps: (holly, Merry Christmas, pine needles, pinecones) Clear Impressions Christmas, *Provo Craft*

Black ink pad

cardstock (8½" x 11"):
   cream, light green, red, tan

Kraft gift bag

Decorative chalk: (dark brown, green, light brown) *Craf-T Products*

Fine-tip pens:
   (black) ZIG Millennium, *EK Success*

   (red) ZIG Writer, *EK Success*

Green tissue paper

Miscellaneous items: scissors, glue stick, ruler, cotton swab or make-up applicator

Finished Size: 5¼" x 5¼"

INSTRUCTIONS

❶ Cut a square of red cardstock to fit the front of the bag. Cut two small squares of light green cardstock.

❷ Apply light brown chalk to the edges of the green squares using the cotton swab or make-up applicator. Draw borders on the squares with the black marker.

❸ Stamp the holly leaf and the pine needles on the squares. Let them dry, color the berries with the red pen, and apply green chalk to the leaf and pine needles.

❹ Stamp pinecones and Merry Christmas onto tan cardstock. Trim the images to small rectangles and mat them with cream cardstock.

❺ Apply brown chalk to the pinecones and the edges of the cream mats.

❻ Adhere the squares to the red cardstock and adhere the completed design to the bag (see photo). Fill the bag with tissue paper.

Christmas Ornaments Bag & Tag

Designer: Teri Andersen

SUPPLIES

Cardstock:
   Black, white, *Provo Craft*
   Christmas Red, *Paper Garden*
   Leapfrog (light green) textured,
   Bazzill Basics Paper

Red gift bag: *DMD, Inc.*

1" circle punch: *Carl Manufacturing*

Accents:
   "God bless" sticker: *Wordsworth*
   Copper wire: *Artistic Wire*
   Copper spiral clips: *Target*

Other: wire cutter, needlenose pliers,
dimensional glaze or metal adhesive

Finished sizes:
   Bag 8¼" x 5¼"
   Card 3" square

BAG

*Adhere all metal pieces with dimensional
glaze or metal adhesive (see "A Tip
From Teri").*

❶ Cut two 4" x 1¼" strips each of white
and light green cardstock. Trim short
ends at angles and adhere to bag.

❷ Cut three thin strips of black cardstock
and adhere between wide strips.

❸ Punch two circles each from red and
light green cardstock. Adhere spiral clips.

❹ Cut ornament tops from black
cardstock and adhere behind ornaments.
Cut four 1" lengths of wire and curl ends
with pliers. Adhere behind ornaments.

❺ Adhere ornaments to bag.

❻ Adhere sticker to red cardstock. Trim
and adhere to bag.

CARD

Make card base with white cardstock.
Embellish with cardstock strips and
ornament (see Bag steps 3–4 for ornament instructions).

A TIP FROM TERI

To adhere the spiral clips, be sure to
use metal adhesive or dimensional
glaze that dries clear. I recommend
Decorator Glaze from Plaid and Glossy
Accents from Ranger Industries.

Bonus Idea

Ornament magnets make clever stocking-stuffers! Just create the ornaments, reinforce the backs with chipboard, and adhere magnetic strips
to the backs. You can even attach the magnets to the bag or card,
using repositionable adhesive.

Classic Santa Gift Bag & Tag

Designer: Kathleen Paneitz

SUPPLIES

Red textured cardstock

Patterned paper: Gold Check, Holiday Floral, Holiday Script, *K&Company*

Red gift bag: Sadie Gift Satchel; Jolee's By You, *EK Success*

Santa stickers:
Dimensional Santa: Grand Adhesions, *K&Company*

Santa with pack: Holiday Traditions, *K&Company*

Dye ink: Sepia, *Ranger Industries*

Accents:
Stickers: alphabet, mini tag, sled stamp; Holiday Traditions, *K&Company*

Epoxy alphabet sticker: "U"; Clearly Yours, *K&Company*

Metal-rimmed tag, "Believe" rub-on word: *Making Memories*

Gold decorative eyelet: *Creative Imaginations*

Ribbon: gold metallic, green gingham, white satin, *Offray*

Gold thread

Eyelet-setting tools

Finished sizes:
Bag 10" x 5½"
Tag 4¾" x 2¾"

BAG

❶ Cut 3½" x 5¼" piece of Gold Check paper. Ink edges and adhere to bag.

❷ Adhere Santa with pack sticker to Holiday Script paper; trim and ink edges. Mat with Holiday Floral paper. Adhere over Gold Check piece.

❸ Spell "A gift for" with stickers.

❹ Adhere "U" epoxy sticker to metal-rimmed tag. Tie green gingham ribbon through hole and adhere to bag.

TAG

❶ Cut tag from cardstock. Adhere strip of Holiday Floral paper horizontally to center. Cut Gold Check paper to fit top and bottom of tag; tear inside edges and adhere in place.

❷ Cut small strip of Holiday Floral paper; ink edges and fold over top of tag. Set eyelet and add metallic gold and green gingham ribbon.

❸ Loop gold thread through mini tag sticker. Adhere sticker to top of tag and attach thread ends in back.

❹ Add sled stamp sticker and rub-on word to bottom of tag. Adhere dimensional Santa sticker to center.

❺ Ink tag edges.

Santa Suit Gift Bag

Designer: Melanie Brower

SUPPLIES

Cardstock: black, white

White textured paper

Red vellum

Red lunch bag

Font: Coronet, *www.fonts.com*

Accents:
  Metal frame, silver spiral clip: *Making Memories*
  Silver eyelet
  White satin ribbon

Metal adhesive

Eyelet-setting tools

Finished size 11½" x 5¼"

BAG

❶ Tear approx. 2" x 9" strip of white textured paper and adhere vertically to top of bag.

❷ Cut 2¼" strip of black cardstock and adhere to bag as belt.

❸ Adhere frame as belt buckle, using metal adhesive.

TAG

❶ Print the following sentiment on white cardstock:

Christmas is Clause for Celebration! Thanks for being part of ours.

❷ Cut into tag and tear bottom edge. Double-mat with red vellum and black cardstock, tearing bottom edge of each.

❸ Set eyelet through top of tag and tie to clip with ribbon. Fold top of bag closed and attach clip.

Bonus Ideas

- Make gift bags in different sizes by simply adjusting the size of the accents.

- Create miniature bags filled with gifts for neighbors, coworkers, or party guests.